I0755878

MEMOIRS

OF THE

REV. WALTER M. LOWRIE,

MISSIONARY TO CHINA.

EDITED BY HIS FATHER.

PHILADELPHIA:
PRESBYTERIAN BOARD OF PUBLICATION,
No. 265 Chestnut Street.

Entered according to Act of Congress, in the year 1854, by

A. W. MITCHELL, M. D.,

In the Clerk's Office of the District Court, for the Eastern District of Pennsylvania.

JESPER HARDING, Stereotyper,

Philadelphia.

CONTENTS.

CHAPTER I.

FEBRUARY, 1819—JANUARY, 1842.

EARLY LIFE—COURSE AT COLLEGE—COURSE IN THE THEOLOGICAL SEMINARY—ACCEPTED AS A FOREIGN MISSIONARY—SAILS FOR CHINA.

LETTERS.

CHAPTER II.

JANUARY 19—MAY 27, 1842.

VOYAGE TO CHINA—JOURNAL IN THE HUNTRESS.

CHAPTER III.

1842.

LANDING IN CHINA—VOYAGE IN THE SEA QUEEN—SHIPWRECK IN THE HARMONY—RETURN TO MACAO.

CHAPTER IV.

1843.

RESIDENCE IN MACAO—VOYAGE UP THE COAST—AMOY AND CHANG-CHOW—RETURN TO MACAO.

LETTERS AND JOURNALS.

CHAPTER V.

1844.

RESIDENCE IN MACAO—CHINESE PRINTING WITH METAL TYPE—ARRIVAL OF NEW MISSIONARIES—THEIR FIELDS OF LABOUR.

LETTERS.

CHAPTER VI.

1845.

DIFFERENT MISSIONS ESTABLISHED—LEAVES MACAO—VOYAGE UP THE COAST—NINGPO.

LETTERS AND JOURNALS.

CHAPTER VII.

1846.

MISSIONARY LABOURS AT NINGPO—HEATHEN CUSTOMS—SUPERSTITIOUS FEARS—PREACHING IN CHINESE.

LETTERS AND JOURNALS.

CHAPTER VIII.

1847.

LETTERS AND JOURNALS.

PREFACE.

This edition of the Memoir of the Rev. Walter M. Lowrie is made up of a selection from the letters and journals printed in the larger editions of the same work. The plan adopted was to let him speak for himself in his letters and journals, and the editor has done little more than to select and arrange the papers of his beloved son. A few remarks have been made with the view of noticing his early years, and connecting the different periods of his short but active and not unvaried life.

His letters, for the most part, were hastily written, many of them in the confidence of Christian and endeared friendship. His journals also were written at the dates mentioned, and his other engagements gave him no time to correct and copy them.

MEMOIR.

CHAPTER I.

February 1819.—January 1842.

Early Life—Course at College—Course in the Theological Seminary—Accepted as a Foreign Missionary—Sails for China—Letters, &c.

Walter Macon Lowrie, the third son of Walter and Amelia Lowrie, was born in Butler, Penn., on the 18th of February, 1819. Until his eighth year, his father was absent from home during the winter months. This left the principal part of his early training and education to his excellent mother, and well and faithfully did she perform this responsible and sacred trust. From his infancy he possessed a mild and cheerful temper. He was a general favourite with his playmates, and always ready to engage in the usual sports of the play-ground. It was often the subject of remark, that he was never known to get into a quarrel, or even an angry dispute with his associates. To his parents he was always obedient and kind, open and ingenuous; he was never known to use deception or falsehood. His brothers and sisters shared his warmest affection and love, and his time with them seemed to be made up of pure enjoyment.

At an early period he was sent to school, where he learned the usual branches of a common English education. It was soon perceived by his teachers, that it required but little effort on his part to get the lessons assigned to him; and the place he usually occupied was at the head of the class. In his tenth year his parents removed to Washington city, and for a part of the year he was taught by his father in the higher rules of arithmetic, in geography, and ancient and modern history. In his eleventh and twelfth years, he spent two terms under an able teacher in a classical grammar school.

At this period the health of his beloved mother was gradually declining, and her physicians advised that she should spend the summers in Pennsylvania, and the winters in Washington. In these circumstances it was deemed best that Walter, although not fourteen years of age, should be sent to Jefferson College. Two of his brothers had already graduated at that college, and his father was well acquainted with the president and the professors. A home was found for him in the family of the Rev. Professor Kennedy, who watched over him with a parent's care. The same month in which he reached the college, in November, 1832, he received the sad intelligence of his dear mother's death. Most deeply did he feel this severe bereavement, and bitterly did he mourn over the loss of one so very dear to him. The account of her calm and peaceful departure, full of faith and trust in her Saviour, which he soon afterwards received, whilst it made a deep impression on his mind, tended much to relieve the bitterness of his grief. After spending a year in the preparatory department, he entered the freshmen class in October, 1833, and continued in the college, with some interruptions for relaxation, till he graduated in September, 1837.

In the summer of 1834, he was at home from the first of August till the last of October. His father was somewhat apprehensive in regard to his health, and believed that some relaxation from his studies would be of service, even if it should require him to spend another year in the college. He retained his place in the class, however, and kept up with the usual studies without difficulty. The family were then spending the summer in Butler. Here he first met with his second mother, and he seemed almost at once to transfer to her the affection he had entertained for his own mother. Nor was this a transient feeling. His affection and deep respect and esteem for her continued till his lamented death, as the letters and journals addressed to her will abundantly show.

During this visit he accompanied his parents and one of his brothers, and a sister in declining health, to the falls of Niagara. He greatly enjoyed the company of his friends on this journey, and was filled with wonder and awe at the stupendous displays of God's power in this mighty cataract. He accompanied the family to Washington, and was present at the calm and peaceful death of his beloved sister, in the last of September, 1834. In November he returned to the college, his health much improved by his temporary absence.

Soon after his return, that seminary and the neighbourhood were blessed with a precious and powerful revival of religion. Many of the students in the college, and large numbers in the congregations of that region, were added to the church. Most of these students afterwards entered the ministry. The history of this revival and its subsequent results, if they were written, would show how important a period of life is the college course of every student. Probably the attention and the prayers of the church have been too little turned towards her young men in the different colleges. The remark will be generally found true, that "as is the piety of the student in college, so will it be in the theological seminary, and in the ministry."

In this revival, after a time of deep conviction of sin, he obtained a hope of peace with God in the Saviour. He was then in his sixteenth year, and he gradually became more and more instructed in Christian experience and warfare. With a number of the students who were admitted to full communion in the church at the same time, he formed a most endeared and lasting friendship, and with many of these he kept up a correspondence till his death.

On leaving college, the subject of this memoir returned home, his father's family then residing in the city of New York. His expectation was to enter the Theological Seminary at Princeton soon after his return. The Seminary year, however, commenced in September, when the regular classes were formed; and his father, still somewhat solicitous respecting his health, deemed it best that he should have a recess from study; and he spent the winter at home. Having few acquaintances in the city, his winter's residence at home was a season of retirement and quiet, and his time was profitably employed in reviewing his previous studies, and in miscellaneous reading. He had also a good opportunity of improvement in vocal music, under the able instructions of Mr. Thomas Hastings. During the winter he took charge of a class of young men in the Sabbath-school, who became greatly attached to him, and were much benefitted by the care he bestowed on their instruction.

In May, 1838, he entered the Seminary, and afterwards joined the regular class formed in September following. In his whole course in the Seminary he pursued his studies very closely. He was never absent from a single recitation; and with his studies, and other necessary duties, his time was fully employed. By persevering industry, he was able to superintend a Sabbath-school at Queenston, a few miles from the Seminary, and also to make a Catalogue of the books in the Library, and arrange them anew.

Before leaving college, as is seen by his letters, he had fully decided to go as a missionary to the heathen, and during his last year in the Seminary, his mind was settled on Western Africa as his chosen field of labour. In December, 1840, he was received as a missionary of the Board of Foreign Missions of the Presbyterian Church. No objections to his preference for Africa were made by his friends, and for several months the question of his field of labour was considered as fully settled. In the spring and summer of 1841, however, the exigencies of the China mission induced the Executive Committee to review the question of his field of labour. The mission to China was then but commencing, and was encompassed with many difficulties. That great empire was at that time closed against the Christian missionary; and Singapore had been selected as the most suitable place where the language of China could be learned, translations made into it, schools established, and other missionary work carried on. The Rev. John A. Mitchell, and the Rev. Robert W. Orr and his wife, had arrived at Singapore in April, 1838. In the following October, Mr. Mitchell was removed by death. The next year Mr. Orr's health failed; a visit to the Nilgerry Hills, in India, did not restore it; and in 1840, he set out on his return home. The same year, the Rev. Thomas L. McBryde and his wife reached Singapore; and in 1841, he was joined by J. C. Hepburn, M. D., and his wife. In one year, Mr. McBryde's health had declined so much, that it was evident he also must soon withdraw from that sphere of labour, and thus leave Dr. Hepburn alone in the China mission. In these circumstances, and having at that time no other suitable man to send, the question in the view of the Executive Committee was clear, that China, and not Western Africa, was the proper field of labour for the new missionary. It was believed, also, that from the tone of his piety, his cheerful temper, his thorough education, his natural talents and untiring industry, he was peculiarly fitted for the China mission. It was, however, with many misgivings, and much reluctance at first, that he contemplated this change in his field of labour; but as there was a perfect unanimity of sentiment in the Executive Committee, the professors in the Seminary at Princeton, and other ministerial brethren, all of whom he greatly respected, he yielded cheerfully to their judgment—viewing these things as a call from God to labour in that great and destitute part of the Saviour's vineyard.

On the 5th of April, he was licensed to preach the Gospel by the Second Presbytery of New York. After leaving the Seminary in May, he spent a few weeks at home, preaching on the Sabbath in different churches. In July and August he was sent by the Executive Committee to the most distant land office in Michigan, to secure the pre-emption right to the mission station among the Chippewa Indians, as the government had advertised the Indian reservation for public sale. The sale, however, was postponed before he reached the land office, and on his return he spent some time among the churches in Western New York. Late in the autumn he visited his friends in Western Pennsylvania for the last time, and by these various journeys his health was much improved.

He was ordained on the 9th of November, 1841, and on the evening of the last Sabbath of the same month, a deeply interesting farewell missionary meeting was held in the Brick church, New York. Addresses were made by the Rev. Gardiner Spring, D. D., pastor of the church, by the missionary, and by his father. These addresses would possess much interest now, but no copy of them was preserved. It was expected that the vessel would sail early in December, but she was delayed till January, and in the interval his time was chiefly spent at home.

Jefferson College, March 10th, 1837.

My Dear Father:—In my last letter I mentioned that as far as I could see, if nothing providential occurred, I had made up my mind on the question, "Should I become a missionary?" It never seemed to present any great difficulty to my mind, and I don't know that I could give any particular account of the reasons, which led me to believe that it was duty on my part to spend my life among the heathen. The question always seemed, though a very important one, to be—Can I do more abroad than at home? There were no providential hinderances to prevent me from going. Indeed Providence seemed rather to point to the heathen as the proper place. My own inclinations and feelings pointed the same way. If I have piety to fit me for being a minister at home, I might hope to have it for being a missionary abroad. Of my talents and qualifications for the work, others must judge. Almost the only difficulty was in regard to my health. My constitution being weak, it seemed almost unable to bear much fatigue; for even the labour of study is preying on it in some degree. But though the case seemed so clear, do not think, dear father, that it was on account of my vanity that it appeared so. For almost always when the duty of being a missionary appeared strongest, I felt my own strength or my own fitness to be least. And even now, when the troubles and deprivations and duties of missionary life come up to view, the question involuntarily occurs, "Who is sufficient for these things?" Yet if I know my own heart, I am willing to live or die for the heathen. It is now nearly two months since I came to the determination expressed above, and never yet has a single emotion of regret crossed my mind on account of it. Nay, a load has been thrown off, and I feel a deeper interest in everything that concerns the extension of the Redeemer's kingdom. Pray for me, dear father; unless I have more piety than I now have, I am not fit for the missionary work, nor for the ministry at home.

Your affectionate son,

W. M. Lowrie.

Pittsburgh, September 13th, 1837.

My Dear Father—We finished our examination eight days ago, but I have been so busy, I have not had time to write to you. At the close of our examination, I expected to be told that I might have my Diploma, but further or higher, I had not directed my thoughts. Judge of my surprise then, when on the next morning, Dr. Brown gave me the enclosed as my standing.* I had never thought of standing more than respectably, but this grade is equivalent to what was once called the first honour. There were two others in the class who were marked equally high. I have been appointed Valedictorian, which is considered here the most important post at the Commencement. I hope, however, you will not consider me to be a very excellent scholar, on account of the high standing I have with the Faculty. In languages especially, I do not consider myself to be much above mediocrity.

As soon as Commencement is over, I shall set out for home. Though I should like very much to enter on the study of theology immediately, yet I do feel almost afraid to commence without a longer recess than common. During my collegiate course, I have not, on an average, studied three hours a day; but at the Seminary, I would wish—indeed, it seems

* Walter M. Lowrie,

	Grade.		Grade.
Languages,	1.	Natural Science,	1.
Moral Science,	1.	Mathematics,	1.

M. Brown.

essential—that at least four hours daily be spent in study. Still, with an opportunity of daily systematic exercise, I should not feel much hesitation about the Seminary studies. Others with far worse health than mine, have gone through as severe a course; and as I may probably never have very strong health, it may not be worth while to delay on that account, especially if my youth be not considered too strong an objection.

I remain your affectionate son,

W. M. Lowrie.

New York, November 21st, 1837.

Mr. John Lloyd—Dear Brother:—Though this method of communication is but a poor substitute for that "sweet counsel" we have so often enjoyed, yet as it is the best that now remains for us, I gladly embrace the first good opportunity that has yet occurred, to renew our friendship. For it does seem as though it had to be renewed, when I think that, though you and myself have often "held sweetest converse about what God had done for our souls," and that though our eyes have brightened and our hearts warmed, as we "talked by the way," yet now we are separated by a distance of more than four hundred miles, and are without the prospect of seeing each other for months, and perhaps years. Yet though separated in body, I trust we are often present in spirit, and especially that, at the throne of "our Father," we can still enjoy communion, and be the means of profit to each other, perhaps even greater than that which our mutual conversations could have afforded. It is surely consoling to know that there is One who watches over us, and over our dearest friends, far better than we could possibly do, and that at all times he will do all things well. Yet, were it consistent with duty, I should like again to spend a few hours with you, and again partake in those social joys that kindred spirits like yours and mine so much delight in. My situation here, though fully as pleasant as I expected it to be, is very different from what it was at Canonsburg. I have as yet very few acquaintances here, and do not expect to have many. Those that I have, I know not what they are, for the rules of fashion are so trammelling, that one cannot at once make those friendly advances which are common among you. Consequently when I would enjoy the holier joys of friendship, I müst draw off my attention from things around me, and return to past days and scenes, in many of which you and one or two others held a conspicuous part. Do you remember that day after our missionary meeting of the Society of Inquiry, last March, when you and I took that long walk "over the hills and far away," and in our conversation seemed to have some foretastes of "glory begun below?" Many and many a time has it risen to my mind, and if it has not drawn tears from my eyes, it has done what is better—encouraged me to go forward, and caused me to gird up the loins of my mind anew for the heavenly race, and made me sometimes to remember a friend, a fellow-expectant of what "eye hath not seen, nor ear heard, neither hath it entered into the heart of man to conceive." I am very glad to find that comparative solitude agrees so well with me; for I was really afraid that after being so used to meetings of one kind or another every night, it would be difficult to get along without them. In fact, it does require some effort to keep alive the spirit of piety, when one has nothing like the Society of Inquiry or the Brainerd Society to excite to action; nothing but the stated ordinances of God's house to nourish the soul. Yet on that very account I prize my present situation the more, because I am thereby enabled, or perhaps I should say required, to live more by faith and less by sight, or frames and feelings. And to a missionary nothing can be more important, than to be able to live without any thing to keep the soul in constant excitement; for, as it has been well remarked, "when he gets to his field of labour, he can attend no crowded meetings to hear some eloquent orator descant upon the magnanimity of the missionary enterprise." All the "romance of missions" must then be laid aside, and in its reality, he may almost be tempted to forget for whom and for what he is labouring, and becoming discouraged, lay down his weapons, and retire vanquished from the field to which his Master called him.

It seems to me, on looking back on the last two or three years of my collegiate course, that we all lived too much by excitement, not enough by simple faith. Our religious societies were precious and profitable, and I should be sorry to give them up, but perhaps we depended too much on them, without remembering that "Paul may plant and Apollos water, but God alone can give the increase;" and this dependence on these means, (at least in my own case,) was productive of a spirit of action more resembling the "crackling of thorns," than the steady, intense flame that consumed the Jewish sacrifices. Oh, my brother! guard against this spirit of trusting to any thing in preference to the revealed will of God, and his ordinances, for animation in the divine life.

What is the state of missionary feeling now among you? Do you yet hear the voice, "Come over and help us," and the wailing cry, "And what then?" as it rises from the death-bed of the Hindoo, and, borne across the waste of waters, reaches our ears both from the east and the west, swelled as it is, and heightened and prolonged by the addition of innumerable others? Oh, does the "cry of the nations," echoed and re-echoed from the distant mountains, still sound among you? Or does it die away among the crumbling ruins of heathen temples, unheard and unheeded, save by the infidel and the deist? Oh, who is there to come up to the help of the Lord against the mighty? There is nothing in all my course for which I reproach myself so much, as that I did so little to excite a missionary spirit at College. I do not mean among those who were already determined as to the path of duty, but among those who had not decided the question; for very rarely did I press upon any of them as I should, the importance of the work, the necessity, absolute, increasing, and alas! almost irremediable necessity now existing for labourers, and their own duty in this great matter. Dear brother, can you not do something? You have the confidence of most of the pious students, and could you but muster courage enough to determine to do something in this matter, unborn millions would bless you for it. Let me transcribe for you a few lines from an appeal of some missionaries in India; you have perhaps seen them before, but they will bear reading and praying over again:

"The soil is ready for the seed, and the seed ready to be sown, but where are the husbandmen? In some places it has been scattered abroad and the fields are white for the harvest, but where are the reapers? Congregations large and attentive might be procured every day, *but we have no men.* Schools might be established on Christian principles, but *we have no men.* Humanly speaking, souls might be saved, but '*how can they hear without a preacher?*' You can increase the number of these queries to an almost indefinite extent, but the answer will almost always be, we have no men! We have gone to the colleges and seminaries of learning, but we found few to answer our demands. We went to the haunts of society, but one was busied about his farm, and another about his merchandise, and another with the sweets of domestic society. We went to the schools of the prophets, and asked if on any of them rested the spirit of Elijah? but there were few to answer the call. Despairing, we looked to the heathen, and as we saw them go down by crowds to the darkness of the second death, we felt as if yet another effort should be made. Oh, who will go for us?"

Wishing you all temporal and all spiritual blessings, and sympathizing most sincerely with you in your afflicting bereavement, (of which I have only just heard,)

I remain your *brother*,

W M. LOWRIE.

New York, January 1st, 1838.

MR. JOHN LLOYD—A happy new year to you, friend John! and may you see many more such, if the Lord will! What are you doing now, whilst I am writing to you? Cousin John tells me you have holidays (old times are in that word) at present; so I will just let my imagination try if she can find where you are, or what you are doing. But as you are pretty much of a home-loving creature, I suppose I need not go far to find you. Probably you are going about, paying some fifteen minute visits, for you were never famous for long ones; or very probably you are standing by the side of the old mill-dam, and watching the fellows skating. I hardly think you would adventure yourself on the ice, for you are almost too grave for that. But no—I forget; this is the first Monday of the month, and of the year, and therefore you are probably stuck up in a corner of your room, reading all the missionary pamphlets you can lay hands on. By the way, have you read the life of Swartz? If you have not, let me "lay my commands" on you to read it immediately. You know how much our experience resembles each other's—now rejoicing, and now, again, discouraged and without heart. Swartz was always on the proper pitch; constantly in the exercise of strong, unwavering, childlike confidence in God, and therefore he was always ready to employ himself in his Master's business. He was always busy, always cheerful, and always useful. Dear brother, may we strive to be like him, and may we have the same success in our labours that he had in his! I can ask for few blessings greater, either for you or for myself, than is contained in that wish. I read Bedell's memoirs some time ago, and have just now finished those of Hannah More. They are both of them most excellent. The former I was delighted with. The memoirs of the latter are also very interesting, indeed. They are compiled from her letters almost entirely, including a great many from various celebrated characters who were cotemporary with herself; and are, I think, excellent models of epistolary correspondence. The style of almost all is very good, and, what is far more important, through most of them there is a strong vein of deep-toned sensibility and piety. I really began to entertain a considerable degree of reverence for her before I got quite through the memoir. She was an extraordinary woman, possessed of more than common talents, and able to do almost what she pleased; yet, so far from indulging herself in this liberty, her whole life was spent in a most quiet manner, without any flashes, or romantic adventures or pursuits, or anything inconsistent with the character of a plain, common-sense woman.

Mitchell and Orr, missionaries to China, sailed nearly a month ago. How soon will you be ready? Do you still think of China in preference to India?

It seems strange that this is the beginning of another year. How the time rolls around! Yet to me the thought that time is rapidly passing away is pleasant. It is solemn, and yet most delightful, to think that my "salvation is nearer than when I believed;" that, if I am a Christian, I am three years nearer to my heavenly home than when first the light of truth beamed on my darkened and distressed mind. True, of many misimprovements and much waste of precious time, I have to accuse myself; yet still the Lord is full of compassion, and the blood of Christ cleanseth from all sin; and through him I can look death in the face, and exclaim, when Satan, and doubts, and fears assail me, "I know that my Redeemer liveth." By the way, I heard a sermon on that text yesterday, from an Episcopal minister. He said that the word translated Redeemer in this passage, was the same as that used in Ruth iii. 9, "A near kinsman," or, as the margin has it, "One that has a right to redeem." The mention that such was the meaning of the word, led me into a train of very pleasing and profitable thought. If we had been taken captive by enemies, and knew that our father, or mother, or brother, were aware of it, we should be sure that they would use every exertion to ransom us. But there is a friend that sticketh closer than a brother: this friend is our Redeemer, and this Redeemer is the omnipotent God. Can there, then, be any doubt of our final salvation?

The last two or three months have been very pleasant ones. I seem to have had more nearness of access to God, greater confidence in the Saviour, and more of the influences of the Spirit, than I have usually had. Among other reasons for these great blessings, I have no doubt but the prayers of my many friends in Canonsburg and its vicinity have had much effect. I still need your prayers very much, for I am prone every moment to fall.

And now, brother, my paper tells me I must close; and commending you to the grace of God, which is able to keep you through faith unto salvation, I remain,

Your affectionate brother in Christ,

W. M. Lowrie.

Princeton, July 4th, 1838.

MY DEAR MOTHER— . . . I get up every morning at half past four, often sooner, but rarely later, and take a walk of one or two miles. It is most invigorating to the whole system, while the fresh air, singing birds, pleasant fragrance of the fields, and the thousand and one nameless pleasures of a morning walk, concur to make it a most delightful custom. When I get back it is near breakfast time. The appropriate duties of the morning over, I commence study at seven, and continue till half past ten, or perhaps eleven, at Latin, Greek and Hebrew, singing a little at intervals by way of relaxation. Dinner is ready at half past twelve, and miscellaneous employments occupy me till two; then some regular reading connected with the course here, till half past four. Prayers and supper at five, and company, talking, walking, singing, meetings, bathing, reading, writing, thinking, and not thinking, &c., till nine. Generally I manage to be asleep soon after ten. My next door neighbour has an alarm clock, which usually awakens me in the morning, and if it did not the *old bell* would at five. Though not pursuing the regular studies of my class, I find abundance to do, and my time generally passes in the way above described.

There is here, as may be supposed, every variety of character. The variety is fully as great, if not greater, than it was at College, excluding of course those who were not professors of religion. There is a good deal of reserve among the students towards new comers, though perhaps not greater than one would expect. As yet I have not made many intimate acquaintances, and do not wish to, for a short time. There are, however, some lovely spirits among these brethren.

Yours affectionately,

W. M. LOWRIE.

Princeton, February 22d, 1839.

MR. JOHN LLOYD—On the subject of personal religious feeling, I suppose I can sympathize with you as formerly. It is distressing to feel that we ought to be more engaged in the service of God, and yet feel a deadness, a numbness of all the moral feelings, when we contemplate divine things. In such a condition, the word of God, while we see that it has force, makes no impression on us; prayer seems more like a task than a pleasure; meditation is a tedious, tasteless thing. And yet we cannot feel happy in the world; that does not satisfy us; that cannot fill the aching void. But it is profitable to be left thus, at times; for then we feel more and more our own weakness, and perhaps it would not do for persons constituted as you and I are, to enjoy too much of mere comfort: we would place our hearts too much on the pleasure, and be in danger of forgetting Him from whom it came. On this subject there is great danger, too, of our making mistakes, and because we do not enjoy religion as much as formerly, of thinking we are not as engaged as we were then. The truth, I suppose, is, that we are not to measure our standard of piety by our enjoyment, so much as by the steadiness of our purpose of self-consecration to God. The more willing we feel to renounce all for him, to submit to him, to be anything or nothing as he chooses—indeed, to have our will entirely swallowed up in his, just so far, and no further, do we grow in grace. Like John the Baptist we shall say of our Saviour, "He must increase, but I must decrease." And there is a pleasure in lying down at the feet of Jesus, and yielding ourselves to him, which may not be accompanied with tumultuous joy, but it brings a calm and holy peace which the world never knew. At such times we look on death and the grave without fear, nay, almost with desire; for, though we are willing to labour our three score years and ten, yet we feel that "to be with Christ is far better." Dear brother, when you feel your heart so cold, does it not rejoice you to think that in heaven it will not be so?—that there you shall know and love as much as you wish, and that these vexing cares and trying experiences will be no more?

> "There is an hour of peaceful rest
> To mourning wanderers given;
> There is a joy for souls distressed—
> A balm for every wounded breast:
> 'Tis found above—in heaven."

Wherefore, my brother, comfort your heart with these words. The Psalmist, in his affliction, remembered God "from the land of the Hermonites, and the hill Mizar." There is a land and a hill to which you can refer with feelings of joy—I need not say where nor when. I commenced the preceding page with my own heart in the dust; but these thoughts have gladdened it and refreshed me.

I think you will be highly delighted with the Seminary course, especially the study of Hebrew; nothing ever delighted me so much, in the way of study, as that venerable language; and the facilities of studying it are now so great that any one may acquire it. Get Nordheimer's Grammar by all means, and don't think of any other; it is a real treat to read that Grammar.

I must close, but only for want of time to write more. The Jefferson students here are all well, and, if they knew I was writing, would doubtless ask to be remembered to you.

Farewell.—Pray for me,

In Christian love, yours,

W. M. Lowrie.

Princeton, June 24th, 1839.

Mr. John Lloyd—Dear Brother:— . . . . I am very sorry you cannot come here in the fall. To me nothing would afford greater pleasure; for one of kindred spirit with myself, to enter fully into all my feelings and sympathize with me, I have not found since we parted—at least, none like yourself. It pains me now at times, when I think how much more profitable we might have been to each other in the Christian life. But it also rejoices me, to think of our seasons of Christian intercourse, and of the long walks we had over the hills, when we talked of heaven, and our hearts burned as our Saviour met with us by the way. Do you ever now enjoy such seasons? Yesterday Dr. Alexander preached on 2 Cor. iii. 18; "We all, with open face," &c. While preaching, a few thoughts of the astonishing condescension and love of Jesus, the great God, taking our nature upon him, and living "manifest in the flesh," seemed to fill my mind. I could readily conceive of a Christian's soul being swallowed up in contemplation of God's character and the Saviour's love. Oh! the riches of boundless, endless grace! Yet it is not often this icy heart is thus melted, and oh! it is much easier for the flame once kindled to die away, than to mount up and reach towards heaven. Dear brother, pray for me. The Christian's life is a warfare, and more and more do I feel that every day must witness conflicts and battles sore and long. Why should the soldiers slumber when the enemy is upon them? Especially why should the leaders be remiss when the danger is so urgent?

The subject of missions receives some attention here, but not what it deserves. Last term the interest was considerable, and there were twelve or fifteen who looked forward to the foreign field as their future destination. How flourishes the spirit of missions at College? You have never mentioned this in any of your letters. I hope the Brainerd Society prospers. That band of brothers might do wonders; they ought to do much. So we all should. But oh! how cold our love, how weak our faith is found. "Ye know the grace of our Lord Jesus Christ."

Most truly yours,
W. M. LOWRIE.

Princeton, August 21st, 1839.

TO MR. JOHN LLOYD—DEAR FRIEND:—Your letter did me good like a cordial. It convinced me, though I did not need that, that there was one person in the world who cared for so useless and insignificant a creature as myself; that I was affectionately remembered when the lowering clouds without were but an emblem of the deeper gloom within; and when despondency seemed to paralyze the energies of the soul, that still there were those who would pray for me, and sympathize with me. It was good news from a far country; and, if you will pardon the comparison, as Jonathan stripped off his own robe and gave it to David, so did the disposition and frame you seemed to be in steal over my mind.

There is not much missionary spirit in the Seminary at present, and few, if any, have lately decided to go abroad. Still there appears to be an undercurrent of feeling on the subject, which, we hope, will soon manifest itself openly. I have not yet decided where to go, and do not expect to, for some time. But let me whisper in your ear, for I don't want it known, that I look to a field nearer home than China, or even North India. Don't hold up your hands in astonishment at this—I mean Western Africa, the white man's grave. There has been a great change of feeling in the Seminary, in regard to this field, since I came here. Last summer, at the first part of the session, there was not one student who even thought of Western Africa as a missionary field. But during the course of the last winter, one, and then another, of the brethren determined to go to Western Africa, and they have now gone. May our Father go with them! I look on this experiment with deep interest;—it is yet an experiment, but I hope it will be successful.

My religious feelings are exceedingly cold at present. It is difficult to be always engaged in the critical study of the Bible, and collateral objects of inquiry, and not have the mind at times drawn away from the spirit to the mere letter of the commands. Yet I do at times, even in recitation, obtain a glimpse of Him whom my soul loveth; and O, how sweet is his countenance! The doctrine of justification by faith has appeared to me in a clearer light this summer than ever before; and though sometimes the "old man" seems to revolt against it, yet it always seems the most glorious to God, and worthy of acceptance. It gives an immovable ground of confidence, and removes every reason for despair. O that we may both heartily embrace it, and be saved for Christ's sake only!

Write to me soon.

Your brother in Christ,

W. M. Lowrie.

Princeton, December 11th, 1839.

Mr. John Lloyd—Dear Brother:—Your very welcome epistle was taken up principally in proposing objections to Western Africa as a missionary field; and I was glad to read them; not that they have altered the current of my desires, but they brought the subject fully before me again.

Your objections were—1st. The unhealthiness of Western Africa, and 2nd. The prospects of usefulness in North India or China. The first is a strong one, and even stronger, perhaps, than you suppose;

in one point of view, and to one ignorant of the facts, it is so. Of one hundred and ten missionaries sent by the Church Missionary Society, in the course of thirty years, a very large proportion died in two or three months, and vastly the majority before they did anything: yet the very first one who went out lived twenty-three years, and several others shorter periods. But the question is, why so many died so soon? Answer: 1st. Because of the unhealthiness of the climate. 2nd. Because far less was known of the climate of Western Africa by medical men than of almost any other tropical country; and therefore their remedies were not so skilfully applied, nor preventives so effectually used in the first instance. 3d. Because many of the missionaries acted exceedingly rashly when they first commenced operations. They came from England and Germany, and, in some cases, with insufficient accommodations on their voyage. They commenced their labours immediately. During the hot summer they preached two or three times every Sabbath, superintended schools during the week, worked at hard work often. Others, particularly females, died of complaints not peculiar to any climate. As to the first reason, it is with me a question whether the climate of Africa is at all more unhealthy than that of India.

Now for the second.—The prospect of doing a great deal of good in India is very flattering. But is Africa to be left until India is evangelized? Perhaps, also, we do not at all know what the prospects are in Africa. I am inclined to think them very extensive. Certainly our missionaries have their hands full, and much more. What else can they say in India? Again, the human heart is the same everywhere; yet I apprehend that there are not so many obstacles in Africa to the conversion of the natives as there are in India. They are a ruder people; they have less to pride themselves upon in the way of science, arts, and wealth, than the Hindus; and we know that not many noble, not many mighty, are called.. True, the Lord is able to convert the learned and proud, just as well as the ignorant and degraded; blessed be his name for it: yet still, do we not commonly find, that among the latter there are more cases of hopeful conversion than among the former? But I have not time now to continue the subject. These are some of the reasons, barely mentioned, and thrown together without any order, that combine to make me prefer Western Africa. China, I fear, is to me out of the question. My life will probably be short at best, and I certainly expect the greater part of it would be gone before I could master that language. Siam I might like on some accounts. I have talked of India often, and while my brother was there, I thought of that country; but it has never appeared to me in so inviting an aspect as it has to some others. My sympathies are awakened for Africa. My judgment, perhaps influenced somewhat by my sympathies, speaks for her; the prospects of usefulness call loudly; objections do not seem so strong to me as to some others; and "Here am I, Lord," is all I have to say about this subject. My mind is not made up, and will not be, till I have more carefully examined the subject. The Lord direct my inquiries, and yours also, my dear brother.

We are now engaged in studying theology—an interesting, delightful, and infinite subject.

Yours in the most cordial Christian love,

W. M. LOWRIE.

Princeton, February 21st, 1840.

MR. JOHN M. LOWRIE—DEAR COUSIN:— . . . . I was reading Turrettin's Theology this morning, about the tree of life, and the comparison he instituted between the tree of life and Christ was really most delightful. I could almost believe I was in heaven partaking of its fruits, numerous and varied and rich as they are; sitting under its shade, and quaffing of the river of the water of life, that flows from the throne of God and the Lamb. Oh for that happy time when faith shall be turned to sight, and expectation to the full fruition of the holy joys of heaven! But alas! the language of mourning and sorrow suits me best. I know but in part, and I am sanctified but in part. I see but through a glass darkly, and eternal things fade away in the distance, while earthly trifles fill the mind. But it will not always be so. The Lord prepare us, both living and dying, to glorify his name!

. . . . With my present views of the holy ministry, I would rather spend four years than three in preparing directly for it, and certainly I think there will be no reason to regret having spent a session extra in reference to it.

I find that in every place I have still the same evil heart, the same proneness to depart from God; and I fear very much, lest after a while, the exercises of this place, admirably calculated as they appear to be for the cultivation of piety, should degenerate with me into a mere round of formal duties. Nothing but constant dependence on God, and constant renunciation of ourselves, can possibly secure us from danger.

I am more and more convinced that the Bible, the word of God, should be the great study of the minister of God, and that all other studies should be subservient to this. Even theology is only valuable so far as it gives us clearer views of what the Bible teaches, and connected views of its great doctrines. With a comprehensive and extended knowledge of the Bible as a whole, and in detached portions, we shall be workmen that need not be ashamed.

Your affectionate cousin,

W. M. Lowrie.

Princeton, September 3d, 1840.

MR. JOHN LLOYD—MY DEAR BROTHER:— . . . . At the time I received your letter I was not very well, and shortly afterwards went home and spent a week there. I was at that time received under the care of the Second Presbytery of New York, and had my pieces assigned me. My Latin piece is, "An Christus pro electis solum mortuus sit?" on which I have written an essay, and translated it into something that professes to be Latin, and is so long that it covers five foolscap pages. This, with many and various other duties, has kept me very busy for several weeks past. My health is now very good, and I hope, Deo volente, to be licensed next April, and ordained soon after.

. . . . I have just been examining a little insect on my window, and comparing its body with those of other insects and with my own. It is wonderfully different from them in shape, size, materials, uses, and objects. It has some members I do not possess, and wants others granted to me. It has life, though not an inch in length, and it appears to enjoy its existence. It is but one of an infinitely numerous class of beings, each species of which is so different from every other, that we can hardly conceive of them as possessing any qualities in common. Yet they have some, for they all live, they all enjoy life, and they were all made by one great and glorious Being. How condescending must he be, who has so curiously wrought their little frames! How wise, thus to fashion their bodies! How kind, thus to grant them life and happiness! How infinite in knowledge, to know all their actions, to direct and govern all their motions, to foresee and provide for all their wants! Will he look with indifference on men! Will he neglect to attend to them when they lift their eyes to him, and cry, Abba, Father? Surely not.

But how humbling is the thought, that with all

our boasted wisdom and vaunted power, we cannot understand the hidden mysteries of these little insects, nor frame another like them! But then it is a glorious truth, that hereafter we shall know all we wish to know; and our knowledge, instead of puffing us up, will humble us, and cause us to love our God and Saviour more. And even now, we may look on these little living things, and say, "My Father made them all." I thank thee, little fly; the sight of thee has filled my soul with pleasant thoughts; and I write them here that my friend may share them with me. . . . .

Farewell.—The Lord be with you and bless you.

W. M. LOWRIE.

Princeton, November 16th, 1840.

MY DEAR MOTHER—Your letter from the distant south, came to me like good news from a far country. You left New York September 30th, I left it the next day, and had a pleasant journey to Philadelphia, Canonsburg, Pittsburgh, and Butler, going and returning, a thousand miles of travel. I spent a most pleasant Sabbath with the church at Miller's Run, where my old Sunday-school is. At Pittsburgh the Synod was in session, and, both in that city and in Butler, I saw and spoke to many dear friends. For particulars, I refer you to the inclosed. On the 5th of November I arrived at my old room in Princeton, prepared to say with gratitude, Hitherto the Lord has helped and blessed me.

I have now got pretty fairly settled down to study. This is my last session; I can scarcely realize that so short a time as six months will finish my theological course. It would not take much to induce me to begin it again. At present, other duties seem to call me hence; but who is sufficient for these things?

I shall probably offer myself to the Board as a

missionary soon, unless something of which I know nothing, should occur to prevent. Don't stay so long in the south, that you cannot be back in time to see me off.

Yours most truly,
W. M. Lowrie.

Princeton, December 10th, 1840.

To the Executive Committee of the Board of Foreign Missions of the Presbyterian Church—It has been my wish and intention for several years to spend my life as a missionary to the heathen. Believing that it is the duty of the Church in her organized capacity to prosecute the work of missions, I offer myself to you as a candidate for that work; and if accepted, shall hold myself in readiness to enter on it shortly after the close of the present session of the Theological Seminary.

I am now in my twenty-second year, and have been a professor of religion for nearly six years. The work of missions has always appeared to me to be identical with that of the ministry, requiring the same talents and preparation, and demanding that those who engage in it should be actuated by the same motives which influence those who enter on the ministry at home. The considerations which have influenced me to believe I ought to enter some foreign field, are, a desire for some such field, considered as a means of being more useful, and the fact, that while comparatively a large number are willing to enter the ministry at home, few will go abroad. The call from heathen lands is loud. It must be answered, and knowing no particular reason why I should settle in this country, I feel prepared with humility, and yet with cheerfulness, to say, "Here am I, Lord, send me." In addition to this, the leadings of Providence, ever since I first joined the church, and particularly since I entered this Seminary, have seemed to direct my course far hence to the Gentiles.

In making you this offer of my services, I shall leave it to the Committee to decide on my field of labour. My own preferences however are strongly towards Western Africa, and I am perfectly willing to take on myself the responsibility of going to that field. It has been before my mind distinctly for two years and a half, and before either of your present missionaries to that field had decided to go there. Still, if it be probable that my usefulness would be greater elsewhere, I shall willingly go to any other field. My health is not robust, yet commonly it is good. I believe myself to be more in danger of pulmonary diseases than of any other, but should probably be less liable to them in a more southern climate than this.

Praying that the Lord would bless and prosper the cause of missions, and all those engaged either at home or abroad in furthering it,

I remain with Christian respect and esteem,

Yours, &c., W. M. Lowrie.

Bedford, N. Y., May 26th, 1841.

My Dear Mother—I have spent the week here very pleasantly. On the Sabbath I preached twice, and attended a funeral, five miles off. These exercises wearied me very much.

I have just had one of the longest jaunts among the rocks I have had for some time. After ascending a number of small hillocks, each higher than the preceding, and each crowned with several large rocks, I reached the top of the highest hill. The prospect was beautiful, and on several sides extensive. Whilst resting, I began to observe more minutely the top of the hill. Several large rocks shot up obliquely from beneath the ground; a few moderate-sized trees were growing among them; and I found several little delicate flowers—a violet, a little white flower, and various kinds of grasses. What a contrast between the everlasting rocks and the fading flowers, and yet both were found side by side! I could not help thinking of the way in which the Bible sometimes groups together the grandest, and at the same time the most lovely of God's attributes; for example—

"Thy kingdom is an everlasting kingdom, and thy dominion endureth throughout all generations. The Lord upholdeth all that fall, and raiseth up all that be bowed down."—Psalm cxlv. 13, 14.

So admirably do the book of nature and the book of revelation agree, when they speak of our heavenly Father. Pursuing my observations further, I found several busy ants tugging away at their several loads, a little wood spider, and several delicately formed little flies, all busy, and all apparently happy. Yet though so small, God—the same God that founded the hills, and hardened the rocks—was watching over them, and supplying their wants. I admired the wisdom and goodness displayed in everything there, and with, I trust, a good deal of the spirit of a true worshipper, I knelt down on the hill-top to offer praises and prayers to him, whom the heaven of heavens cannot contain, and who yet dwells in the humble and the contrite heart. Such seasons are like foretastes of heaven. I may never revisit that solitary place, yet I hope often to remember it. . . . .

Yours most affectionately, W. M. Lowrie.

Ogdensburgh, July 31st, 1841.

My Dear Father—I have just received yours of July 28th, and as it was the first news I had from home, it was a very agreeable visitor. I have made appointments to preach to-morrow at Morristown, and at the second church of Oswegatchie, and the

Sabbath following at Evans' Mills, so that I shall not be able to leave for home until the 9th or 10th of August. I hope, however, to be home about this day two weeks. Thus far my visit has been very pleasant, and profitable to myself at least, if not to others. The people have everywhere received me cordially, and seemed quite gratified at my coming.

In regard to the object for which Mr. Orr wishes to see me, I suppose I know what it is, and am half inclined to think that it can be settled as well in my absence as otherwise. My mind was turned very strongly to Africa three years since, and the considerations that induced me to wish to go there were —that very few are willing to labour in that field, and that my talents seem to fit me peculiarly for such a people as the Africans are. I like to deal with an ignorant and yet affectionate people, who are not self-conceited. My acquirements, preparations, &c., seem to qualify me for that field. Another consideration that weighs a good deal with me is, that every one expects that I shall go to Africa. It is not vanity that induces me to believe, that both Canfield and Alward will be greatly disappointed should I go to any other field; and I fear that many of those who know what my intention has been, will attribute any change in my destination to fear of the climate. For myself, I should not care about any such suspicions; but the effect on others may be unpleasant, as it may induce some who have thought of going to Africa to hesitate.

There is still another consideration of a personal nature. The mission to Africa is considered rather a dangerous experiment, and if I should now decide to go elsewhere, would it not give some captious spirits the opportunity of saying, that the Corresponding Secretary was willing to let others go there, but not to let his own son expose himself? These considerations make me unwilling, with my present views, to take on myself the responsibility of determining to go to any other country. If the Executive Committee, however, think my services are more needed in China than in Africa, and that, all things considered, I will be more useful in the former place; then I have nothing further to say, but will cheerfully submit to their decision; and shall hold myself in readiness to go this fall, if necessary. I shall, in that case, wish to have it stated in the Chronicle, that "my preference was for Western Africa, but the wants of the China mission being such as to induce the Executive Committee to change my destination, I consented," &c. Such a statement, I think, would not be improper, while it would shield me from the charge of "lightness," or wishing to avoid an exposed station.

This letter you may consider either as addressed to yourself personally, or to the Executive Committee. Mr. Orr's statements may perhaps induce me to take some other course than the one above mentioned, but at present, I do not see that I can do otherwise.

I remain your affectionate son,

W. M. LOWRIE.

Steamboat St. Lawrence, Lake Ontario, July 13th.

DEAR MOTHER—When riding in the wild woods of Michigan, I found so many ideas coming up, that I concluded to write you a long letter. I have it all to write yet, and the steamboat shakes so, that I write like Mr. Hopkins in the Declaration of Independence.

From Detroit by railroad to Ann Arbor, it is a dreary country part of the way, heavy timber and thick underbrush, and any quantity of marshes. I left Ionia July 1st, and took the road on the north side of Grand river. Next day the road lay through a beautiful country, though thinly inhabited, and with a profusion of flowers, some of which were very beautiful. I saw whole fields quite blue with the "four-o'clocks," which Reuben watches so carefully in your little garden. Then there were wild roses, red lilies, sweet-williams, yellow marigolds, wild peas, and many others, red, blue, and white, which I had never seen before. Some were very beautiful, especially the mocassin flower. It is a large lady's-slipper; the flower is red and white, and has a very fine appearance. All this was in the wilderness.

"Full many a flower is born to blush unseen,
And waste its sweetness on the desert air."

But are they *unseen?* Is their *sweetness wasted?* Would this be consistent with wisdom in that glorious Being who makes nothing in vain? Yet of what use are they? Well, they are the houses of a great many insects. It is said that several different kinds live in every plant. Then, their seeds are food for the little birds. Who can tell us, too, what effect their perfumes have upon the winds that sweep over these solitudes, and visit, in all their freshness and healthful influences, the abodes of men? Then, how do we know but that these wild woods are the school-houses of other beings, who come down and learn lessons from the flowers as they spring up in their beauty, and open towards the pure light of heaven? It is a very contracted view of things to suppose that the productions of the earth are intended only for man, and are lost if he does not use them. But there is another thought of far more weight—these flowers are grateful to God himself; he "delights in the work of his hands." What skill, and wisdom, and goodness are displayed in these little flowers! He "clothes the lilies of the field." Surely, if God delights in these works of his hands, they were not made in vain—their beauty is not unseen—their sweetness is not wasted.

The following Sabbath I spent in Buffalo, and on Monday I started off for the Falls of Niagara, determined that this time, I would see both sides. I spent several hours on the Canada side, and got my face wet with the spray on Table Rock, but did not feel inclined to go under the Horse-Shoe fall. I soon began to drink in the spirit of the place, and to feel my soul expanding with the emotions it was so well fitted to produce. I will not inflict a description on you for several very good reasons. I spent the night and the next day till 2 P. M., on the American side. Every step about the falls was as familiar as if I had traversed them but yesterday, and yet it was seven years since our hasty visit to the place. The little bridge on the Terrapin rocks, where we all sat down, and looked over into the boiling abyss, is broken down. You will recollect how we all admired that magnificent scene. I felt melancholy almost all the time. Where were those with whom I had formerly walked over these scenes? Two of them were already in their graves. I saw many others there, like our party was seven years ago—husbands and their wives,—parents and their children,—brothers and their sisters. As we did then, they seemed to enjoy their visit the more from the society of each other. But I was now alone,—I knew no one, and scarcely spoke to any one. "A stranger and a pilgrim," my thoughts turned to our everlasting home. Here I was surrounded with the evidences of the power and glory of God. The dashing, roaring waters; the foam and the silver bubbles that floated on the waves; the bright rainbow that played in quietness over the scene; the old trees on the island; and the little flowers that grew out of the fissures of the everlasting rocks—each seemed to have a tongue to speak the praises of the great Creator. My heart was full; and as I felt almost overpowered by the solemnly joyful feelings of my soul, I could not but ask—will there be such scenes as these in heaven? The only answer I could give was, if not, there will be that which will produce the same emotions that these do, in a

4*

more enrapturing degree. We can know the character of God only in his word and in his works, for himself we cannot see. Here we learn his power, wisdom, and goodness, by such sights as these. In heaven we shall know far more of these same attributes. What the works which shall declare those attributes shall be, we may not presume to say. But if they are not such as we see on earth, they will be so much more glorious, that we shall not wish again to see these mighty displays of his power.

From the falls I went to Ogdensburgh, and was most kindly received by the Rev. Mr. Savage and his lady. I remained in this neighbourhood from the 20th of July till the 3d of August, and preached in a number of the churches. Some of our meetings were seasons of deep interest, and I formed acquaintances which I will remember while I live. With Mr. and Mrs. Savage and their children, I could not but feel at home. I saw a good deal of that dear patriarch, the Rev. Mr. Rogers, and preached for him several times. I enjoyed our intercourse very much, and I trust was profited by the privilege of being with him. When speaking of the Saviour he said: "Whenever the Bible speaks of Christ by way of metaphor, it is always with some term expressive of divine excellencies. If he is called a tree, then it is the tree of life. If he is called a vine, then it is the true vine. If he is called a shepherd, then it is the good shepherd. If he is called a plant, then it is the plant of renown." The remarks may not be new to you, but they were new to me, and they brought to my mind the idea, that the flowers of the Bible are like the flowers of the field, the more closely they are examined, the more beautiful do they appear.

The river St. Lawrence is the noblest river I have ever seen. Opposite Ogdensburgh it is about a mile and a quarter wide. I had a good view of it from the window of my bedroom. It flows on in its majestic calmness; the waters are beautifully clear, and very deep. The opposite bank looks well in the distance, much better indeed than when you are close to it.

July 31st. A letter from home; all well. Mr. Orr has returned from China, and wishes to see me. I suppose he wishes me to go to China. Well, I am ready if it be necessary, but I would rather go to Africa. However, here am I, and God is everywhere, and I will go wherever he sends me.

August 2d. My time in this pleasant neighbourhood is nearly up, and in two days I set off for home. Yet why do I talk of home? "Strangers and pilgrims"—such we all are, and who more than I? I don't know whether this lonely feeling that so often comes over me is the cause of it, but I love to walk in graveyards, and read the names on the tombstones. The influence of such places seems to come over my soul with a quietness and calmness that is really pleasant. When I was in Rochester I visited Mount Hope cemetery—a beautiful place. The inscription on a grave of a mother and her daughter, struck me as very beautiful:

"The night dew that falls, though in silence it weep,
Shall brighten with verdure the grave where they sleep;
And the tears that we shed, though in secret they roll,
Shall long keep their memory fresh in the soul."

Denmark, N. Y., August 9th. I preached yesterday three times at Evans' Mills, and was pretty well tired. These ministers have no mercy on a wayfaring brother when he comes along. I left early, and arrived here at eight P. M. I have now before me sixty-one miles by stage, ninety-six by railroad, and one hundred and forty-five by steamboat; three hundred and two miles, to be passed over in thirty-six hours. However, rest after labour is sweet. If we were all as eagerly anticipating the rest of heaven, as I am the close of my present journey, it would be well.

Most affectionately yours, W. M. Lowrie.

Pittsburgh, September 24th, 1841.

My Dear Mother—Since leaving New York on this, most probably my last visit to this side of the mountains, I have been so constantly on the move, I have not been able to write to you. Indeed there has but little occurred that is worth notice. I came by way of Washington and Canonsburg, spending a Sabbath at Miller's Run, my old parish when I was a student in college. It was a time of deep feeling both to them and to myself, especially when I told them I never expected to meet them again in this world. I preached on Monday in Canonsburg, and on Tuesday came to Pittsburgh. After two days with our friends there, I set off for Butler and Venango counties. I spent the Sabbath in Butler, and preached once for Mr. Young. I need not go over my visits to our friends. Very pleasant and very painful they were. O how affectionate and kind my dear aunts were; and painful as was our parting, it was brightened with the blessed hope of meeting again in peace, when time shall be no more.

I returned to Butler on Saturday, and preached for Mr. Young on the Sabbath. In the morning, on "I am a stranger in the earth;" and the afternoon on missions. In the evening, a very large number came to the Monthly Concert meeting, and Mr. Young and myself both addressed them. Much feeling was manifested, and many tears shed. My text in the morning seemed to my own feelings to be appropriate, even in this the place of my birth. I left the place so young, and have been so long absent, that my earliest playmates are strangers to me. I walk through its streets, and feel myself almost alone. I meet but few I know, and the houses of old friends are filled with strange faces. The school-house looks unnatural, from the changes in the neighbouring buildings, and the thickets and the forests where I played have been cleared away. Even the church, with which some of my earliest recollections are associated, has been removed, and another stands near its former site. In the graveyard alone, I felt at home. How my deepest affections clustered over the grave of my own sainted mother; the letters on her tombstone are not more faithful to their trust, than is my memory to her pure and lovely virtues. There, too, were many whom I knew slightly, or of whom I have learned much from others. How sweet the thought that many of God's children are sleeping here, and their dust is precious to that Saviour who never sleeps, and who has the keys of death in his hand.

Next day I came to Pittsburgh, and after staying a few days with my sister, I will set out for home. . . .

Affectionately yours,

W. M. Lowrie.

Princeton, September 3d, 1841.

THE PRESENCE OF CHRIST WITH HIS PEOPLE.

(*Written in a book of Extracts, for Wm. H. Hornblower.*)

That Christ Jesus is constantly with his people, is a fact declared with surprising frequency both in the Old and New Testaments. It was he who appeared to Isaac, and said, "Sojourn in this land, and I will be with thee, and bless thee:" Gen. xxvi. 3. It was he who appeared to Jacob, as he lay upon the cold ground, and said, "I am with thee in all places; I will not leave thee:" Gen. xxviii. 15. It was he who appeared to Moses in the burning bush, and sending him to the court of Pharaoh, said, "Certainly I will be with thee:" Ex. iii. 12. And when David, in the sweetest strains of poetry and piety, sang, "The Lord is my shepherd, I shall not want; yea, though I walk through the valley of the shadow of death, I will fear no evil, for thou art with me," there is no doubt but it was the presence of the Saviour which he so gratefully acknowledges.

For a time Christ was with his disciples in the flesh, and they saw his glory: but it was "expedient" that he should depart. And yet he is with his people still. By his Spirit, by his providence, by his own personal and abiding presence, he is with them still, and will ever be with them. Almost the first thing recorded of him by Matthew is, that his name is "Emmanuel, God with us." His own last words on earth to his disciples were, "Lo, I am with you always." And this is not all. His prayer to the Father is, "Father, I will that they also whom thou hast given me, be with me where I am, that they may behold my glory."

That this Saviour may be ever with you, my dear brother, enlightening you, sanctifying you, sustaining you in sorrow, temptation and trials, making you useful in life and happy in death, and glorifying you with himself for ever,—is the earnest prayer of the writer of these few lines.

We have lived and laboured together pleasantly and profitably I trust, for a few short years. We must soon separate, but we will meet again. Till *then*, pray for me.

W. M. Lowrie.

New York, November 30th, 1841.

Mr. John O. Proctor—Dear Brother:—You will probably begin before now to suppose, that amid the many cares and labours preparatory to a final farewell to home and country, I have forgotten you; but I have not. I often think with great pleasure of the few days spent in Carlisle a year ago. How soon our pleasures vanish! yet when they are rational, and especially when they are Christian, they leave a savour behind them that survives their freshness, like the rose, which, though withered, still yields its fragrant perfumes.

My ordination took place Tuesday, November 9th, and the farewell meeting was held last Sabbath night in Dr. Spring's church. Addresses were made by Dr. Spring, my father, and myself. I feel at present very cheerful, and think I have seldom passed my time so pleasantly as within the last two months; yet it is not insensibility, nor want of affection to home and friends, that makes me so cheerful; for tears will flow at times at the thought of going far off, no more to return. Who knows what a day may bring forth? I am going out into the wide world, expecting to be gone for life; yet I know not but that a very few years may see me again at home. However, that is not probable; and now I do not desire it. It is a responsible step I am taking, and I never felt more in need of sustaining grace, and of the prayers of my friends to secure that grace for me.

Dec. 9th. The time of sailing is still uncertain. However, such a disappointment is not very grievous, for it gives the opportunity of being more at home; yet *I* should not talk of *home*, for there will soon be no such place in the wide world for me; and, indeed, for many years, I have spent but little of my time at home. Long a wanderer, I am a stranger in the place of my birth, where I spent my boyish days. When I was out there this fall, I felt alone as I walked through the streets, for a generation had grown up that knew me not, and almost all my old playmates were gone: some were dead; others married and settled in life; others moved far away; and, save here and there a gray-haired patriarch or a mother in Israel, I knew very few. I went into the church where my grandfather preached, and my parents had worshipped, and felt that I was almost alone; and I preached on the text, "I am a stranger in the earth," for no other passage of Scripture seemed to suit my own feelings so well. Now "the world is all before me, where to choose my place of rest, and Providence my guide;" though the poet was wrong there, for men can no more find a place of rest in this fleeting world, than the dove could find rest for the sole of her foot, when the waters of the deluge rolled round the earth. Like her we must fly, and that towards heaven, if we would avoid being buried in the waves of worldliness and spiritual death. Blessed be God, there is for us, also, an ark, where the weary may resort for shelter and defence, when the storm is abroad; and when the heavens and the earth shall have passed away, we may still repose with unshaken confidence on him who now walks on the waves that threaten to engulph us, and who then shall be our everlasting portion! I did not intend to have talked so much about myself, but at present nothing else occurred to me that I thought would interest you. I shall hope to hear from you very soon after I get to Singapore. Pray for me.

Your brother in Christ,

W. M. Lowrie.

New York, December 29th, 1841.

Mr. John Lloyd—Dear Brother:—I expected long ere this to have been on my way, but I am yet detained, and having a spare hour this afternoon, I can spend it very pleasantly in having a talk with you; though, unfortunately, the talking must be all on one side. The Huntress, which was to have gone a month ago, will hardly get off in less than two weeks from the present time. I am now all ready, or could be ready at a few hours' notice; and as my mind has become familiarized to the idea of departure, I begin to wish that it were over. As to my "feelings" in the prospect of departure, which you are so anxious to know, they are really so commonplace that they are scarcely worth the writing. I could hardly help being amused at the way in which you asked me to tell you what my feelings were at present; you seemed to attribute so much importance to them. I did not say much about my feelings, &c., in my last letters to you, because I had not time, and did not feel then just in the humour for that kind of writing. To tell the truth, there are so few persons to whom I care about telling my feelings, either orally or by letter, that lately I have got much out of the habit of saying anything about those deeper feelings that are known only to God, and my own soul.

Another thing that makes me say less about them is, that I have learned not to rely upon them so much as I once did; and indeed, I so often find it necessary to act without, and even against feelings, from a sense of duty, that this makes me less careful about them. They are certainly important; when we are in a proper "frame," and our "feelings" are urged on by a favourable impulse, there is a great deal of pleasure connected with them. But too much dependence upon them will often unfit us for duty. A man's feelings may take their colour from many things besides his religious state. He may be melancholy, from a low state of health, when he thinks it is a sense of sin that makes him sad. He may be cheerful and feel very grateful, as he supposes, from a sense of God's favour; and yet the greater part of his joy shall be caused by the mere flow of animal spirits. Our feelings arise very often, indeed, from something in ourselves; but our standard of duty is not anything in ourselves, but the eternal word of God. That is liable to no changes, and does not fluctuate with the ever-varying tide of human passion, but flows on ever the same. I do not undervalue the importance of feelings; they are like the perfumes that sweeten the gales which waft us on our course; and at times they may even be compared to the gales that assist the galley-slave, as he toils at his oars. But we are rowing up stream, and it will not do for us to lie on our oars, every time the breeze lulls. "Time and tide wait for no man," and we, on the other hand, in our heavenly course, must toil on without waiting for time or tide, or wind or wave. "Faint, yet pursuing." As John Bunyan says of religion among men, so may it be said of religion in the heart, "We must own religion in his rags, as well as when in his silver slippers, and stand by him too when bound in irons, as well as when he walketh the streets with applause."

But I did not intend to write so long a lecture on the feelings, nor do I want you to understand that I will not tell you my feelings, nor be glad to hear yours:—far from it; for some of the pleasantest hours I have ever spent, have been when communing with you, as we told each other what the Lord had done for our souls. I do think, however, that you attach more importance to the state of your feelings, than you ought; and hence, one reason why your harp is so often tuned to the notes of woe. I have often been struck with the remarks of Dr. Doddridge, in his Rise and Progress, chapter xxii. § 2,—"Religion consists chiefly in the resolution of the will for God," &c. That section is well worthy of your attention. But I must stop writing on this subject, or it will fill up my whole letter, and I have a good deal more to say.

This (December 29th) is the ever-memorable day in my history, when a "hope of heaven first budded in my heart." Seven years have rolled away since then. It seemed a long time then, to look forward seven years; now, to look back, how short! I have been looking backward to-day, and, amidst much that is painful and humiliating, I find also much that is very pleasant. I think that the most delightful object on which I fix my eyes, during all that time, is the walk you and I had one early spring morning, over the hills about Canonsburg. We talked of heaven, and it seemed as if while we talked, heaven was opened, and we could see its glories. Perhaps you have forgotten the time, but it seems to me I never shall. Every time I think of it, the scene comes up vividly before my mind. "I remember thee, oh my God, from the hill Mizar." Shall we ever enjoy another such hour? I almost fear at times, that added years have taken from me the power of appreciating so sensibly the pleasures enjoyed in the days of my "first love." Perhaps it is best they should. At any rate the instability of youth is well exchanged for the sobriety of riper years, when the latter adds to our capacity for glorifying our Father in heaven, even though it may take away the sense of novelty and delight once experienced. I have been trying to look forward seven years, but who knoweth what a day may bring forth? I can see nothing certainly, yet I can imagine enough to make me tremble. What should such creatures as we are do, if we had not an Almighty Saviour near?

I feel very much disappointed at not having seen you, and would ask you to come over new year's day, but I shall be out of the city for two or three days about that time. Farewell.

Your brother in Christ,

W. M. Lowrie.

New York, January 18th, 1842.

Mr. John M. Lowrie—Dear Cousin:—After long delay, the Huntress is to sail to-morrow. We are all well here, and I believe all in good spirits. Very seldom have I found my own mind so perfectly calm and peaceful, as it has been since last Friday. The Sabbath was to me one of my bright days, or rather, as I very seldom have bright, dazzling days, it was one of those calm, peaceful days, when the soul rises insensibly above the world, and dwells with the assurance of faith on unseen realities. Unexpectedly to me, but very gratefully, it was communion Sabbath in Mr. Smith's church, the church of which I have been a member here. He preached an excellent sermon in the morning on "As oft as ye eat this bread," &c. After communion, I made a few remarks, and the exercises were closed with prayer by my brother John. It was good to be there, and one of the elders remarked to me afterwards, "Truly we have had a feast, and a good day."

Yours in haste, with true affection,

W. M. Lowrie.

CHAPTER II.

January 19 to May 27, 1842.

Voyage to China—Journal in the Huntress.

Ship Huntress, Wednesday, Jan. 26th, 1842.
At sea, N. lat. 33° 38′, W. long. 54° 04′.

My Dear Mother—As it is just a week to-day since leaving home, and circumstances are favourable, I shall commence my promised journal; though I have so much to write up from my pencil notes, that the very idea of it almost appals me:—so much by way of preface.

We got under weigh at half past twelve last Wednesday, and, with three hearty cheers from the crew, proceeded down the bay. The novelty and excitement of my situation kept me from any very unpleasant feelings at parting. I ought to say more than this, however. The conviction that I was in the path of duty, and the felt presence and sustaining influence of an all-gracious Saviour, upheld me and carried me safely through a scene that I had dreaded almost as much as death itself.

As there was little or no wind, the captain and pilot thought it best to anchor for the night in Prince's Bay—a large and very beautiful and safe bay, just inside of the Hook, and wait till morning. Accordingly the steamboat left us at 3½ P. M., and I felt really glad, when I saw Mr. B. parting from his father and brother, that I had come alone. The quietness and deliberation of such partings are killing. Farewell speeches read very well, but when one is swallowing his feelings and choking almost with emotion, and doing his utmost to retain his calmness and composure, the sooner in such circumstances the better. A silent shake of the hand and away is enough for me. It is bad enough to think of it now.

After reading my Bible with more than ordinary interest, I went to bed at ten P. M., as quietly and calmly as if I had been at home, and dreamed of you all before morning.

Thursday, January 20th. I was wakened early by hearing the men at work on different parts of the rigging, weighing anchor, &c. I dressed and went out on deck before sunrise. I found Mr. K. there, and the captain soon came out. There was as yet no wind, but the pilot, who was "wide awake," thought a breeze would spring up about sunrise, and they were preparing sail, to catch the first breath. We did not get fairly started, however, until after nine A. M., when a light breeze filled the higher sails, (topsails and top-gallants,) and we slowly moved away. Several other vessels, outward bound, had anchored near us, and they followed close in our wake. We soon got outside of the Hook, and when fairly under weigh, the pilot left us, at a quarter before twelve. I had hastily written a few lines to you and father, which I sent back by him. He sprang lightly over the side of the vessel into a row boat that was waiting for him, and the last link was broken! We kept on in somewhat of a south-east direction, and soon the only object that could be seen, was the Highlands, south of the entrance of the channel to New York. I could hardly realize my situation.

I soon found Mr. B. standing at the stern, looking rather pale. I could not help laughing, though I pitied him, and wrapping myself in my cloak, as there was a fresh breeze, I sat down on a stool in the stern of the vessel. The motion soon began to affect me, and when I went to dinner, there were none at the table except the captain and Mr. K. I found I was "too far gone" to eat anything, and feeling very dizzy, went out into the open air. Though I felt more and more sick, I could not help being struck with the extreme ludicrousness of the appearance of a sea-sick passenger. How the old sailors must laugh among themselves at the pale faces and wo-begone countenances and staggering gait of the "men with gloves on!" I was quite sick on Friday, and till three P. M. on Saturday, when I went out on deck, and staid about two hours. We were then about the middle of the Gulf Stream, and the air was quite mild and pleasant. Thermometer, about 63°. I saw a shoal of fish playing in the water. Mr. K. said they were porpoises, but I could not see their shape.

I felt a great deal better; went to table and ate a light supper, and immediately after turned in for the night and slept pretty well. Dreamed about home, and my trip to Ogdensburgh, and fifty other things.

There! I have got safely to the end of last week, and I'll now turn in for this night. It is now past four bells, i. e., past ten o'clock, P. M., with us, while my watch, which I have not altered since leaving home, says it is a little past nine with you. I suppose you are now at family worship. Am I right in thinking, that the absent one is remembered at this hour? But I need not ask the question, for I know it. Good night.

Sabbath morning, January 23d. Rose and went out about six o'clock, New York time, but here it was past sunrise. The air was very mild and pleasant, and I found little use for my cloak. Temperature of the water 71°; air, about 63°. Was out on deck most of the morning, when it was cool and pleasant. The sky was covered with clouds almost all day. I thought of trying to preach in the afternoon, but felt almost too weak. The captain, too, was quite unwell; and as he and I had concluded nothing definite when we spoke of the subject before, I did not like to make any move, without consulting him further. Could not read much; it made me light-headed to read more than two or three pages.

Monday, 24th. Quite a gale rose soon after midnight, and took us all aback. The captain was just getting into a refreshing sleep, when he heard the sound, and, rushing out on deck, he was wet through in an instant by the rain and the sea; and though he came back soon, yet he was much the worse for the exposure. I heard the loud and rapid orders of the mate, and the quick tread of many feet about deck, but, knowing I could be of no use, I kept my berth. Went out about seven o'clock, though there was so much motion in the ship, that I was nearly sick, and could hardly dress myself. It was blowing quite a gale, and the ship was driving on, and rolling like an egg-shell. Only think of a vessel whose weight must be several hundred tons, probably 1200, tossing about like a cork! What immense power to produce such effects! And how great and powerful must He be who holds the winds in his fists, and the seas in the hollow of his hands! I stood and gazed on the dashing and rolling waves, and thought of Him who "walked on the waters." How sweet to think his name is "Emmanuel, God with us."

The gale continued all day Monday and Tuesday, and, as may be supposed, we had a dreary time. Not being perfectly recovered from sea-sickness, we all felt it more or less. There was a constant gale, the wind roaring and groaning through the rigging, the foam and spray breaking over the forecastle, and sometimes over the after-parts of the vessel. The decks were dripping wet all the time, and showers of rain falling every half-hour.

During the morning the wind tore our jib to ribbons, and we were obliged to take in most of the sails, and drive on under close-reefed topsails, and reefed mainsail. (To "reef a sail" is to take in about-one third of it; to "close-reef" is to take in two-thirds.)

I do not know what our crew think of their passengers, but many sailors think that ladies and clergymen are very unfortunate people to have on shipboard. We tried to talk some in the evening, but it would not do, and we turned in to hope for better days.

Tuesday, January 25th. Gale still continued, though not so hard, perhaps, as yesterday; but still severe, and the motion of the ship, if possible more unpleasant. I could eat but little at breakfast, and after it was over, I leaned my head against the mizzen-mast, which comes through the table just aft of my seat, and felt very uncomfortable. The Bible was lying just under my face, and I opened it almost mechanically. It opened at Job xiv., and I read that touching and melancholy passage with a deeper experience of its truth than almost ever before:

"Man that is born of a woman is of few days, and full of trouble.

He cometh forth like a flower, and is cut down: he fleeth also as a shadow, and continueth not.

Man lieth down and riseth not, till the heavens be no more. They shall not wake, nor be raised out of sleep.

Thou prevailest against him and he passeth, thou changest his countenance and sendest him away."

Wednesday, 26th. A splendid day! After a few light showers, it cleared off gloriously; the sea became smooth, and the sun shone out pleasantly; and with a pleasant breeze, that soon dried up the moisture of the decks and rigging, we held on the "even tenor of our way." We sat in the sun, and all felt decidedly better. The captain was out, and seeing me reading, "Two Years before the Mast," he said, "That's one of the greatest books ever written. It is a real masterpiece. There's a great many men, and officers, and captains, just as they are there described, though they don't all like to own it."

A pigeon or gull followed us for several hours to-day, flying with almost no exertion. It was as large as a duck, though longer, ash-coloured above, and white beneath, with a long bill.

Took the opportunity of speaking to the captain about religious services. He was perfectly willing to have service on the Sabbath, and seemed anxious to know if we could have singing. He said there was no objection to the passengers having prayers as often as they chose in the after-cabin; but when I spoke of having the men attend once a day, (which the mate recommended,) he answered in such a way, that I considered it prudent not to afford him the opportunity of giving a direct refusal, at least for the present.

A light shower in the afternoon cooled the air a little too much. Thermometer during the day ranged from 68° to 72° in the shade. The wind has increased some, and the vessel rolls a good deal. Saw a sail on our stern to-day, a great way off, which may have been the same one we saw yesterday.

Finished "Two Years before the Mast," and lent it to the captain, who wants to read it. Overhauled some of my papers, and began to lay out brother Owen's route to India. Read a page of the Brother Jonathan, gazed at the deep blue sea for a long time, listened to the canary bird, and talked with Mr. B., whom I find a very pleasant companion indeed. Saw a gull flying about and sporting in the waves. Its flight was

> "O'er the mountain wave,
> Its home upon the deep."

Yet methinks like the dove that Noah sent out from the ark, or like the Christian pilgrim in the world, it would here "find no rest for the sole of its foot."

Saturday night, January 29th. How many thoughts of past, of distant, of high and holy and heavenly things it brings! It speaks of the Sabbath—of rest. But I am tossed on the wide and heaving sea; there is no rest on earth, not till we come to the heavenly world, where "there is no more sea." Now the ship is rolling in the waves, everything here is moving. I am a stranger and a pilgrim in the earth. I look about in vain for some solid, unmoving foundation, but I see none below the skies. Upwards, I see the heavenly host, and they appear fixed. I know that the things of the invisible heavens are firm. That city hath foundations. Its builder and maker is God.

> "Heaven is the Christian pilgrim's home,
> His rest at every stage."

Our passengers have begun to amuse themselves with talking and planning about their return home, but I do not join them in this. Even now, my outward condition is better than His, who "had not where to lay his head;" and for his sake, willingly do I "confess that I am a stranger in the earth." Good night; I am pensive, but happy. It is now near your time for family worship; and though absent in body, in spirit I will join with you. The peace of God keep you all!

Monday, January 31st. Yesterday was the Sabbath; the sun rose clear and bright, and the day was fine, with sufficient wind just to keep the sails tolerably full. The men were all free soon after nine A. M., and soon after ten, we met for preaching in the fore-cabin.

I took my station by the door of my room, where I could hold on to the back of the seat round the table. The two ladies sat on the bench just before me, and the mate next to them, the captain on a chair at the corner of the table, Mr. B. and Mr. K. on my right hand, and the men along the side and end of the room opposite me. They were all present, I believe, except the man at the helm and the second mate, who had to keep on the lookout. The room was quitè full. The services were commenced by reading 2 Kings v., then followed prayer and singing. I set the tunes myself, and was pretty loudly accompanied by several of the crew, some two or three of whom knew the tunes, while others guessed at them; on the whole the singing was tolerable, but I hope it will improve. After singing the hymn, I preached on Luke xvii. 11—19; Christ's healing the ten lepers. My hearers were very attentive indeed, especially one of the men, whom I had spoken to several times, and whose jolly air and hearty singing at the ropes had attracted my attention. I was, however, a good deal embarrassed. My head almost touched the ceiling. My audience was almost within arm's length; some were in fact so; the room was small, and not being sufficiently accustomed to the motion of the vessel, I had to hold on all the time to the back of the seat to keep my balance. Then by having to lead in the singing, there was no time to compose my thoughts, and I suppose I made but blundering work of it. After preaching, there was prayer and singing again, and the benediction—the whole exercises taking about fifty minutes. I wanted to have them as short as possible, and not knowing exactly how much time they would take, this contributed a little to embarrass me. I assure you, I felt for a while after the services were over, as though I should like to hide myself from the sight of everybody. However, I could not but believe, that I had endeavoured to do right; and though for a while half tempted to think that such services were of no use, yet on the whole I was glad that a beginning had been made. We shall probably do better hereafter. Soon after service, Mr. Gillespie told me that just before service, he had gone into the forecastle to see if all the men had come forward. He found one there who was not quite ready, but said he was coming. "Ah, Mr. Gillespie, it is seven years since I heard a prayer." It was the same man who appeared so attentive.

Saw a couple of flying-fish to-day, and thought at first that they were little birds; one of them flew with an irregular flight more than forty yards before it touched the water. The sight of them made me think of a passage in Henry Martyn's diary, where he says that he thought his own aspirations after holiness and heaven, were short and low and uncertain, like the flight of the flying-fish. The sight and the thought made me condemn myself.

Had prayers in the cabin at eight P. M., and afterwards a long talk with Mr. Gillespie about the Wall-street and Middle Dutch churches, and about a voyage Mr. G. made from Liverpool to New York with 135 steerage passengers, several of whom died on the voyage. He had almost the whole care of them, and dates his first serious impressions to what he then witnessed. Then we talked about the difficulty of maintaining the life of religion on shipboard, and in places of trial, the danger of worldliness, &c.

Friday, Feb. 4th. Another glorious day. Up and out before the sun; saw him rise. My vocabulary wants words to express the richness and beauty of the clouds

"Which sat about the East,
And wantoned with his golden locks."

After tea, looked over a little school-book in astronomy, with maps, &c., and concluded to try some of the constellations; was quite charmed with my success, for I made out the whole constellation of Orion, and single stars in four or five others. The ladies, who were promenading the decks, joined me, and after showing them my newly acquired knowledge, we spoke of him "who loosed the bands of Orion, and sent forth Mazzaroth in his season." I became quite enraptured with the study, and promise myself a good deal of pleasure in pursuit of it. Do you remember how, one night, as we were going to church, I pointed out to you the North Star, and Orion's belt? I have been looking up so long, that my neck fairly aches. How little we know of the stars! They are, doubtless, at least that is my own firm conviction, inhabited worlds,—all displaying the power, and wisdom, and goodness of our Creator. What wonderful and varied displays of his attributes would be seen by one who could visit them all! I am inclined to believe—though, of course, it is mere conjecture—that every one of them is arranged in a different order, inhabited by different kinds of rational and irrational beings, with different genera and species of plants and minerals; aye, and different kinds of things for which we have neither names nor conceptions. Who shall limit the works of Him, whose understanding is infinite, and who is wonderful in working?

Monday, Feb. 7th. Yesterday was a very calm, delightful day. Sufficient breeze to carry us on from five to seven miles an hour, and so steady, that there was very little motion. Had service in the morning, at ten o'clock. Preached on Psalm xxxvii. 5; and being less embarrassed, I got on much more comfortably than on the preceding Sabbath. The attention was very good indeed. After service it was quite pleasant to look to the forward part of the ship. The forecastle doors were open, and some of the men were lying in their berths or sitting on their chests, reading. Others were sitting on the windlass and spars, or standing by the sides of the ship, reading or talking, all neatly dressed, and apparently all at their ease, and very comfortable. I think our crew are a very good-looking set of men indeed. One of the boys was sitting by the ship's side, doing nothing. The mate went past him, and as he passed, pulled out a tract from his pocket, and gave it to him. Afternoon and evening passed off pleasantly and pretty quietly. The passengers were talking together in the lower cabin, in the evening, where they had cakes and nuts, &c., and sent for me to join them, but I excused myself, and retired to my own room. It was Monthly Concert evening, and I thought of the many Monthly Concerts I had attended,—of the last one, and of the work before me. Commenced an essay, or address, or—I hardly know what yet, —but something for Sabbath-schools, which, if it is ever finished, I'll try to have published, provided I think it worthy of that honour.

This morning I mustered np courage enough to climb up to the main-cross-trees. You may be sure I held tight to the ropes, when I had got so high. I was surprised to find how small everything looked on deck. The ship seemed no broader than a common row-boat, and the men on deck only like children.

Saturday, Feb. 12th. Trade-wind still continues, and we have come over a thousand miles in five days—pretty good sailing that. Calm, pleasant day, and rather warm; looked very much like rain for several hours, but it has cleared off beautifully, and we have the promise of another pleasant Sabbath. This afternoon, as I was standing by the gangway, I observed another kind of fish, the "skip-jack." There was a large shoal of them, playing about in the water, and leaping sometimes ten feet, though commonly not more than three or four. I could not observe the shape or size very distinctly; they were perhaps as large as a shad. Saw a very large flock of dark-coloured birds, but they were too far off to be distinctly seen. Star-gazing to-night, and saw a couple of stars you never see in the United States—Canopus and Acherner. The north star is fast sinking, and we shall soon lose sight of it.

Saturday night again! The past week has fled away swiftly and pleasantly. Soon the Saturday night of life will come, and the unending Sabbath of eternity will dawn.

Sabbath, Feb. 13th. A calm, beautiful, and glorious day. Quite clear all morning, and light fleecy clouds in the after part of the day, which tempered the air. Preached at ten, A. M., on 2 Cor. v. 21. Audience very attentive. I still lead in singing, and must say, it was to-day quite respectable. Sung the last hymn (we only sing two) to Old Hundred, and almost every one joined in. Heard a voice I had not heard before singing, and, looking up, found it was the captain, singing with a good deal of earnestness. After dinner went up to the main-top, where I could feel myself alone, and, sitting down, read and sang, and looked out on the blue sea for an hour. It was good to be there. I was above the cares and the business of the deck. A light breeze made my station pleasant, and I looked out on the calm and gently heaving sea, where the sun shone down with bright and yet undazzling rays. I felt as a Christian sometimes feels when all around is calm, and the Spirit's influences, like gentle breezes, move upon his soul, and the favour of God, like the sun's glad beams, comforts his heart. Yet still it was not home; the rolling sea was still there, and no one could say how soon the calm might become a storm. It was not heaven, it was only a foretaste of the eternal rest. My meditations, however, were disturbed by the sight of a large fish making his way after the ship.

The sailmaker said it was probably a shark, because we were now in the "shark country."

Tuesday, Feb. 15th. Rain during the night, and quite a heavy shower in the morning. Caught about 100 gallons for the stock, and the men and boys washed a good many of their clothes, and hung them about the rigging to dry. It then fell dead calm, and the ship lay like a log on the water. The captain said it was just the kind of weather for sharks, and he got the shark-hook rigged out, and baited with a piece of pork, and hung it out astern. Very soon a small shark showed himself, and seized it; the line was drawn in, and he was quickly on deck. He floundered about at a great rate, but was soon hauled to the middle of the vessel, and a handspike thrust down his throat; he then received several blows on the back of the head with a heavy iron hammer, and lay quite still. Although he was dead, and the second mate opened him, took out all the entrails, and washed the inside of his body—would you believe it?—after all this, he floundered about, and beat the deck violently with his tail, and looked so savage, that it was found necessary to thrust the handspike down his mouth again. He very soon became quiet, and we looked at him. He was five feet four inches from the nose to the end of tail; fore fins, fifteen inches long; back fin, nine inches; tail, eighteen inches: quite a young one. He had evidently been feeding pretty heartily, because in his stomach we found several large pieces of squid, a fish that is said to grow to as large a size as any in the ocean. There were a couple of little fishes swimming about him and clinging to his back, while in the water, and one of them clung so tight, that he came up on deck with him. It was a sucker, which I have in spirits, and will try to send home.

In the afternoon the mate caught a bonito, a fish about two feet long, and perhaps six inches in diameter in the middle. He was perfectly round in every part from the head to the tail; on the back he was of a most beautiful purple, and the belly was white and golden yellow in streaks, the colours gradually mingling with red. Altogether I do not wonder that the Portuguese called him bonito, the beautiful. The fins on the back and side fold up like a fan, and can be laid so close to the body that you may pass your hand over them without feeling them. Its great peculiarity, however, consists in the heart, which is double, the largest part being red and the other white. The abdominal cavity is very small, and the fish is almost a solid mass of flesh. We had part of it cooked, and it formed a not unpalatable dish.

Thursday, Feb. 17th. To-day I paid a visit aloft, and went out to the end of the main-top-gallant-yard, which is considerably higher than the cross-trees; but the reason I did it was, I found they had fixed a ladder from the cross-trees to the royal-mast, so that there was no difficulty. Being now used to being aloft, I sat on the yard-arm for some time and enjoyed the prospect. It is like being at the top of a steeple. I went up again by moonlight, and the view was very beautiful, even sublime.

We crossed the line sometime last night, and were at twelve M. in lat. 27′ south. That is a very good passage. It was just four weeks yesterday since leaving New York, and four weeks to-day since leaving Sandy Hook. This is one of the great divisions of our voyage. We shall now begin to ask how long it will be before we pass the Cape, and then, how long to the straits of Sunda.

Friday, Feb. 18th. Took the south-east trade-wind, about four o'clock this morning, and we are now moving off gaily in a south-west course. We shall run down now towards South America.

This is my birth-day. Another mile-stone in the journey of my life is past. I have come by a smooth road so far, and it does not seem long; but I cannot tell what my road shall be hereafter, nor how long. I often feel, when I look back, as Milton did on a similar occasion.

> "My hasting days fly on with full career,
> But my late spring no bud or blossom showeth."

But let them fly—

> "If I have grace to use them so,
> As ever in my great Taskmaster's eye."

Aye—and let them speed their flight. I would not be impatient, I would not desert my post, however incompetent to fill it, nor however great its dangers, till my discharge comes. But if they hasten on,

> "They'll waft me sooner o'er
> This life's tempestuous sea,
> Then I shall reach the peaceful shore
> Of blest eternity."

This has been a very pleasant day; too warm to be in the sun, but in the upper cabin we had a cool breeze all day, and the awning and sails keep the sun from beating on the roof. A shoal of porpoises were playing under the bows of the vessel for some time, but they were "old fellows," and kept out of the harpoon's way. In the evening, saw the Southern Cross for the first time. It has not been visible before, until after I had gone to bed. I do not think, however, that any of the constellations I have seen are as splendid as that of Orion.

Sabbath, Feb. 20th. A very delightful day, except that we are becalmed most of the day. However, that made it all the pleasanter for me, on account of its being the Sabbath, and thereby giving us a quiet time. Preached on Ephesians v. 16, "Redeeming the time,"—a duty greatly neglected on shipboard. In the afternoon we did see a sail, homeward bound, but ten or twelve miles off, and the breeze so light, that there was no chance of our speaking her. The captain was greatly disappointed. He came away from home almost sick, and is very anxious to write to his wife. He is a very kind-hearted man, and often speaks of his family with very great affection.

Our sunsets now are very splendid. The sky is quite as beautiful as I ever saw it at Princeton; and if there were only the green fields and waving forests to receive the last rays of light, the prospect would be quite as fine as it commonly is on land. Captain Lovett is a great admirer of such scenes. After tea, I sat out at the stern alone, and sang over a number of our old favourite tunes. No one here cares much about music; and I generally go by myself when I wish to sing; but in a ship, with so many around, it is impossible to be all alone.

Thursday, Feb. 24th. A delightful, pleasant day. Captain "never knew so much fine weather at once on an outward-bound voyage." Having finished Neal's History of the Puritans, I commenced Bancroft, which is quite a relief. The evenings are so beautiful, and the moon shines with such brightness, that I have spent several of the past evenings on deck; sometimes gazing on the evening sky, and suffering all kinds of calm imaginations to float through the mind, remembering and repeating scraps of poetry, like this—

"How many days with mute adieu,
Have gone down yon untrodden sky,
And still it looks as clear and blue
As when it first was hung on high;"

sometimes learning the names of different stars, and comparing their colours and positions. You know what the Apostle says—"one star differeth from another star in glory." I often wonder I never observed that before, for the glory of Sirius, with its more than lunar brightness, differs widely from the red blaze of Arcturus; and Canopus and Capella, and Regulus and Aldebaran, have colours that the vocabulary of the earth can hardly name. Truly the heavens declare the glory of God. At other times I walk on deck, and think of the past, and the present, and the future. Sunshine and showers, and smiles and tears, and lofty oaks and little flowers, mountains and valleys, and rich and poor, —where was the one ever seen, that the other was not near?

Had a long talk with the sailmaker to-night. He is by birth a Swede, but left Sweden at the age of four years; has been at sea twenty-eight years; shipwrecked three or four times; once, off Cape Horn; once, seven days without a mouthful of food; another time, seventeen days on so short an allowance, that at the end of that time hardly one of the crew could walk; once, nearly dead from an attack of fever caused by giving up tobacco, the use of which he was obliged to resume. He seems to be a serious sort of a man; has a number of pious phrases, and said that, "he could spend two Sundays as easily as one; always plenty to do on Sunday,"—meaning that the Sabbath never hung heavy on his hands. He says he reads his Bible a great deal, but often wishes he could get a great many parts of it explained, "which worry and bother" him. This was just what I wanted, and it was in fact the reason why I commenced talking with him, that I might propose the formation of a Bible class. I accordingly did so, and he seemed very glad, and said he would try and get some more to join him, and we shall probably make a commencement next Sabbath.

Monday, Feb. 28th. Fine weather still continues. On Saturday, saw a "Portuguese man-of-war," *i. e.* a little semi-transparent bubble, of a pale rose colour, floating on the water. It is a sea animal substance; is something like jelly. In fine weather, a great many are occasionally seen about ships. They are of a triangular pyramidal form, and are very pretty little things. The captain prophesied that we should see land on Sunday, and also a sail. Sunday came

—a fine day. "We always have fine weather on Sunday." Preached in the morning on the Messianic prophecies of Genesis; attention not so good as heretofore, and I was afterwards a good deal disappointed when the sailmaker told me that he had spoken to several of the men about forming a Bible class, but they were ashamed to be seen in such an employment; several "would like to, but if they did all the rest would be at them." However, I have not given up hope yet. We had hardly got through with the service in the morning, when the second mate, whose look-out it was, said that land was in sight. It was the Island of Trinidad, and the rocks of Martin Vas—Lat. 20° 28′ S. Long. 20° 50′ W. When we saw them first, they were twenty or thirty miles off; but we afterwards, in the course of the afternoon, passed within ten or twelve miles of the rocks of Martin Vas.

Wednesday, March 2d. Rain in the morning, and a much pleasanter day. Progress slow. Have already lost all the comparative advantages of our speedy passage to the line, and the officers would now be willing to compound for ninety days to Angier, or even more.

After prayers I went out to gaze at the stars, paying particular attention to those about the south pole. I think that this is the most splendid part of the heavens; or at least, that it will very well compare with that part of which the constellation Orion is the centre. These stars are all seen at one view. The Southern Cross is a very beautiful object. It is more like a boy's kite, however. And the Southern Triangle is also very conspicuous, because there are almost no other stars near it. The most remarkable, however, of all these stars, is Bungula. It changes colour every two or three minutes, from a bright red to a beautiful sea-green, and is constantly twinkling. Looking at it through the captain's spy-glass, it showed the red and green colours combined. The captain says he can see only the twinkling, but Mr. B., the mate, and myself, have all remarked the alternations of red and green. These stars, however, are not the only wonders of this part of the heavens.

In clear nights when the moon is not shining, we see also the Magellan clouds. These are three in number, in the form of the letter V.

A, at the vertex of the letter, is situated between Acrux and Beta in the cross. It is black, but right in the middle is a single star or luminous opening, that may be seen with the naked eye, and, examined through the telescope, is quite bright. B, is a large white cloud, but no stars are seen in it, at least not with the naked eye; and C is about one third as large. B and C are about as bright as the milky-way.

After gazing at these wonderful objects, I turned the spy-glass to look at the Pleiades. One has no idea on looking at them with the naked eye, of the number and beauty of the stars in the cluster, as seen through a spy-glass.

Thursday, March 3d. A little rain and wind in the morning; a dead calm from ten A. M. till after sunset; a sea as smooth as glass, all the while; showers after dark, and a light wind afterwards, which continued all the night, were the external appearances of this day. A solitary porpoise showed himself under the bows of the boat, but after playing about a little, as if in mockery of our motionless condition, he swam away. The motions of the porpoise are exceedingly rapid, and when the ship is going ten miles an hour, they will frequently collect together and sport in the foam directly underneath her bows.

Saturday, March 5th. The men were at work on the rigging all day yesterday and to-day, and their long-drawn and strange cries, the development of the muscles of their limbs as they pulled and hauled about the rigging, and the numerous knots and splices and contrivances to secure the rigging, have afforded me a good deal of instructive amusement. A sail has been in sight all day; an English top-sail schooner, going the same course with ourselves, but not so fast; she has fallen astern.

It seems strange how the time passes away. I have never on land found it fly more swiftly than it has done this voyage. Sabbath comes and Monday, and, almost before I know it, Saturday night is back again. My employments still occupy all my time. I commonly prepare a sermon every week; and as I meet the ladies in a Bible class on Sabbath afternoon and Wednesday morning, that also takes time. I had hoped to have a class formed among the men, but am afraid I shall not succeed. They seem ashamed to be seen engaged in such an employment. I stand very much alone as to religious exercises; and the worst of it all is, that though I am engaged in the business, I have not the spirit of Paul. I look forward with much fear at times to this Chinese mission. It hardly seems possible, that I should do anything in less than twenty or thirty years; and yet I have never seriously allowed myself to anticipate that length of life. But "sufficient unto the day is the evil thereof." I do not regret in the least the course I have taken. I have never wished since I left home, that my face were turned back to the land of my fathers.

Not that I have forgotten you, not that I do not prize its privileges. I feel most sensibly even here, that I should rejoice to go up once more with the great congregation to the house of God. I feel most deeply that there is an influence in the society of Christians to sustain the man of God, which he is not aware of, till removed from it. But when I look back on my short life, smooth and unruffled and unvaried by any striking occurrence as it may seem to others to have been, I can mark the way in which I have been led along by an unseen hand, severely tried and almost bowed to the earth, when others thought me gay and unconcerned. Yet upheld and impelled onward, time after time, when the indolence or the quietness of my own temper would have kept me back, I can say, "Thus far hath the Lord helped me;" and surely I can say, "Not unto me, but to thy name give the glory." If my Master has so long led me and fed me in the wilderness, if he has so long guided me on the voyage of life, and has showed me so many favours hitherto, he will surely still keep me and bring me at length to my "desired haven." If I might but give some proof that the religion I profess is not in vain, if I might but glorify in some feeble degree the Saviour who has so graciously redeemed me, then I could rejoice and die. Yet perhaps it is best for me to see little fruit of my labours in my lifetime, that I may not depend on anything short of the righteousness of Christ Jesus. It would be dangerous for me to be looked up to as some great one. "The Lord reigneth—let the earth rejoice." It is well that he chooses our lot, and appoints us our work. My life has not been long, but it has been amply long enough to show me that I should fail most wofully, if I had the sole care of my own course.

Monday, March 7th. Yesterday was a beautiful day, and my mind was at peace. I preached on Phil. ii. 6—11, with more ease and fluency, and was listened to with more attention, than at any time since coming on board; and when the evening shades came over the sea, I was happy still. During the day I brought out a copy of the Pilgrim's Progress, and laid it on the table. In a very short time Mr. B. was reading it very busily, and when he laid it down, the captain took it up. "The Pilgrim's Progress!" said he, "I read this a long time ago; I think I would like to read it again." He commenced right away, and has been reading at it very busily since. He said this evening that he liked his book very much. Yesterday evening the sunset was very beautiful. I would try and describe it, but can give you no adequate idea of it. You will perhaps wonder that I write so much about the sky and stars, but except in our own little world on board there is nothing but sea and sky to write about.

I went up to the cross-trees to look out on the ocean, and the scene was indescribably grand. For several miles all around, the sea was covered with large waves, each wave breaking into masses of foam many yards in extent, and the noise of the winds and waves together made it impossible for me to hear Mr. B., who called to me to "go up higher." The sun was shining almost all day, which added greatly to the splendor of the scene. Several albatrosses have been flying about the ship, and, though she goes eight or ten miles an hour, they make nothing whatever of flying around her, sailing off a mile or two on each side and astern, and then coming up again. It is wonderful with what ease they fly. They will go a mile without any apparent motion of their wings, and that too in the face of a gale, that sent us ploughing up the waves at the rate of ten or eleven miles an hour. In fact they fly better when there is a gale than in a calm. It is very hard for them to rise off the water, unless there is some wind going, but if there is any wind, they turn their heads to it, and are speedily in the air. They will skim over the water when it is rough with waves six or eight feet high, and never wet a feather. The captain says they have several joints in their wings, (which are prodigiously long,) and when the wind is strong, they "take in a reef and shorten sail." I used to think they were all of one size and colour, but they are not. One that I saw was of "the first magnitude,"—wings extending ten feet or more. There are others of the second, third, and fourth magnitudes. They do not appear, however, nearly so large when seen flying as when on deck. Some are white, some are dusky brown, some are brown on the backs of the wings and white on the body above and beneath, and on the lower part of the wings. Some have a dark belt or ring round the neck, and some are somewhat mottled. I have not seen any other varieties of colour. One old brown fellow flew so close to the ship's stern, that I could see the white of his eyes.

Monday, March 14th. Preached yesterday on Phil. iii. 1—11. But it being quite a calm, the swell caused the ship to roll so much, and the rudder creaked so constantly, as it always does in a calm, that I had not much satisfaction in the exercises. Bible class as usual. Mr. B. always attends, though he takes no active part. I find this quite an interesting and profitable service.

The weather, after being very cold for three or four days, began to moderate yesterday morning, and now is very comfortable. The wind is from the north; which in this part of the world is our warm wind. I think the sunsets in this part of this hemisphere are different from those in the United States, but I have not yet observed them sufficiently to state wherein that difference consists. It would be endless to describe every sunset, to say nothing of the impossibility of giving you any idea of sights which I can find no words in any language I know to describe.

It is just eight weeks to-day since leaving New York. I hardly feel as if I ought to say, "since leaving *home*," because it seems as if I had no right to say "home." Psa. cxix. 19.

Yesterday evening as I was looking up at the stars, one of the sailors, a young man of very intelligent countenance and pleasing manner, with whom I had exchanged a few words several times before, came up to me and began to speak of the stars; then of the delight one finds in knowledge. This led me to remark, what a proof that was of the immortality of the soul, that it was constantly expanding in capacity. He then asked me in a very serious manner, what I thought of the question, "Are any of the heathen saved who never heard of Christ?" I told him I thought not,—speaking of adult heathen; and mentioned several passages in Romans, that induced me to think as I did. This led him to say, that he had been in the habit of reading the Bible every day on this voyage, but he found a great many things he could not make out or understand. I offered him any assistance in my power, for which he seemed very grateful, and said he would avail himself of it. He then said, "What is it to be religious? A young lady asked me when in New York last time—'Are you religious?' I said 'Of course I am. I believe in Christ,—that he is the Son of God,—that he did live on the earth, and that he died to save men's souls'—was I right in saying I am religious?'" I told him that what he believed was not all that was necessary; that many bad men, and even the devils, could say they believed that much. "That's true," said he, with a good deal of emphasis. I then went on to explain what true faith was, but much to my regret the watch was soon changed and he had to leave me. I hope to see him again, however, before long. I could not help thinking at the time, how little one can tell of what is passing in the minds of others. A few weeks ago, as I was thinking over the character of the men on board, I had set it down in my mind, that this young man would be the least likely to think of religion of almost all on board. There seemed to be a sort of "don't care about it" air in him. I regret that I have very few opportunities of much intercourse with the men. There are almost always several of them together. Indeed I scarcely ever see one alone, except the man at the wheel; and it is against the rules to talk with him: consequently I have few means of influencing them except on the Sabbath. The ship is so well supplied with tracts, through Mr. Gillespie's care, that I find but little use for mine.

Sabbath, March 20th. A fair pleasant day to commence with, but soon clouded over. Preached on 2 Tim. iii. 16; but as there was some wind, and a heavy sea, which there is constantly here, the mizzen-mast creaked dreadfully, and I had little satisfaction in the services. Besides, I saw it was growing darker, and the men were looking out occasionally, as if a squall were coming. The services were no sooner over than they were called to the ropes to take in some of the sails. So we had it, showers and sunshine, the rest of the day. About 9 A. M. the breeze freshened, so that we went on ten miles an hour. This has continued till the present time, Monday, P. M. About dark, things looked so squally, that it was thought necessary to send down the main royal-yard—the fore and mizzen-royals had been sent down several days ago—and we had showers and squalls till I went to bed, after ten P. M. Going out about seven A. M., I found that the greater part of the sails were furled, and we were driving on under close-reefed topsails. The ship looked very bare with so many of her sails taken in, and as the sea was high, she rolled more than I ever knew her to do before. The wind whistled through the rigging, and our ship dashed on like a frightened bird; but everything is snug and secure, and as far as we can see, there is no reason for alarm. Several little birds are flying about, and apparently enjoying the commotion of the water. As I looked at them, several times to-day, I thought of the words of our Saviour, "one of them shall not fall on the ground without your Father. Fear not therefore; ye are of more value than many sparrows." It is pleasant to be thus reminded of the presence of our all-gracious God.

Tuesday, March 22nd. The waves were even higher than yesterday, and were much broken, so that to look out astern, or off from the side of the ship, there seemed to be a large number of rocky hills in the sea, and the ship was making her way over and between them. I have seen nothing so grand since the voyage commenced. The waves would mount up twenty feet or more, and burst into a wide sheet of foam; while still further off, the white foaming tops of others would lift themselves up in the horizon, and the constant dashing and roaring of the waves combined together to fill the mind with exalted ideas of Him, who holds the waters in the hollow of his hands, and stilleth the noise of their waves. "An undevout astronomer is mad," but surely a careless sailor is worse: with the tokens of God's power and presence everywhere around him, one would think he could not move a muscle without thinking of his Maker and Preserver. Yet alas! he does not like to retain God in his knowledge. But though the scene was grand, it was not very comfortable on board. Such constant rolling and tossing and pitching of the ship, made it almost impossible to study; and it was very fatiguing either to sit, stand, or walk. To lie down was useless, unless one was bolstered up on both sides.

I think the sailing of the albatross is one of the most beautiful sights I have ever seen, and when several of them are together, it is really grand. The other day I saw eight of the largest size close together, and they flew up and down, and one way and the other, and in circles, and crossed each other's paths so rapidly, that the eye could hardly follow them in their flight. They move with such perfect ease, and have such complete command over their motions—at one time darting off like an arrow from a bow full bent, then slowly rising in the air and floating almost motionless in the sky, then careering round the ship when at her full speed, as if contemning her comparative sluggishness,—I have watched them by the hour. The beauty of their motions amply compensates for what may be called the ungracefulness of their bodies. I do not think their shape handsome, though, doubtless, it is the best for their modes of life. How pleasant it is for the Christian to think, when he looks at these birds, that they are not beings in which he need feel no interest; they are made by his best Friend, and he sees in them new proofs of the wisdom and goodness of God. It is transporting to be able to say, "My Father made them all."

Saturday, 26th. Last night we had a strong wind, which kept the ship steady. This afternoon the wind gently died away; for an hour we had a perfect calm. The ocean, however, even in the most perfect calms, is never still. The surface may become glassy, but there is a constant heaving; and commonly, in calms, we see what Edwards calls "continual, infinitely various, successive changes of unevenness on the surface of the water." The sun is setting in a cloudy sky, and we shall probably have a gale in a very short time.

Tuesday, April 5th. Strong breeze and very heavy swell. The sea is "troubled, and it cannot rest," but the sun is shining down brightly, and we speed on our way across the foaming waves. A shoal of porpoises were playing about the ship this afternoon. The vessel was going nine miles an hour, and dashing the foam away in immense volumes, but they played about under her bows and in the foam, as if she were at anchor. The mates tried to harpoon some of them, but did not succeed. The harpoon went into one of them, and he was hauled several feet out of water, but the iron did not hold, and he got off. Sailors say the porpoises play about that way before a gale of wind. Saw also an albatross sailing up very high in the air; another sign. Quite a flock of albatrosses showed themselves a little after sunset. I saw seven of the largest size flying close together; but it was too cold to stand and watch them.

Thursday, April 7th. Yesterday was a very pleasant day, though rather cool; sun shone all day, and a moderate wind carried us gently on. To-day the wind is strong, and in fact is increasing so that we have had a reef taken in each of the topsails, and all the sails above furled. The wind is so nearly ahead, that we cannot keep our course, but are going more to the northward than is desirable. It is surprising to see in how many different directions one can go with the same wind, or how one may make winds that blow in opposite directions send him forward in the same course. This is done by shifting the yards, so that the sails may obtain the full benefit of the different breezes. Thus, one going from west to east, as we are, can proceed with any one of the winds represented by the arrows A, B, C, &c., to G. Of these winds, C and E are the best, because they strike all the sails, while a wind from D would not. Pilot boats can go with the wind H and J, i. e. within "four points;" ships cannot go within "six points." Each of the quadrants above is supposed to be divided into eight points, as in the mariner's compass. The wind we have to-day is G, or S. S. E. I'm at a loss to know how you will receive this disquisi-

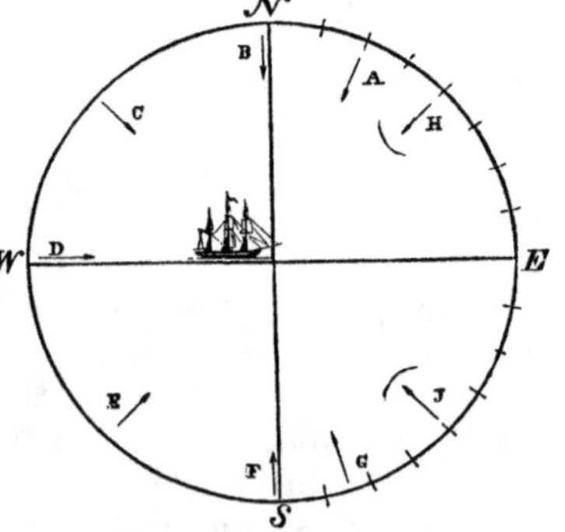

tion. If you did not know these things before, I take it for granted you will be glad to learn them; but if you did, then I beg pardon for troubling you on the subject.

Saturday, April 9th. After rather a restless night, owing to the ship's rolling so much, I went out in the morning and found all sails set, and studding-sails out; so we are "out of the woods now," with a fair prospect before us. This has been a very pleasant day, though our course has been rather slower than usual. However, "we are glad, because we be quiet," and hope soon to be brought to our "desired haven."

Sabbath, April 10th. Preached on John iii. 3: the nature and necessity of regeneration; and was very attentively listened to. The mate told me afterwards he was talking with "Boston Bill" about my sermon, and asked him if he did not think there was a great deal of truth in it. He answered, "he believed there was;" but he quoted from my sermon the remark, that Christians would try to do good to others, and then said, "Now I've been with men who said they were Christians, and yet they were trying to injure others all the time." This is one of the many excuses men make for continuing in impenitence. Another that has equal weight with the better educated part of our company is that "Christians are always quarrelling among themselves." I think I shall prepare a sermon on the text, "And they all began with one consent to make excuse." Bible class as usual in the afternoon; so pass away our Sabbaths. I sometimes wish I could again go up to the sanctuary with the great congregation; but I find that that God, who is "the confidence of all the ends of the earth," is also the confidence "of them that are far off upon the sea." I have taken "the wings of the morning and dwell in the uttermost parts of the sea." Yet, even here "his hand leads me, and his right hand upholds me." What a glorious thing it is to serve such a God! to be able to say, "This God is *our* God for ever and ever!"

Tuesday, April 12th. Pleasant weather still. A sail in sight about two o'clock; soon came near enough to make out that she was a whaler. She ran up the star-spangled banner, and we the same; presently she crossed our bows, and coming, or rather falling nearer, ran up her flag again—a sign that she wanted to speak; so we took in all our light sails, and put the yards round so as to make the ship go slower, and she came up astern but in speaking distance. Asked us where we were from, and if we had any papers to spare. Captain answered, "Yes," and we held on till her boat could come alongside. They speedily lowered one, and half a dozen men jumped down into it, and came dancing over the waves to us. Their boat was sometimes almost hidden by the waves, but they did not seem to mind them at all. They were soon alongside, and their mate and a couple of men came up on deck. They were rough-looking customers compared with our crew, though the latter were in their every-day dress. It was the ship Palladium, of New Bedford; out eight months; had 1000 barrels of oil from sixteen whales; had not seen land for four months; had been south among the icebergs; were going to New Holland soon; crew of thirty men. I asked the mate if they had any books. "Well, yes, some; but what we have, have been read pretty often." Captain gave him two or three dozen of newspapers, and I hastily wrapped up a handful of Tracts, and Doddridge's "Rise and Progress," and Pike's "Religion and Eternal Life," and with a silent prayer for a blessing on them, gave them to him. He then asked the captain if he could spare them any vegetables; and got a keg full of potatoes and onions, &c., and then off again. They have men constantly aloft, one at the fore and one at the main-mast-head, who are relieved every two hours. In this way they saw us several hours before we saw them.

Friday, 15th March. A strong breeze was blowing all day yesterday, and had not the news been almost too good to be true, we should have thought it the south-east-trade. However, it continues to-day, and there can be little doubt that we have the looked-for wind. Thus we are going gaily on our course, without having to beat about among the variable winds that are commonly found between the regular western winds in lat 40° and the trade-wind, which commonly is taken in lat. 28° South. We had anticipated being delayed thus for three or four days, whereas we had no sooner lost the western winds, than this wind took us up. These are very curious things. In lat. 40° north and south, and for several degrees on each side, the wind blows from the west almost constantly; from about 30° to 10° or 5°, north and south, they blow from the north-east and south-east respectively; these are the north-east and south-east trades. On each side of the equator for a few degrees, variable winds prevail; and commonly between the western winds and the trade-winds there is a space of several degrees where the winds vary a good deal. It has been by these regular winds that we have made the greatest part of our voyage.

What grand things these winds are! Just to think of one breeze blowing steadily for days together over a space of a thousand or fifteen hundred miles, ruffling the surface of the old ocean, and playing with a giant strength among his hoary locks! And then when the rain comes down in wide-spread torrents, and the voice of the thunder sounds along the waves, how does the grandeur of the scene put to shame our bellows and our watering-pots, our mimic experiments, and our boasted inventions for controlling the laws of nature! Who can talk of the greatness of man, when surrounded by such proofs of the omnipresent power of God? True, it is a wonderful thing to see a little ship urge onward her course among such mighty elements, and some may say, "Behold here the power of man! superior to the winds and the waves." But who filled man's heart with the wisdom to invent and guide a vessel over such abysses, amid such contending forces? He may laugh when it is calm, but when storms arise, and he is "at his wits' end," he will acknowledge that there is a God who reigneth in the earth; and, blessed be his name! he is "*Our Father.*"

Saturday night, ten o'clock. We are now directly on the opposite side of the globe from you, or within one degree of it, so that with you it is ten, A. M. Saturday night, and the Sabbath draws near. If I could spend every week as pleasantly as I have spent the past, I could rejoice in long life; but it is pleasant to think, that there remaineth—after all the privileges of this world—still, "there *remaineth,* over and above them all, a rest—a σαββατισμος,—a keeping of Sabbath, for the people of God." Rest is sweet; and O, to think of rest from sin, rest from temptation, rest from disappointment, rest from sorrow, rest in the peaceful haven after long toiling over the uncertain, restless ocean, and long struggling with adverse winds! Surely it is well we have thus to labour and to suffer, it will make the end more joyful. Yet it is hard at times to resist the desire to "fly away and be at rest." But it is well that the all wise God holds our times in his hands. He will give the signal when it is the best time to cease from labour, and therefore—

> "Here my spirit waiting stands
> Till He shall bid it fly."

Sabbath, April 17th. A dull, rainy Sabbath, with a light wind; pleasant enough, however, in other respects. Saw a flock of flying-fish, the first I have seen for several weeks. Cleared off beautifully before sunset, and the trade wind came back again strongly.

Preached on Luke xiv. 18, "And they all began with one consent to make excuse." Spoke of the principal excuses men make for not repenting and believing: as, 1. "I have not time." 2. "Religion is a gloomy thing, and a hard and mean service." 3. "The Bible is so hard to be understood, and some of its doctrines, as election, &c., so absurd." 4. "Christians are hypocrites, and there are so many sects, so that there is no truth in religion." 5. "There's time enough yet—I do not mean to die so." The attention generally was better than I have yet seen among the men, and several of them I observed watching me very closely all the time. I understood they had rather an argument about the sermon afterwards in the forecastle, though I did not hear the purport of it. Yet alas! it seems almost hopeless to preach to these people. Like the prophet of old, I seem to be "in the midst of the valley of bones and, lo, they are very dry. Can these dry bones live? O Lord God, thou knowest." Yet in his name would I "prophesy upon these bones, and say unto them, O ye dry bones, hear ye the word of the Lord." And I would also "prophesy to the winds, and say, Come from the four winds, O breath, and breathe upon these slain." I wonder if Christians at home, who know that a missionary is on his way to the heathen, ever think of praying that he may be a blessing to the almost heathenish sailors, as he sails with them week after week. How little success would commonly attend the minister's labour at home, if he had not the prayers of his people to assist him! Yet in cases of this kind, the missionary most commonly stands alone, and has to preach to some who scarcely know what are the very first principles of Christianity—to some who, like one of our crew, "have not had a Bible for many years, nor heard a prayer for seven years;" to some who, like another, "know not that there is any difference between the "faith the devils have," and the faith that "works by love, and purifies the heart;" to some who, like another, think that "if a man goes to church, he is safe enough," and that "those Christians are mistaken, who say that men are naturally averse to religion;" to men rendered reckless of danger by long familiarity with it; who will curse and swear when out in a little boat on a raging sea, seeking if they may find a comrade who had just fallen overboard in a dark night. This is a fact that occurred in this ship on the last voyage!—to say nothing of the evil habits they acquire on shore, and the evil examples they there see, and of the effects these must have upon them. They have long felt that "no man cared for their souls," and they make this an additional excuse for continuing as they are. Surely it is "casting bread upon the waters" to preach to such. Yet God is all-powerful, and some things that have come to my knowledge of late, make me think that the Holy Spirit has not yet left this ship's company to themselves.

Tuesday, April 19th. Warm sultry day, and several heavy showers. What is the use of rain on the sea? why should the water, after having been so carefully drawn up by the sun, be poured down again to the place from which it came? Surely this was all foreseen by him who causes the rain to fall, and he had some design in it. It is hardly a sufficient answer to say, that these showers at sea are of great service to sailors, for vast quantities fall where no ships are, and fell for thousands of years before ships sailed over the ocean. Yet surely they are of use. I have been puzzling my brain for a long time to find out the final cause, as theologians say, of this phenomenon, but I fear with very little success. Perhaps fresh water is as necessary for the inhabitants of the sea, as salt is for us along with our food. Perhaps those winds which, after sweeping for so many thousands of miles over the salt water, and in such hot climates as this, need to be purified and to have their unwholesome qualities thus acquired removed, by having the rain come and pass through them, filtering away, if I may use such a figure, their impurities, before they blow upon the land or influence at all the air men breathe. Who knows what influences are necessary to preserve the atmosphere of the earth in its purity?—and what part of those influences is excited by the rains that fall on land, and at sea, and "in the wilderness where no man is?" But this is one of the "things that are too wonderful for me." Men pass over such things oftentimes as uninteresting, because of their ignorance of what is really in them. So it is in regard to everything. We are often told that the life of such and such men is uninteresting, void of incidents, and dull. Professors of rhetoric, and critics, tell us that only great subjects and the lives of great men, furnish suitable themes for an epic poem. But surely the life of every man, however poor and mean he may be, could we but know it all, would furnish such a subject for an epic poem as would astonish even Homer and Milton. There would be the secret counsels of God respecting him from all eternity; the unnumbered and almost the innumerable incidents in his birth and in his after life, when good and evil angels watched over and influenced him, and when the providence of God was busied about him; the narrow escapes from evil; the woful falls, or the triumphant victory; all the feelings in his own mind, and their varied causes; the plans of others with respect to him, and their influence over him; the effects of his actions, outlasting his own life, and reaching far off amidst almost infinite ramifications to the end of time; the various crises of his life; and the endless realities of the eternal state. What created intellect could fully comprehend, or rightly describe, all these? God knoweth them all. We hardly ever even think of them, and yet our whole life is spent in influencing and being influenced by such wonderful beings. Verily this is a fearful and wonderful thing.

About sunset the ship was very nearly becalmed; her motion was barely perceptible; and I was leaning over the gangway, looking down at the little bubbles on the deep blue sea. While thus engaged, my attention was arrested by a number of little insects, no longer than the gnat you sometimes see sporting in the evening air. They moved about over the calm surface of the water with great rapidity, just as the little water-bugs and spiders play about in the eddy of a brook in summer. Where do these little creatures come from? whither do they go? where shelter themselves when storms arise? Or are they, like ourselves, mere creatures of a day, floating about on the fathomless ocean of eternity, one moment sportive and busy, and cherishing great hopes, the next swallowed up by the dark waters, and seen no more? *

It was a lovely night, calm and clear, a few clouds in the sky; but the moon shone down brightly, and the large stars beamed out, like a queen in her royal robes with her maids of honour around her. Underneath was the boundless sea, quiet and smooth—"a great still mirror-sea," and the moonbeams and starlight were reflected back from the surface of the water. But how different the direct and the reflected light! The one came down and gave a clear image of the heavenly bodies; thus we see the glory of God in the face of Jesus Christ. But the other was distorted and broken by the constant swell of even that calm sea; so it is with all our views of things in the invisible heavens. If our faith can only gaze steadfastly thereon, our hearts will burn within us; but the moment we turn our sight to earthly things our vision becomes confused, and we see no more clearly; at best it is but "through a glass darkly." I could hardly

* "Light mortal, how you walk your light life minuet, over bottomless abysses, divided from you by a film."—CARLYLE.

think of going to bed; again and again as I turned off to retire, a new appearance of beauty or a brightly shining star arrested my attention, and kept me under the open sky. Once the moon was slightly obscured by a white cloud, that passed like a veil over her face; but that only made her more beautiful, for immediately a triple circle was formed around her, of white, bright orange, and pale green.

Saturday, April 23d. Raining almost all the night. Towards four o'clock this morning I awoke; it was pouring down heavily. Several very loud claps of thunder, that came roaring and reverberating over the waters, reminded me of the words of the Psalmist:

> "The voice of the Lord is upon the waters:
> The God of glory thundereth;
> The Lord is upon many waters.
> The voice of the Lord is powerful;
> The voice of the Lord is full of majesty."

April 27. In the Straits of Sunda. Altogether it has been an exciting and interesting day. The sight of inhabited land, and those inhabitants being heathen; the effort to enter the straits, and failure; the mortification of seeing others pass us with a fair breeze, while we, not half a mile off, were becalmed; then the pleasure of catching up and passing again; the sight of so many ships, and of the native prows; the smell of land; the sight of noble mountains; the preparing of letters for home; and the lifting up of the heart in gratitude to God, that through so many dangers, and along so lengthened a course, he has led us and fed us,—surely here will I raise an Ebenezer, for hitherto the Lord hath helped me. And then to think, that in precisely one year from the day I was first licensed to preach the gospel, I was permitted to see the land of nations sitting in darkness, to some of whom at least I hope to preach the gospel! Is it not a day much to be remembered? The host of the enemies are numerous and powerful, but I may well use the words of king Asa and say, "Lord, it is nothing with thee to help, whether with many or with them that have no power; help us, oh Lord our God; for we rest on thee, and in thy name we go against this multitude. Oh Lord, thou art our God; let not man prevail against thee."

But if the day had so many things to be remembered, the evening was still more magnificent. About sunset, we were about two miles from shore, directly off from the Karang mountains. We were gliding swiftly over the smooth waters; nine other ships of different nations, English, American, and Dutch, were in sight on the western side, and six of them in full view. On the other side, a dozen Malay prows were hugging the shore. Some shoals were to be passed over, which required close watching: dark and thick clouds, many and large, were overhead, but most of them tinged of the deepest orange and red by the sun's rays; high mountains, five or six in number, loomed up in various directions, and above the highest, Crockatoa, was the darkest mass of clouds; but beyond all these was the evening star, "mildly beaming on the forehead" of the calm blue sky, diversified and enriched as it was with the glorious sunset tints. I looked and gazed with almost speechless, certainly with an unutterable admiration; and as the bright colours faded, the ardour of my thoughts subsided to a quiet comparison of the varied scene before me, with what may perhaps be the course of my future life. What is before, I know not; but I thought that a swift, though perhaps a long voyage over the uncertain sea of life, was before me; that I should have fellow-labourers, perhaps of different nations, striving together to benefit the poor heathen whose representatives we here saw on the same sea with ourselves; that secret dangers might be in my way, which it would require prudence and care to avoid; that many sorrows are impending over me, but they shall be tinged and beautified with the favour of God; and thus the

"Clouds I so much dread,
Are big with mercies, and shall break
In blessings on my head;"

that difficulties are before me like mountains, and over the greatest and the least of them, it may be, the most impenetrable darkness now overhangs; but that above them all, shines brightly the star of hope; and, having at last surmounted them all, the peaceful and glorious rest of heaven will open upon my delighted view. However I may be mistaken in some of these anticipations, I trust and pray that the last may prove true.

After dark my attention was called to the many fires kindled along the coast, probably by the natives, catching fish. They looked very cheerful, after having been for so long without seeing any traces of human beings, except those in our own little vessel.

Walked out with my umbrella; saw some men catching fish with a long net, but they caught only about two gallons full of them, and all very small, none, I suppose, more than an inch and a half long, shaped mostly like sun-fish, and coloured like silver-fish; I should suppose that they are very delicate eating. There were a large number of children playing on the beach, either entirely or nearly naked, and all bareheaded and barefooted; their greatest amusement seemed to consist in pursuing and catching a small crab, that ran with exceeding swiftness and burrowed in holes in the sand. I was surprised to see how very quick it could run—much faster than they could. When they had chased one to its hole, they would sit down and try to dig it out, if the hole was not too deep. I began to pick up some small shells on the beach, and among the stones at the water's edge, and half a dozen of them gathered round me, and began talking, and asking me questions. Some of them were quite good looking, and had very beautiful teeth; but they will soon spoil them by chewing betel nut, as all the grown-up people, men and women, do here, at least among the Malays; I did not observe whether the Chinese use it or not. I did not understand a word they said; but they were evidently in great spirits, and very good natured; so I talked away to them, asking questions, and making remarks, and laughing and talking with as great glee as any of them. They helped me to pick shells, crying out "Gubboosh!" "Yes!" "Karang!" &c. I felt almost sorry to part with them, and having nothing else to give them as a reward for their services, I took out my pin-cushion and gave them *a pin a piece*. They were quite eager to get them, and stood round me in a half-circle, holding up their little hands and chattering away. They waited very patiently, each till his own turn came, and followed me some little distance afterwards, till I turned and waved my hand—and then off they went.

Sabbath morning, May 1st. When I went out before breakfast, we were away out in the Java Sea, and the only land in sight was the high peaks of Rajah Bassa, which must have been seventy miles off. During the day, saw a ship to the eastward that looked very much like the Oneida. A pleasant breeze all day, and tolerably good progress; out of sight of land all day. Sea about thirteen fathoms deep; it varies from eight to thirty fathoms, all the way from Java to the island of Banou; is generally about eleven to fifteen fathoms.

Preached on Luke xxiii. 33; "There they crucified him." On the death of Jesus Christ. Was favoured with great fluency and good attention. In the afternoon, one of the men came and asked me to lend him a Greek Testament. He said he could read it. I was just preparing for my Bible class, and could not talk with him about it then. I got it for him, and he took it off to the forecastle, and seemed to be reading it very busily for some time. In a day or two afterwards, he came back with a translation he had made from the Greek to Latin, of Matt. ii. 1—12, which was very well done. He had been at some German schools and universities, and understands more languages than any one on board; Greek, Latin, English, French, Danish, German; yet he is not more than twenty two years old.

Monday, May 9th. Preached on John xvi. 7, to an attentive audience, though they were not so much interested apparently, as they were for two or three late days. It is hard at times to repress unbelieving fears, or to avoid giving way to the suggestions of the enemy, that "it is of no use to preach to such people." Truly, it is like casting bread upon the waters. How many difficulties of the same kind must I experience in China! My heart sinks within me at times, and then again I am encouraged. But, so far, I have had no desire to go back, but constantly a willingness to go forward and see what God would have me to do. Looking over the account of Dr. Morrison, in the Chronicle, I could hardly tell what to think. I cannot plod away as he did at a language.

We hope to be at the end of our voyage in two weeks, and you will perhaps think I must be very glad of it. I can hardly say, however, that I am. For a few days after leaving Angier I did wish pretty heartily that we were safely moored; but now I feel almost sorry to think of ending the voyage so soon. Having been now nearly four months at sea, I feel quite at home; and I know, on arriving in China, I shall then again be a stranger, with responsible duties to perform, and no fellow-labourer to counsel with in regard to them. My faith and hopes fluctuate considerably in regard to the future. When I cast my cares upon the Lord, I can wait with calmness and peace, knowing that he will bring it to pass; but too often I suffer my mind to dwell upon the future, without reflecting that my strength is all from on high, and the consequence almost invariably is, that I am disheartened by the prospect. When shall I learn to live by faith, and not by sight? I am sad, and almost sick at heart, to-night, for I have been thinking of difficulties, and of myself. But that it would be wrong, I could wish, "Oh, that I had wings like a dove, for then would I fly away, and be at rest."

Monday, May 16th. Preached yesterday on Luke xviii. 19, to a very attentive audience. I have rarely seen in America a more attentive and well-behaved congregation, than our sailors here. Yet the truths they hear from me are as plain and evangelical, and as much calculated to bring down one's high thoughts of himself, as I know how to make them. I believe they sometimes think I preach hard doctrines, yet they are very respectful. Yesterday there was hardly an eye turned from me for the whole time, though I was not conscious of being more than usually interesting or fervent. But, alas! "who hath believed our report, and to whom is the arm of the Lord revealed?" "They came before me as the Lord's people come; they hearkened to my words, but their heart goeth after idols." How can any one think that almighty power is not necessary to change the hearts of men? How can any one take credit to himself, if success attend his efforts? I lent my "Holy War" to the sailmaker the other day. He was greatly pleased with it, and was telling me last night how much he liked it. I asked him if he understood it all. "Oh, yes, sir! it's very plain; and if it were not, I could understand it, by overhauling my Bible a little." He seems to be a good man, and I am always sure of having at least one attentive hearer on the Sabbath. I believe he never takes his eyes off me while I am preaching.

Friday, May 20th. A fine breeze for two days past has carried us on finely, and if it holds out, we shall probably be at our "desired haven" in a week. Consequently all are in fine spirits, and it is quite amusing to see how eager every one is to hear the latitude. For my own part, I cannot say I am anxious either way. The responsibility of my station, and of the steps I may take at Macao, sometimes weighs me down a good deal; and, like Jeremiah, I say, "Ah, Lord God! I cannot speak; for I am a child." With a very slight change, I find Solomon's prayer very appropriate for myself. "Oh Lord God! thou hast made me a messenger to a people like the dust of the earth for multitude; give me now wisdom and knowledge, that I may go out and come in before this people: for who can instruct this people that is so great?" But the promises to Moses, and Joshua, and Jeremiah, and Paul, have sustained me, and the recollection of the providence of God in times past, cheers me, and I am going forward. A great work is before me, and its greatness appals me at times; but the reflection of the pendulum, "I have to tick so many thousand times, that I cannot count them all, but then I have a moment for every tick," encourages me again.

Monday, May 23d. Preached yesterday what I suppose is my last sermon on shipboard, from 1 Cor. i. 23, 24, with as much fluency and feeling, and as good attention as at any time yet. The seed is sown: how or when it shall spring up, or what shall be the final results, I know not. Sometimes I hope it may spring up and produce much fruit; but I never think so, when I recollect the unworthiness of the instrument by whom it was dispensed.

Tuesday, May 24th. Had our last Bible class, probably, this morning. I have been writing up various things; among others, a preface to my journal.

Thursday, May 26th. Yesterday was a pretty gloomy day. We had gone on so finely during the night, that we expected to have been at Macao by noon. About six o'clock, however, A. M., the wind increased to a gale; had to double-reef the topsails. There was a heavy sea, and the ship groaned, and rolled, and pitched after the fashion of the Cape of Good Hope. We had had so much fine weather, and so smooth a sea for six weeks before, that the change took us all aback, and all the passengers were quite sea-sick. About eight o'clock, A. M., yesterday, we saw land ahead, probably the great Ladrone Island, a few miles south of Macao; but just then the gale came out dead ahead, and we had to put back to sea. Two or three other ships, that were nearer in than we, had to do the same. Wore ship, and stood in for land again at noon; saw it very distinctly about four, P. M.; but the wind being still ahead, had to put off to sea again, and soon lost sight of it. We are now trying again to go in, but the wind is unfavorable. It may be several days yet before we can get in, though we are not probably six hours' fair sailing from Macao. "The worst coast," says the captain, "in the world; nobody knows when we will get in, and yet, I dare say, the gale does not extend fifty miles." I could not help thinking how often we see such things in common life. Just as we are on the point of acquiring what we long labour and hope for, we are disappointed, and again made to urge on our rough and stormy course. What a blessed place heaven will be, where "*there is no more sea!*" no more storms; no more wearisome calms; no treacherous shoals; no disappointments. It is the haven of eternal rest, and doubly sweet, because entered "through much tribulation."

China Sea, May 26th, 1842.

MY DEAR MOTHER—So here it is, the long promised, and I flatter myself, the long expected journal. Before you decide that it is too long, just imagine yourself in my situation, with a charge to tell you all I do, and see and hear, seeing and hearing a great many things new and strange, or amusing; and having hardly any connection with home, or home folks, except this journal. As long as I was writing it, I seemed to be holding intercourse with you; sometimes sitting down for a long chat, sometimes running in to tell you a little story, sometimes pointing out a splendid scene on the sky, sometimes giving you a picture of social life on shipboard,—was it any wonder that my pen sometimes loved to linger on the paper, when it thus brought up before me so many tender, and so many pleasant associations; and when it caused me to think the oftener of one—yes, of many whom, though I love, I dare not expect to see any more on earth?

If you find it badly written in some places, you must consider, that it was sometimes so damp, that my paper seemed to be almost wet; and especially the ship often rolled so prodigiously, that in my efforts to maintain my own position, I had enough to do without minding whether I wrote backhand or slopehand, or whether the strokes went perpendicularly or horizontally. I think, if you had seen me sometimes, laying my writing desk in my berth, bracing my foot against the sides of my room, and holding on with one hand to the berth board, while I wrote with the other, and after all getting knocked, now against the berth, and now against the partition of my room, you would think I did pretty well. This is no fanciful description, for such things happened to me again and again, when off the Cape of Good Hope.

As to publication of extracts—No. I set my foot down there. Keep it out of the way of that little *omnivorous* monster that they keep in the Mission House—[the Missionary Chronicle.] There is not a line of it that was written for publication. and very few lines in it that I think fit for publication, They are mere unstudied and unlaboured accounts of what happened to myself, in a voyage that contained few or no striking incidents. I have not that squeamishness about the publication of letters and journals that some missionaries have; but still I would rather not appear in print for several years yet. The less I am known for a while—at least until it is known whether I am likely to be of any use in this part of the world—the better. If I should prove a worthless vessel, a useless labourer, there will be fewer disappointed in me. I know that some would laugh at me for feeling such an anticipation, but with me it is no laughing matter. My coming to this part of the world is but an *experiment.* If it succeeds, there will be time enough to become as prominent as is needful; if it does not, it will be better by far, both for myself and the Church, that as little be said about it, and as few expectations disappointed, as possible.

What more shall I say? I might fill page after page with expressions of attachment and affection. I might say how often I think of you all, and recall to mind the many, many proofs of love, and tokens of kindly feelings, I have received from you. I may say how much I would delight to hear from you, and about all that concerns you, especially those things that relate to the spiritual welfare of each and every one of the family, and of other dear friends. But why should I? You already know all this nearly, if not quite as well, as I could tell you. When you think of me, or speak of me, do not think or speak of me, as if you thought I were unhappy, or repented of the course I have taken. I may be sick I may be in outward distress, I may be, I often am dejected and despondent, but I never yet have regretted that I am away from home, and never yet felt the wish (however much I should like to see you all) to leave the path I am now treading, and turn my back upon the heathen. What may be my feelings hereafter, I dare not presume to say. I may be "troubled on every side;" "perplexed," oftentimes; "persecuted," it may be; "cast down," even. But, I trust not to be "distressed," not to be "forsaken," and, far from being "destroyed," to come off at last conqueror, and more than conqueror, through him that hath loved me. With such a confidence, and with the hope of being sustained by many influences from the land of my birth, more precious than gold and silver, I may well rejoice; yea, I do rejoice.

Most affectionately yours,

W. M. Lowrie.

CHAPTER III.

1842.

Landing in China—Voyage in the Sea Queen—Shipwreck in the Harmony—Return to Macao.

At the period included in this chapter, hostilities existed between Great Britain and China, and the result of the contest, or even its duration, could not be known. On reaching China, the new missionary was instructed to inquire particularly, in view of the state of things then existing, the practicability of establishing a station at Hong Kong, or any point on the coast further north. Having obtained this information, and joined his colleagues at Singapore, they were authorized to decide the question of removing from Singapore, and concentrating the whole missionary force in China. On landing, he found that the Rev. T. L. McBryde had been at Macao for some months, having left Singapore in hopes that a sea voyage would recruit his health.

Having made himself acquainted with the existing state of things in China, Mr. Lowrie left Macao on the 18th of June; and after four months of unavailing efforts to reach Singapore, he returned to Hong Kong on the 18th of October. The account of these distressing voyages, and his perilous shipwreck, is fully given in the following letters and journals. It is matter of regret that one-half of his journal in the Sea Queen was some years ago destroyed by fire, when the house of one of his relatives was burned down. The loss cannot be supplied, as no copy of this impressive journal was taken.

During the time of these disastrous voyages, the providence of God had made the question plain, on which the missionaries were seeking for light. The war between Great Britain and China had been terminated by a treaty of peace, with which the contending parties appeared to be satisfied, and by which five cities on the coast were opened to the commerce and enterprise of Western nations, as well as to the labour of the Christian missionary. The time had now fully come when the labours of the church of God, in behalf of China, needed no longer to be carried on at a distant outport.

Macao, May 28th, 1842.

My Dear Mother—We anchored yesterday at four P. M. in Macao roads. Here I found Mr. and Mrs. McBryde, who had reached China several months ago, having taken the voyage from Singapore on account of his health. I was greatly delighted to find him here, and was much relieved by having his counsel and assistance in deciding the various questions before us. I was most cordially received by the different missionaries here, and found a temporary home with the Rev. Mr. Bridgman. At a late hour I got to bed, under musquito curtains, but could not sleep for a long time. It was so strange to be lying in a large or wide bed, to be in a large room, to feel that I was on heathen ground. I greatly missed the ship's bells, which strike every half hour on board. The noise of the gongs, and drums, and rattles, and other strange sounds in the town, and the many, many thoughts of hundreds of things, past, present, and to come, that crowded rapidly through my mind, kept me long awake. It is Saturday night again;—

I am a stranger in the earth, but Ebenezer—Emmanuel.

Hong Kong, June 7th, 1842. I stayed in Macao from Friday evening till Wednesday morning, and saw a good deal of the place. The population is about 35,000, principally Chinese, with perhaps 5000 of Portuguese descent. The streets are narrow and crooked; very few are more than ten feet wide, and some not more than six. They are commonly full of persons passing along, hucksters and pedlers, with their wares and cries of various kinds. I saw a poor girl, who had lost both her feet by the leprosy, and was moving about on her hands and knees. Very few women are seen in the streets, except that in the mornings and evenings a number of well-dressed Portuguese women, with a servant behind, holding a large umbrella over them, go out to walk. The ladies, and a good many of the foreign male residents, commonly pay their visits in sedan chairs, borne by two Chinese. I used to pity some of the bearers as they went panting along under the weight of some fat fellow. These bearers commonly go in a little short trot, though it is very seldom that you see a Chinaman run. The houses of the foreigners are commonly large and roomy; the servants live in the basement, and the owners in the upper floor. Few or none of them are more than one story high. Most of them have one or more *punkahs*. I went out one morning to bathe, in the place where Mr. Stanton was captured, and in the way passed through a large Chinese burying ground. Most of the graves were very carelessly attended to. A great many of them had pieces of Chinese paper at the head. It is but a short time since the Chinese had their ceremony of worshipping the graves of their ancestors. It is their custom then, to put such a piece of paper on the graves, to serve as money for their departed ancestors in the other world. I also visited the Protestant burying ground, where Dr. Morrison and his first wife are laid. It is a small, and rather a pretty place, now nearly full. I suppose, however, it will not be much used hereafter, as probably most of the Protestant foreigners will remove to Hong Kong.

There is a little chapel owned by the British in Macao, where one of the missionaries usually preaches every Sabbath, using the forms of the Episcopal church. Mr. Boone preached on the Sabbath, on "Train up a child," &c.—He had first baptized the daughter of Mr. Swords, an American Episcopal merchant there. This, I believe, was the first public baptism ever performed by an American in Macao. The missionaries usually have their children baptized privately. There were two punkahs in the church, so that, though the day was warm, we were quite comfortable. There were probably forty persons present. The Chinese, however, have no Sabbath, and were going about vending their wares, and uttering their cries as usual. As for the Roman Catholics here, their Sabbath is over after mass, which is performed early in the morning. In the evening I preached to an audience of some twenty or thirty, at Mr. Brown's house,—on Psalm cxix. 19. As Mr. McBryde was to leave Macao for Amoy on Wednesday, June 1st, together with Mr. Boone and Dr. Cumming, we had a missionary meeting at Mr. Brown's on Tuesday night. The vessel in which they were to go to Amoy, was lying at Hong Kong, and I accompanied them to this place.

Having a head wind the whole time, we had to beat all the way, and were twenty-nine hours coming forty-five miles, the distance from Macao to Hong Kong. I suppose in our beating about, we went at least a hundred and fifty miles. Mr. B. and Mr. McB. were neither of them well; their wives were even more weakly, and in addition were sea sick; their children were uneasy and fretful, and two ayahs or female servants, whom they had engaged to go with them to Amoy, were so sea-sick they could not hold up their heads. There they were, among tables and boxes, and chairs, and plates, with scarcely room to stir, sick, going to a strange country and far away from the comforts of home and friends. I assure you I began to think more seriously than before of the personal trials and discomforts of missionary life. Yet there was not a murmur uttered, nor as far as I could see, an emotion of impatience or regret felt. We arrived at Hong Kong harbour about three P. M., on Thursday.

On Saturday morning I tried to go up one of the hills—I assure you that it was up-hill work, and I had hard tugging to get myself up. It was so steep, I concluded to go no further, and sat down to rest on a rock before descending. My toil in ascending the hill, naturally reminded me of the circumstances of the mission, which we were trying to establish here, and of the work that is yet before us. The difficulties are great—high as the mountains, and, apparently, as hard to be removed as the granite upon them; and after all, what is it to the eye of man but a barren prospect, like the bare side of the hill I had been climbing? And yet, as I ascended I had seen little plants and flowers, and insects, and shells, and recognized in all of them traces of the presence and power of God; and as I looked around I saw that some Chinese women had ascended the hills to gather firewood to sustain their earthly lives, and that civilized men were toiling at great expense to found a city here, where apparently, there was so little prospect of one being founded. If they spare no expense for a mere earthly object, why should Christians grudge their money or labour in endeavouring here to build the temple of the Lord? There are great difficulties in the way, but when I looked round, and saw these vast hills piled up on all sides, and covered over with the immense blocks of granite as if in sport, just as a child heaps up little sand hills in its play, and disposes its pebbles and its shells on their sides and their tops, I could not but exclaim, The God who formed these hills, and placed these rocks upon them, is all-powerful; and though they seem immovably fixed, yet even men, by slow and patient labour, may take them away; and he himself, by means that he can well employ, can remove them at once. The difficulties of our mission, God could remove at once; but if he chooses to employ us in this work, the probability is, that for the present we shall proceed by slow, and perhaps for a time, almost imperceptible steps. But the work shall be done, for the mouth of the Lord hath spoken it. The granite rocks around were a little sanctuary to me, and I did not regret my toil in climbing up the hill.

The Sabbath-day to me was a very pleasant day, though I saw many things to pain me. I could not but feel that I was in a worse than a heathen country. It is a heathen land under the control of Christians, where the heathen are allowed, and even required by the Christians, to work for them on the Sabbath-day. How can the missionaries urge the natives to keep holy the Sabbath-day, when the merchants and the Government send them to count money, store away goods, open roads, hew granite, and build houses, on that day; and when the Roman Catholic priests, who are now exerting the greatest influence on the natives of any of the foreigners, consider that the Sabbath is over as soon as a mass is said? The merchants go to their counting-rooms as usual, and the Sabbath is emphatically the day for visiting.—"Woe is me that I dwell in Mesech, and sojourn in the tents of Kedar!" My heart is sick at the sight of the wickedness around. O Lord, show thyself. I felt almost afraid to establish a mission here, for how can a city prosper whose foundations are laid in the desecration of the Sabbath-day? "Sin is a reproach to any people," and how much more to England and America!

China Sea, June 24th, 1842.

MR. JOHN LLOYD—MY DEAR BROTHER:—I am often thinking of you, and, especially of late, often wishing I had you out here along with me. You must come out to China. . . .

Here I am all alone, and rather lonely, going down the China Sea against the monsoon, and wishing most heartily that I were on *terra firma* again, and settled down at my Chinese studies. Excepting sea-sickness, and a very slight attack of fever at the commencement of this last trip, I have been uniformly very well since leaving New York; and have been enabled to see and hear a good deal, and to collect a good deal of information respecting China as a missionary field. I know you will be anxious to hear what I think of it in that respect, so I propose to tell you, in as few words as possible, what I think of it. You know how very unexpected it was to me that I should ever be a missionary to China. It is not a year yet since my station was assigned to me in this part of the world; and I came out with many fears and misgivings, and many doubts as to my fitness for such a station, and as to its suitableness for missionary labour at the present time. But what I have seen and what I have heard has shown me many things I never knew before, has opened up to me views of its vastness as a field for labour almost overpowering, and has taught me that many of its difficulties have been greatly overrated. It has its difficulties, and some of them, such as the evil influence of foreigners, though I knew of them before, are far greater than I expected; but on the whole I am greatly encouraged. There is a great work to be done, and the men are now wanted to perform it; and it is not required that these men should be angels "greater in might and excelling in power" the rest of mankind, in order that they may perform it. The language can be learned, the people can be approached; and I verily believe that

China is *now opening;* certainly it is more open now than it has ever been before. Missionaries can now labour in Macao much more freely than ever before. Hong Kong will soon be perfectly open. Missionaries are now at Amoy and Chusan, places where no Protestant missionaries have ever been before; and those at Amoy and Chusan, where the people have not been as yet corrupted by the evil influence and example of foreigners, represent them as an uncommonly interesting people, easy of access, and free in their manners. They are heathen of course, and have the vices of heathen; but I am inclined to think that there is no people except the native Africans, among whom I would more readily labour, and with more hope of success, than among the Chinese; and this I think is saying a good deal. You know how promising a people I have always thought the Africans are.

I am not able now to give you the facts on which I base the above conclusion. Perhaps I may at some other time. But I never felt so anxious to live long as I have several times in China, when I saw the Chinese around me, and wanted to preach Christ to them. I think I should rejoice to wear out a long life in Christ's service in China.

I formed some very pleasant acquaintances among the missionaries in China, most of whom I have seen, and some of them frequently. . . .

There is an infinite fund of wisdom in our Lord's saying to his apostles, "Be ye wise as serpents." Missionaries above all other men, it seems to me, need to be men of prudence; not actuated by impulse, but influenced by steady and enlightened principle. Certainly nothing else will atone for the want of prudence, in a missionary to China at the present time. A "prudent counsellor" is invaluable, especially now. And yet there is very great danger of having prudence degenerate to timidity, and thus overpower our zeal. Surely we have need of wisdom from on high to direct us. I often think of

Solomon's prayer for wisdom, when he was appointed to rule over the numerous people of Israel.

How are you coming on in matrimonial affairs? Let me whisper in your ears a good piece of advice. Keep your eyes open; if you see one who would make you a good and prudent wife, by all means try and secure her. If you cannot find one that would be an helpmeet for you, consider it an intimation of Providence that you are to remain unmarried for the present, and come out single. Such was the principle I acted on in the United States, and after all I have felt and seen, I am more and more convinced that it is the proper course to be taken. The missionaries here all recommend that a man should be married, but I believe they all abhor what are sometimes called "missionary matches," and I think most justly. I hope you will by example and precept discountenance all such things.

How I should like to see you, and chat with you for a while! Where are you? what doing? How are you getting on? What are your prospects? When will you be licensed? Are you ready to come out here? or do the Nestorians still call forth your sympathies? Do you still remember "the love of your espousals?" and that bright and happy season at Jefferson College, with our many pleasant interviews, and the walks we took, and the prayers we offered, and the many conjectures and plans for future usefulness we laid? Some who started with us, and for a while promised as fair, have already gone back; while others have already entered into rest. Why are we spared? What are we doing? Could we now rejoice to give up the account of our stewardship?

Farewell—and may the Lord we have so often delighted to worship together, still watch over and bless thee.

August 12th. Dear brother, if you ever come to China, I hope you may not have to go up or down the China sea against the monsoon. After fifty-three days' hard work, we have been obliged to abandon the effort, and are now going to Manilla, to lay in fresh provisions, and prepare for another effort. The monsoon will be nearly over in a month, and then perhaps we may succeed. How often have I thought of you on this voyage, and wished you were here!

Affliction is a good thing to make one study the Scriptures. I never understood them half so well before, nor relished so much their precious promises. This has been a pretty severe trial to me: alone, with no Christian friend; a boisterous sea; hope deferred until the heart became sick, and then entirely cut off. But I have become pretty well reconciled to it, and can even rejoice, "for the Lord reigneth." Why he has thus disappointed my expectations, I cannot yet tell; but no doubt for wise reasons. This affliction I trust is doing me good, and I shall yet justify him in all his ways.

Very truly yours

W. M. Lowrie.

China Sea, June 22d, 1842.

My Dear Mother—I have a prospect of a long, lonely, and perhaps tedious passage. And I know of nothing that may contribute better to cheer at least a few of its lonely hours, than to keep a quiet journal, connecting me once more with "home and home folks;" so I pray you to receive this *little* manuscript, as another proof, if proof were needed, that I have not forgotten you, and do not think of you with the less affection, though my letters may not at all times be composed with so many laboriously sought expressions of affection, and longing desires to see you again, as you may sometimes meet with in the case of home-sick travellers.

Late on Saturday, word came that the "Sea Queen goes to-morrow morning at daylight, and you will have to go aboard to-night." There was no help for it; so I hastily packed up my trunk, said good-bye to my kind friends, to all of whom, and especially Mr. and Mrs. Brown, I had become very much attached, and at half-past six, got aboard another Chinese boat to go out to the vessel. It rained several times pretty hard, yet we got out in two hours and a half. It was rather a stormy, uncomfortable preparation for the Sabbath; and I could not think without longing remembrances of the many pleasant Saturday evenings on board the Huntress, and particularly of the "preparation," as "the Sabbath drew near," at home. I wondered what you were all doing; and whether you had any idea of my situation,—alone, weary, and half despondent. However, my troubles seemed to be over when I got safely on board, and I thought I should now in these "splendid accommodations," have at least a quiet and pleasant voyage to Singapore. But I began to think very soon, that I had reckoned without my host. My room is a good, large, airy apartment, and high enough for me to stand upright; but it has no berth, though a large transom supplies the place of that; no table, no wash-stand; not even a wash-basin; no lamp, no shelves, only one or two hooks, and one stool; these are its "accommodations." The first thing I saw when I went in at night, was a host of large cockroaches, which made themselves perfectly at home there; a quantity of spiders and spider's webs in every corner; and a very unpleasant odour, caused, I suppose, in great part, by the cockroaches, to which, after three or four days' experience, I have not yet become accustomed.

We were to have sailed at daylight Sabbath morning, but did not get off till ten o'clock; had a head wind and a rough sea; and by ten o'clock, P. M., we had gone only ten or fifteen miles, and had to anchor just outside of the great Ladrone Island. Next day we did very little better, and beat about in sight of land all day. Meantime I felt very poorly, Sabbath morning, though not unwell. I could not fix my thoughts on anything. The business of our mission, and various plans, kept crowding into my mind. I tried to read the Psalms, Life of the Martyrs, &c., but could not with any ease or pleasure. Afternoon, my head ached, tooth ached, hands and face were sore from being sun-burnt the day before, and I had a good deal of fever, which kept on me for several hours. I was tired lying down, yet too weak to sit up; and it was too wet and unpleasant to be out. The officers were too busy to attend to me; and Chun Sing, who is going with me to Singapore, was quite sea-sick himself.

Oh, how often I thought of the Huntress, with her nice clean sweet cabins, her kind captain, pious mate, intelligent and quiet crew, and pleasant passengers! Everything seemed different here. I could hardly avoid murmuring, though at the same time I felt that I had many, many more comforts than I deserved, and after a while I became rather more satisfied. Next day, I kept getting better; got several refreshing naps, and in each of them had a sweet and pleasant dream. I dare not tell you the first,—it would amuse you too much. In the second, I dreamed that father and yourself had come out to Macao to see me. He wanted to go to Singapore in the Sea Queen, but I told him to go in the Huntress by all means. We had to part for a while, and I was very anxious for him to read the letters, and particularly the official one, which I had that morning left in the hands of a young friend to be sent to America by the first vessel. I hope you have got them before now. I had some trouble to get the letters for him in time, and just as I got them, I awoke, and behold it was a dream.

Next day, Tuesday, I was better still; and to-day, Wednesday, June 22d, I am quite well, and have things a little more comfortably fixed. I have told Chun Sing to come to my room every day, and read the New Testament, and learn the Shorter Catechism, &c. This is the strength of the S. W. monsoon, so that we have the wind strong and right ahead, and shall have it so all the way. Consequently, we have to sail one hundred and fifty miles at least, in order to make fifty on our course.

Saturday, June 25th. Here we are still beating down the China Sea, but on the whole making very fair progress. As good success as we have had thus far would take us to Singapore in twenty days, and I should be pretty well satisfied to be assured we should be no longer. My situation, on the whole, is tolerably pleasant; though I do sometimes feel sadly out of sorts. In the Huntress, when I had no other employment, I could sit and watch our sailors; they were always busy, either working, or talking, or reading; and what they did, they seemed to do heartily. But these Lascars are the poorest set of human creatures I have ever seen; they are not to be compared to the Chinese. There must be near fifty of them aboard, though the vessel is not much more than half as large as the Huntress, which had only twenty men and boys; and yet these fifty do not do their work half as well as those twenty. So many of them seize hold of a rope, that they are actually in each other's way, and they pull as if they were afraid of hurting the rope's feelings. And then, so dirty; I have not seen one of them with a clean article of dress since I came on board. I must except the carpenter, who is a pretty decent looking-fellow. He is a Chinaman. It does me good to look at him. I do not want to see our butler at all, however, and least of all when I am eating,—with his soiled turban and faded shawl, dirty trowsers, and apparently unwashed face and hands. I was always fond of potatoes, but I like them now better than ever, for they come to the table with their coats on, and I am sure they are clean; cannot say the same of anything else at table. But, a man must eat, and there is no use of being so squeamish; besides, I am usually hungry at breakfast time, half-past eight, and at dinner, half-past two; and these are the only meals I eat. At tea I take but little, the tea is so abominable that I can not drink it. And the dry ship biscuit, the only bread we have, is not very inviting by itself.

I could bear these little matters if other things were right. Our officers are to me quite gentlemanly, and personally, I have no complaint; but, they evidently consider the men as of an inferior caste. And the men feel that they are looked upon as such. Some of the men have rather fine countenances, but almost all of them betray vacant minds, or, at least, minds filled only with the least important cares of this passing and perishing world. How can I be sufficiently grateful that I am made to differ from them? As to religious services, at present there are none; and this, more than anything else, makes me feel alone. The most pleasant occupation I have, is to spend an hour every morning in teaching Chun Sing the New Testament, and the Shorter Catechism. And perhaps I may give another hour hereafter to other studies. Then I read Hengstenberg's Christology, History of Scotland, The Middle Ages, &c.; study a little Chinese, and about China, &c. I write some every day; expect to have a host of letters written when I get to Singapore; and if a vessel should be going thence to the United States direct, they will arrive sooner than those I wrote at Macao.

The thermometer has stood about 84° all week; to-day, 85°, but owing to the strength of the wind, the air has been quite pleasant. Numerous flocks of flying-fish are constantly starting up, as our vessel in her course disturbs them. What immense numbers there must be! We probably startle some thousands every day, and yet the course of our ship is a very narrow line in the midst of a very wide sea. Sea sights have lost much of their novelty for me now, and I have to seek amusement and employment principally in myself. It is well for me that I can do so, and still better that there is One above me to whom I can always go. For three or four days after the voyage commenced, I could hardly bear the thoughts of its lasting thirty or forty days;—but now I am disposed to say with cheerfulness, "The Lord reigns, let the earth rejoice!" Let him hasten or retard the end of this voyage, as seems best to himself, for He doeth all things well.

Sabbath evening, June 26th. At the close of a silent Sabbath, my thoughts turn back to the land of my birth, and I cannot help asking, how are you all? And what are you doing? In a few hours I suppose you will be going up to the house of God. You have opportunities of communion with fellow Christians. Your hearts are cheered at the sight of churches, and though pained at the prevalence of wickedness, yet you can believe that the Lord has much people around you. It is not so here. I am alone, as far as Christian society is concerned, and almost alone as far as any society is concerned; surrounded on all sides by lands where there is no Sabbath, few churches, few Christians. In such a situation I find it a very hard thing to keep up the life of religion. At home one depends for the state of his religious feelings very much on the general tone of the churches around him; here there is nothing of the kind to depend upon. Perhaps this is an advantage, for it causes one to feel more entirely his dependence on God, the great Author of all true religious emotions; but it is hard at first, to become reconciled to such a state of things, and like David of old, I can well say, "I had rather be a door-keeper in the house of my God, than to dwell in the tents of wickedness." When you go up with the great congregation to worship God, do not forget those that are in the ends of the earth, and that are far off upon the sea. True, God, your God, is our confidence; but it is pleasant to think that we are thought of by you, in the midst of your privileges. The tears fill my eyes, and my heart is full, when I think of you and your enjoyments; but I have no wish to go back. Blessed be the name of Christ for that precious promise, "Lo, I am with you always."

And yet it is good to be in such circumstances occasionally. There are passages of Scripture that cannot be understood otherwise. I have often read over, and dwelt upon the eighty-fourth Psalm, and yet all my previous meditations, and all the commentaries I have read upon it, have not shown me its sweetness and beauty, so much as this day's experience.

Truly, "Blessed are they that dwell in thy house; they will be still praising thee." But those who enjoy these external privileges, do not monopolize all the blessings. "Blessed is the man whose strength is in thee, in whose heart are the ways of them." Even in the most unfavourable circumstances, when far removed from the refreshing dews of God's house, they shall enjoy his favour. "Passing through the valley of Baca, (weeping, Bochim,) he maketh it a well; the rain also filleth the pools." ("As the rain cometh down from heaven, so is my word," &c.) Such are the consolations of wanderers here; and hereafter, after they have gone from strength to strength, "Every one of them in Zion appeareth before God." Such truths and encouragements may well strengthen a lonely wanderer to run with patience the race set before him; and while he cannot but feel, that a day in the Lord's courts is better than a thousand, yet even here "the Lord God is a sun and shield; no good thing doth he withold from them that walk uprightly." How far superior is such a lot to that of the proudest of this world's favourites! Truly "my soul doth magnify the Lord, and my spirit rejoiceth in God my Saviour."

Monday, June 27th. I did not expect to have been becalmed in the strength of the monsoon; but we are. Have hardly gone twenty miles in the last twenty hours. I do not think, however, it will last long, but it tries the captain's patience a good deal. I have been busy to-day, and happy, though alone.

Tuesday, June 28th. We made eight miles yesterday, and from present appearances shall not make much more to-day; though a little squall we had this afternoon, may have carried us on perhaps five miles. I was very glad the squall came, for in the rain our dirty Lascars got a washing, that improves their appearance very much. I have now got to feel pretty well contented and at home, but would notwithstanding be very glad to be at Singapore, and better pleased still to be at Macao, or some place nearer China.

As you wanted to know what we live on, I will give you the account of one day's fare. It has been precisely the same, every day since I came on board. Breakfast, at half-past eight; tea, fowl or duck, salt beef, salt tongue, potatoes, rice and curry, guava jam. Our only bread is ship-biscuit. For dinner, at half-past two; soup, commonly pea soup, fowl or duck, salt beef, salt tongue, potatoes, rice and curry, pudding, generally of some kind of dough and rather heavy, cheese, preserved ginger, or some similar sweetmeats. For tea, at six o'clock; tea and biscuit. I have a wonderful appetite at present, and eat my salt beef and potatoes with very great relish. I suppose the above bill of fare will last all the voyage, unless the fowls and ducks should happen to give out.

Wednesday, June 29th. With reading and writing and eating and sleeping, my time passes quite comfortably, though I often catch myself wishing to be at Singapore. Yet there is no use of being impatient. My principal reason for wishing to be at Singapore soon, is that I may the sooner be at my appointed business. But surely the Master on whose business I am sent, knows best when I ought to be there, and it is in his power to hasten or retard my arrival. He holds the winds, and can cause them to waft me on speedily, if he sees best.

If he does not choose to have it so, certainly he has wise reasons for doing as he does, and I ought contentedly to submit. With such considerations, I try to allay the impatience I sometimes feel, at being delayed by these calms.

Saturday, July 2d. Still progressing slowly. Had calms every day of greater or less duration, from Sabbath till to-day. Though, as we commonly had a little wind at night, and that such a wind as enabled us to proceed directly on our course, we have probably gone quite as far as we should have done, had the monsoon been blowing in its strength. Yesterday we did uncommonly well. We had a good breeze during the night, that carried us eighty miles directly towards Singapore. To-day we are going perhaps faster, but not so directly; we are running now between south-east and south, or to speak according to the compass, we are going S. S. E. Having been pretty busy, my time has passed away rapidly and pleasantly, though I do at times feel the monotony of this voyage quite sensibly, and often think of the Huntress. To increase my pleasure, the captain said that two months ago, as he was going from Singapore to Macao, he was becalmed ten whole days in sight of a small island near Singapore, and he believed he was fated to make long voyages in the China Sea. There! while I am writing I see the sails flapping against the masts, and we are becalmed again! What is so helpless a thing as a ship at sea in a calm? How vain is all human power in such a case! and oh, how much more dreadful, is the spiritual case of those who are deprived of the influences of that Spirit, which is like the wind that bloweth where it listeth! If Christians were half as anxious to obtain the influences of the Spirit, as sailors are to catch the breeze, what a different appearance the church would have!

Wednesday, July 6th. The calm I spoke of Saturday P. M. lasted but a few minutes, and we have had the monsoon strong ever since; strong wind, heavy sea, and slow progress. Yesterday we went fifteen miles west and fifteen south; to-day, thirty miles west and twenty north; so that, as far as latitude is concerned, we are worse off than we were two days ago. This morning the wind was so strong that it broke our main top-gallant-mast, and the men have been all day employed making a new one. There has been so much motion yesterday and to-day, and that of so unpleasant a kind, that I could not study Chinese. Just as I get my pencil ready to make a neat stroke, away goes the ship; and while I am busy holding to whatever I can catch, the ship staggers off, and leans over on the other side, and a wave rushes in at one of the lee ports. Still, on we dash on our foaming way, and as yet no harm has befallen any of us. My situation is as pleasant as that of any on board, indeed more so; a good large room, plenty to eat and wear, plenty of books and papers, and at present no responsibility. Yet I would like to be at the end of this voyage. We have now been out sixteen days, and are not half way yet.

These poor Lascars have rather a hard life; their only food is rice, with a very little curry. They sit on the deck, and eat with their fingers, three or four out of the same dish. They sleep on deck, in the open air, with only a coarse piece of flannel for a covering. No provision at all is made for their accommodation in the "country ships," no forecastle nor berths. If it rains, they must let it rain, and sleep through it, or else keep awake. All hands are employed all day, and no watches are kept, as on board vessels manned by English or Americans. They may sleep all night, unless they are wanted, when the "tindals," or overseers, of whom there are four, answering to boatswain and boatswain's mates, sound their whistles, and call all hands. Six of them, however, at a time, watch for two hours during the night, and when the bells are struck, every half-hour, the one nearest raises a yell, for I can call it nothing else, which is repeated by the next, and so on through the whole six. This is to show that they are awake; but, for all the watch they keep, they might as well be asleep.

The "*glorious fourth*" passed away without a word being said on the subject. I thought of it, and of the last fourth of July I had spent at Marshall, Michigan, and how little I then expected to have ever been tossing about on the China Sea. Who knows what a day may bring forth?

Saturday, July 9th. The close of the third week of our voyage, and we hardly can say that we have gone half way! We have come ten degrees of latitude, but we have ten degrees more of latitude, and eight of longitude, still to traverse: if we run west, we cannot go south; if we run south, we must also run east; thus making our distance in longitude greater. But why should I complain? If hope is deferred, should my heart be made sick thereby, when I know that a Father's kind hand defers it? I felt greatly reproved this afternoon, as I sat on the stern, and saw a large sea-fowl slowly sailing over the waters. Our heavenly Father cares for it, and feeds it, even on these wide and rolling waters. Am not I of more value than many such? Is not the work I am engaged in more for his glory, than the preservation and sustenance of the fowls of the air and the fish of the sea? And if he cares for them, will he not much more care for me and carry me on? Surely he knoweth what is best for me, and most for his own glory. I will therefore commit my way unto the Lord, and trust also in him. He will bring it to pass. Forgive me, dear mother, if I bring these things improperly to your eye; I have no one here of kindred spirit with myself, and it is pleasant, even though on paper, and afar off, to give utterance to sentiments that I know will find a response in your own feelings. It seems to me, were I once more in the society of fellow-christians,

I should prize much more highly than I have ever done, the opportunity of talking of these things,—of "speaking one to another."

Monday, July 11th. For two days we have been running west, and have made over three degrees; but a strong current yesterday carried us more than a degree to the north of our position on Saturday. The officers are beginning to shake their heads, and predict a long passage. We have all, I think, made up our minds to six weeks instead of four. The mate told me to-day, that the Sea Queen had never had a fair wind for a whole day since she was launched, about fifteen months since! However, I do not know but that this voyage will prove a very profitable one to me. It reminds me of several facts that had almost entirely escaped from my memory. I had quite forgotten that the Apostle Paul, after being in journeyings often, in weariness, in painfulness, &c., had also "thrice been shipwrecked, and spent a night and a day in the deep." So it seems even the best of missionaries did not escape from some troubles on the seas. I wonder if he had as fine a state-room as I have, and whether, in his voyages, he had to live on salt provisions and hard biscuit! We have no journals nor diaries and the like, from the times of the Apostles, to tell us how they managed on such occasions; but the more I think of the matter, the more I am inclined to believe that I am better off as to outward things, than Paul, or almost any of his fellow-labourers; and therefore, so far, I have not much reason to complain. Still, I must say, I should not be sorry to exchange this ship's fare for a short residence in Singapore. However, the Huntress has spoiled me. The Sea Queen is a great deal better ship than the Anna Watson, in which Mr. McBride went to Amoy.

I have since found a passage of Scripture much more to the point than the one above. Acts xxvii. 7. "And when we had sailed slowly many days, and scarce were come over against Cnidus, the wind not suffering us," &c. It has taken such hold of me, that I have laid it up for future consideration.

We had quite a gale last night, with a very heavy sea; so much tossing and pitching, that I scarcely slept the whole night. For the time it lasted, it was more uncomfortable than the gale off St. Paul's, where we had to lie to for twelve hours. We were almost lying to, the greater part of the last night, but now (P. M.) we are going on rather pleasantly.

Monday, July 18th. About six A. M., on Saturday, the wind rose again with great force, and it was the middle of the day, yesterday, before it abated. In the gale on Friday, the wind split our fore-topsail and jib, and others had to be put up in their places. On Saturday the wind split the second fore-topsail, main-topsail, and spanker. Ship rolled prodigiously, and for a while things looked rather dark, as you may well suppose. A strong gale and heavy sea, and the wind dead ahead, are not very pleasant things. At the middle of the day on Saturday, we were not more than one degree further on our course than we were seven days before; with a slight variation, we might almost have adopted Peter's words: "We have toiled all night and caught nothing."

The wind is such to-day, that we could go almost in a south course—S. by E.—but unfortunately there are a number of shoals in that direction, and this wind would carry us among them in twelve hours; consequently, we are obliged to put off to the north-west, and the wind being strong, we "lose a point" in our course, by lee-way. Such are some of the troubles of the voyager's life. Do not forget to pray for the sailor.

Tuesday, July 19th. Wind more favourable still; we can go south, and sometimes even S. by W., but being still too near the shoals have to run W., and N. W. by N., more than half the time. Yesterday was the best day's work we have made in a long time, thirty miles west and sixteen south, equal to about thirty-three on our course, i. e., if the captain's observation was a good one, of which he is doubtful. We are now very seriously expecting that our trip will be of two months, instead of one month. But the Lord reigneth. I trust I can rejoice thereat. We certainly have evidence that He is watching over us. To-day, as I was lying on the transom, (there has been so much motion for a week, that it is very unpleasant to sit, and I spend more than half the time lying down,) very quietly reading one of Irving's sketches, I heard a great and unusual cry on deck. As it continued, I ran out and found a man had fallen from the bowsprit into the sea. Most providentially, he caught one of the ropes thrown to him, before the ship had gone too far, and was drawn in. The sea was so rough, that the captain could hardly have let a boat down for him. Had it been night; had the sea been rougher; had he fallen on the other side of the vessel, where the waves would have carried him from her; had he not been able to grasp the rope; in any of these cases he would have been lost. But the poor heathen, if he thinks at all about it, will ascribe his escape to chance, or to some of his idols, as blind and helpless as chance. These poor fellows have a great horror of the sea. It is only for high wages that they will serve as sailors. These men get fourteen rupees monthly, or nearly seven dollars, a large sum for such sailors; and after all, the greater part of the crews of the "country ships" are impressed by force, and carried off without their own consent.

July 21st. Here we are, fifty miles north and thirty miles west of our station day before yesterday. Quite a gale came on yesterday afternoon, and we have been almost lying to for twenty-four hours. We have one duck, and ten fowls left, and nearly a certainty of having only salt meat for a few weeks to come, unless Providence so order it that we get to Singapore next week, which might be done, even in this monsoon, under favourable cir cumstances. The captain has begun to talk of allowances of wood, water and provisions. Outward things look gloomy. I do not say these things by way of complaint, for I feel less disposed to complain now, than at any previous part of the voyage, but to give you some idea of our situation. As to myself, I find the promises increasingly precious, and I think I shall soon have Acts xxvii. by heart. It becomes more and more instructive. Still, hope has not yet left me, that we may make a reasonable voyage as to time, though the prospect is more and more discouraging. Such times as these, head winds, tossing tempests, and adverse currents, make me think of that happy place, where "there is no more sea."

The most unpleasant thing about our present situation, is its uncertainty. We may have a favourable wind to-morrow, and soon reach our "desired haven." We may toss about here for weeks, and at last not be able to make the port after all. But "the Lord reigns, let the earth rejoice. Clouds and darkness are round about him, but righteousness and judgment are the habitation of his throne."

July 22d. Worse and worse; after running for eighteen hours to the N. W. and W. N. W., and six hours S. S. E., at the rate of four miles an hour all the time, we find ourselves twenty miles north, and ten miles east of our station yesterday! The current here must be tremendous. We are almost at our "wits' end." We have now been beating about for a week, most of the time under double-reefed topsails, and have made almost no progress. Indeed, we are very little farther on than we were two weeks ago. Yet I am thankful to find that my own mind is calm and peaceful most of the time. I should greatly regret to be obliged to put back to Macao; and should be most heartily glad to be at Singapore, or to be assured of getting there in three weeks; but it is the Lord who has "raised the stormy wind," and he has wise ends in view. It is not very comfortable being here. My health may suffer for want of exercise; there being so much motion, it is hardly possible, with safety, to take any; the affairs of the mission may be retarded somewhat by my detention; Dr. Hepburn may be in need of the funds I have with me, so may Mr. Buell; our removal to China, should that be resolved on, may be delayed a good while, &c.; but all these things are known to Him who controls my course, and He will care for his own cause. Cowper's hymn,

> "God moves in a mysterious way,"

is a very precious one, especially the last lines:

> "God is his own interpreter,
> And he will make it plain."

Saturday, July 23d. Twenty miles to the east of our station yesterday; same latitude.

Monday, July 25th. I see the China sea in an entirely different aspect this voyage, from what it was in May, when we went up. Then all was calm; now all is stormy. We are lying to to-day again, after splitting three or four more sails. Yesterday and to-day have been so cloudy as to allow no observation, and we know not where we are. I almost begin to doubt whether we shall arrive at Singapore at all, during this monsoon. We have now been out the usual time required to make the trip, and the prospect is darker than ever. The captain talks of going to Manilla to lay in fresh stores. We shall be obliged to do this before long, if we do not soon arrive at Singapore, as we have provisions for but little more than a month longer. However, I am not discouraged. "*Jehovah Jireh.* In the mount it shall be seen." God is accustomed to reveal himself when his creatures are at their greatest extremities. I have been comparing my condition with that of the Lascars on board; ill-fed, ill-clothed, ill-treated, working hard, few social, no intellectual, and, worse than all, no spiritual privileges. How much is my condition better than theirs!

Friday, July 29th. We are now near two hundred miles further north than we were last week, and about sixty miles further from Singapore than we were fifteen days ago. I thought that I undertook this voyage in obedience to the intimations of Providence, but hitherto they have almost all been against us. One gale this week drove us eighty miles to the northward in less than twenty hours; head winds and adverse currents make it nearly impossible to proceed. Our provisions will last us but a month longer, and it would require almost all that time in favourable circumstances to make the remainder of our voyage.

To be sure all anxiety, even on these points, is quieted by the recollection that Christ is "head over all things for the church," and that all things shall work together for good, to them that love God; but sometimes I forget these things.* I would not willingly undertake another such voyage as this, and yet I must say, so great have been the benefits which I have received from this trial, that they far more than counterbalance all the inconveniences hitherto endured. Still we are not required to seek afflictions, and I should greatly rejoice to be once more on solid ground; yet while detained I hope to be sustained.

Saturday, July 30th. The pleasantest day we have had for weeks: a light clear sky, blue sea, little motion, and pleasant breeze. At noon, the captain put his head into my room, crying, with great glee, "Hurrah, she springs it again! We have made ten miles southing!" The first time we have been able to get to the south for a week, though we have had more favourable winds. This is a "little reviving in our bondage," among these currents. If

* I am not quite sure that I recollect right, but I think Bunyan makes Mr. *Forget-good* Mayor of Mansoul in place of my Lord Understanding, which is very appropriate.

it will only continue! In a case like this, one is in danger either of building too much on such a prospect as we have to-day, or, on the other hand, of "despising the day of small things," and being cast down, because it is no better.

I was much struck with Isa. xxvi. 4, yesterday evening. The literal translation of the Hebrew is, "Trust ye in Jehovah even for ever, for in Jah Jehovah is the rock of unending ages." No translation, however, can give the force of the original. It is, I think, even more emphatic than "the five negatives," Heb. xiii. 5, on which you may have seen some very delightful remarks in Nevins's Practical Thoughts. I think if I ever know enough of Chinese to be of any service in translating the Bible into it, I shall find it a very pleasant employment. I find that in proportion as I closely examine almost any passage, it presents gems more and more sparkling. Thus, in the above passage, in addition to the triple mention of the name Jehovah, the peculiar name of God, as the Covenant God of his people, the first "for ever" is literally "eternities of eternity;" and the last expression is "the rock of everlastings." Well might the Psalmist (Ps. cxliv. 15,) say, "Happy is that people" (literally, O the blessednesses of that people,) "whose God is *Jehovah.*"

Monday, Aug. 1st. Delightful weather and fair progress; yesterday, forty-six miles direct; to-day, fifty-six to the east, and three to the south; and wind getting more favourable. If this weather continues, we hope to be in Singapore in less than three weeks.

Tuesday, Aug. 2d. Still progressing at a very fair rate. Saw the coast of Cochin China to-day, about thirty or forty miles off. It is high and mountainous, but we have not gone near enough to see its features very distinctly. The part we saw was Cape Varela, or the Pagoda Cape—so called from a very large rock on the side of the mountain, just behind the cape. It has a very singular appearance.

Saturday, Aug. 6th. After going on swimmingly for four or five days, we found ourselves beset by a current yesterday, which became very strong to-day, and has sent us a long way to the eastward. This casts rather a damp over our spirits. Where we are now, Lat. 11°, is the narrowest part of the sea, and if we meet a current anywhere it is likely to be here. Could we only get two degrees further down, we should probably be safe enough. To-day finishes our forty-ninth day, and yet we are hardly more than half way; yet the weather is fine, and we still hope for the best, though I assure you it is quite trying. What shall the end of these things be? Here I am all alone; no, not alone; for God is here, and He whose Providence did so remarkably arrest me a year ago, and turn my course from Africa to China, and has brought me hitherto, will not now desert me. Nothing encourages me so much in regard to my labours in this mission, as the recollection that I have been sent here. I should never have come of my own free choice; and I am sure that He who has sent me has work for me to do, for which he will strengthen me. It may be he has sufferings for me to endure, and though the thought of them almost makes me tremble, for the rod I have felt on this voyage has been hard to bear, and for the present grievous, yet will his grace therein be sufficient for me. If he has neither work for me to do, nor trials for me to bear, then my course is almost done. And it is no further from this rough sea to heaven, than from the soft beds, and the kind and soothing attentions of home; and never, I trust, either in this world, or in the world to come, shall I regret that I have left father and mother, and brethren and sisters, for the kingdom of heaven's sake.

I could wish I had a Christian friend near. Even this communion with you on paper, with "pen and ink," when I "have many things to say," and c . write but a very few of them, is refreshing. How often I think of you!—of the hasty breakfast that morning; how Reuben was like a silent cricket all the time; how Jane burst into tears when I came away; of the meeting in the Mission rooms, and the kind friends there; of the walk down to the ship, when the sun shone out so clear; of the crowd, and the bustle, and the hurry there; *the parting!* I can see you yet, waving your handkerchiefs for the last time; brother John's last blessing yet sounds in my ears; and I think how poor Elizabeth was watching over Samuel's sick couch at the time. Again, I see you, and father, and Reuben. Now, the ship has moved, and I see you no more! It is too much. I do not often weep; but sometimes: and yet they are not tears of sorrow, but of affection, and fond remembrance. In this world there are partings and sorrow. In this world there is perplexity and disappointment; in this world we "shall have tribulation." But in heaven there is no more parting, and "no more sea;" no more tribulation, for "sighing and sorrow shall *flee* away," not *go* away, but *flee* away.

* * * * * * *

[The rest of this Journal was destroyed, as stated on page 99.]

Manilla, September 1st, 1842.

My Dear Mother—. . . When my journal comes to hand, which I hope it will before very long, you will have a fuller account of the various adventures and hair-breadth escapes, of the voyage from Macao to this place. It is rough and uncouth in many ways, but it has been a companion to me in loneliness and in dangers, and in pleasures. It made me think of home and of friends when the storm howled around me, and the billows tossed our ship as if they would overwhelm her and us in the black gulf beneath us. It made me think of home, too, in the calm sunset hour at sea, and it brought the tears to my eyes more than once, as the quiet hours of the Saturday and the Sabbath closed around me. I have laughed over some of its little tales, and wept over others, and insensibly it grew like a friend in whose welfare I was deeply interested, and when I sat in my silent cabin and was sorrowful that I had no friend to feel for me, or sympathize with me in my solitude, I laid my hand upon its pages, and said, Wait awhile; when she to whom it is addressed has read it, I shall lack no sympathy; and the very anticipation relieved me. Thus, though in itself it has small merit, yet its associations and nameless influences give it a value in my eyes, that I trust will not be wholly wanting with you.

The houses here cover a great extent of ground, and are two stories high; the ground floor is used for offices, storage, servants' rooms, stables, &c., and the people live on the second floor. A verandah from four to six feet wide runs all round the second story of the house; about four feet of the verandah from the floor is boarded up, and the rest up to the eaves of the roof is occupied by sliding frames, which are glazed, if I may use that word, with mother-of-pearl shells, instead of glass. The shells are cut into pieces about three inches square, and being semi-transparent, admit abundance of light, even when the verandah is all closed up. Glass windows are not used at all, and as there is no winter here, there are neither stoves nor fire-places. Just before my window there are two or three plantain trees, shooting up their broad leaves. One of the leaves before me, I should say, is nine feet long, and two feet and a half broad, of a beautiful green, and gently waving with the wind. By the side of the plantain is an areka tree, with branches of leaves of a much darker green, the branch of leaves being about half as long as a single plantain leaf. Half a dozen or more plantain leaves grow from the top of a plantain tree, and half a dozen branches of leaves from the top of an areka tree. Among the leaves of the areka tree, a couple of little brown sparrows are now building their nest; beyond these are a few tropical plants, the names of which I do not know. By the side of the house, in front of my window, flows a branch of the river Pasig, in which I see a custom-house boat, with its sail-cloth awning; several bankahs, or row-boats, with mat awnings; several canoes, and several heavy boats for carrying off cargo to the ships. On the other side of the water are several houses, with their shell-glazed verandahs, red tile roofs, and each house is surmounted by a cross; while over the roofs of the houses I see the high steeple of the Binondo parish church, once white, but now blackened and discoloured by age, with grass growing out of the cornices, and several bells in the cupola. One of the houses opposite is the place for depositing cocoanut wine, where several large boats are loading and unloading. This being a government monopoly, several sentinels are keeping guard at the gates. This being one of the hottest parts of the day, eleven o'clock, A. M., very few Europeans are to be seen; but there are a number of native men about. They are very cleanly: their dress consists of a pair of trowsers and a shirt, which hangs outside, and either a handkerchief or a hat on the head. They use a variety of colours for shirts and trowsers, but are always very clean. . . .

Yours, most affectionately,

W. M. Lowrie.

Manilla, Sept. 14th, 1842.

REV. J. C. LOWRIE—DEAR BROTHER—After spending about three weeks in Macao, and Hong Kong, very busily, but very pleasantly, and accomplishing all that seemed necessary at that time for the prosperity of the mission, a rather more than usually favourable opportunity of proceeding to Singapore was offered, which it seemed proper that I should embrace. It was a clipper bark, built near Calcutta, expressly for the trade between India and China, and intended to run up and down the China Sea, both with and against the monsoons. It is probably known to most persons, that the monsoons are periodical winds that prevail in the Bay of Bengal, and among the islands that separate the Pacific and the Indian Oceans. Those that prevail in the China Sea, are called the north-east and south-west monsoons. The north-east monsoon is commonly preceded by about a month of variable winds and frequent calms, and commences blowing from the north-east steadily in October. It continues till some time in April; then follows nearly a month of variable winds and calms, and about the first of May the south-west monsoon sets in, blowing till the middle or end of September, and sometimes to the middle of October. This is the general division; but these winds are subject to great irregularity in their commencement and termination. For example; when we went up the China Sea in May, in the Huntress, we expected to have had the south-west monsoon steadily, though gently, in our favour; but, to our great disappointment, experienced calms and light and variable winds during the whole of that month. It was formerly thought useless for vessels to attempt a passage through the China sea, against either of the monsoons, but of late years fast-sailing vessels, and particularly clippers, and clipper-built ships, have very frequently succeeded in making a passage in the course of from twenty-five to thirty-five and forty days. In the year 1841, several vessels passed down the China Sea, from Macao to Singapore, in the months of June, July, and August, without any difficulty. Among others, the captain of the Sea Queen, in which I took my passage, who was then chief mate of another vessel, had made the passage in thirty days, with delightful weather the whole time.

The prospect of another month at sea, after having just finished a four months' voyage, was not very pleasant; but the instructions of the Committee and the state of the mission seemed to require it, and full of hope, and anticipating a pleasant voyage, and safe arrival at Singapore, I embarked in the Sea Queen, June 18. Our progress for two or three weeks, though slow, was still tolerably good; and as nothing else of special interest occurred to occupy my attention, I had an opportunity of learning something of the character and regulations of a "country ship." This is a term applied, not to vessels belonging to the natives of these countries, but to vessels built in the East Indies, owned and commanded by Europeans, and manned by Hindus or Malays. The greater part of them are built in India, of the teak, and other hard woods of that country, and their cordage is made of the fibres of the husk of the cocoa-nut. They trade principally between India and China, touching, however, at the intermediate ports. They carry rice, opium, and other articles to China, and return with teas, silks, Chinese manufactures, and the like, to India; frequently making two, and occasionally three voyages in a year. . . .

It is of course necessary for the officers to acquire some knowledge of the Bengali language, as the crew cannot be expected to learn English. A very small smattering, however, commonly serves their purpose, consisting simply of the nautical terms necessary for the regulation of the ship: (*barra bras*, mainbrace; *garva bras*, topsail-brace; *deman*, sheet; *stringee*, clewline; *bobber*, weather; *barraka*, sea, &c.)

The *serang* and *tindals* are supposed to know so much of what is needful, for the management of the ship, as to require but little direction from the higher officers. . . . . .

For ten days we made tolerably good progress; we then had a week of calms. Nothing is more trying at sea than a calm: yet it is true that scarcely any sight is so beautiful as that of the ocean in a perfect calm,—provided it does not last too long. The water then becomes of a blue colour, as beautiful as that of a field of flax in bloom: a few light or golden clouds float in the sky, or mirror themselves in the sea: while all around the surface of the water is calm, and smooth as glass, varied only by a heaving, as gentle as that of a sleeping infant's bosom. Now and then a faint light air causes a gentle *simmer* or a ripple on the water, like the smile on an infant's face when dreams are pleasant in its soul. Especially is the sight beautiful in the evening, when the sun's last rays are reflected from the resplendent wave, and a sea of liquid gold seems to mingle with the bending heavens. I have sat by the ship's side for hours, gazing around, and mentally exclaiming: No earthly painter, and no earthly pencil, ever drew such gorgeous, such delicate, and such beautiful scenes as these, and yet, they are but transient reflections of that glorious place, where, though "there is no more sea," such as here we cross, yet there is a "sea of glass, clear as crystal," and that glass not frail and perishable as ours; but "pure gold, transparent as glass." Surely to stand on that sea of glass, having the harps of God, and to sing the song of Moses and the Lamb, will amply repay a few years of toil, and disappointment, and suffering, on the restless sea of life.

Yet, beautiful as were many of the scenes witnessed in the calms, nothing is more wearisome, and we were soon so tired of them, that we wished for any other kind of weather. The S. W. monsoon

soon recommenced, and blew very strongly. The weather became unsettled, and during the course of a month, we had almost constant gales, during which we lost our maintop-gallant-mast, and had so many sails torn by the wind, that sometimes we had not a topsail to spread. In addition to the strong wind and heavy sea, (for three weeks we had not a dry deck to walk upon, on account of the constant breaking of the sea over it,) we were exceedingly embarrassed by adverse currents. Several days, when we thought we had made tolerably good progress to the south-west, we found, by observations, that we had actually been carried ten and twenty miles to the north-east. If our ship had not been almost new, she could scarcely have sustained the strain that came upon her. As it was, it was necessary to have the men at the pumps two or three times every day. As may be supposed, in such circumstances, our progress was exceedingly slow. We frequently lost as much in one day as we had gained in three or four; and after beating about for thirty-one days, we found ourselves, August 11, only one hundred miles nearer Singapore than on the 10th of July preceding. . . . .

It has often been said, and with truth, that no trial which a missionary experiences, is greater than that of being deprived of the advantages of Christian society, and of the privileges of the sanctuary. Such I found to be the case; and it was difficult at times to refrain from tears, when the Sabbath came round, and the recollection of its peaceful and hallowed scenes at home rose before me, in contrast with the solitude of the dark and foam-crested waves, where, alone, I had no fellow-Christian with whom to worship God. Truly, "blessed are they that dwell in thy house; they will be still praising thee." But it was pleasant to think, and to *experience* that those who enjoy these external privileges, do not *monopolize* all the blessing.

"Blessed is the man whose strength is in thee, in whose heart are the ways of them." . . . .

Finding at last that we could not make head against the currents, and that our provisions were nearly exhausted, we very reluctantly turned about, and shaped our course for Manilla, where we arrived safely, August 3d, sixty-six days after leaving Macao. And yet, great as was our disappointment, we found abundant cause for gratitude. The bad weather we had experienced had extended over a large part of the China Sea. An English vessel had been wrecked, not far from ours. Her captain and mate were drowned, and the crew obliged to go to Manilla, in their boats. Several other vessels had been driven back with damage, and almost all the vessels in Manilla Bay had dragged their anchors, while one or two of them were driven on shore. Yet we had escaped without any serious injury.

I arrived at Manilla a perfect stranger, not knowing even the name of a single person here. There were no Protestant missionaries in the Philippine Islands, and Manilla is almost the only port from Chusan in China to Calcutta in India, where I could not have found persons whom I knew, or with whom, from similarity of pursuits, I could not speedily have formed an acquaintance. Yet I had not been ashore an hour, before I found myself most perfectly at home in the house of Mr. Moore, a merchant from Boston, and at present acting as United States vice-consul.

Such, dear brother, is my story. It may give you an idea of some of the difficulties of the navigation of the China Sea, and lead you to unite your thanks with mine for the goodness of God which has so manifestly attended me. . . . .

Your affectionate brother,

W. M. Lowrie.

SHIPWRECK OF THE HARMONY.

Having engaged a passage from Manilla to Singapore in the Harmony, I went on board with the captain about noon, September 18, 1842, and found Messrs. M. and G., my two fellow-passengers, already there. It was quite calm, and we did not start till eight o'clock, P. M., when a fine breeze sprang up, and as the moon was shining brightly, we got under weigh, set studding-sails alow and aloft, and went off in full sail. The ship was deeply laden with more than six hundred tons of sugar, and drew nineteen feet of water. She was counted one of the fastest sailing British merchantmen in the Chinese waters; but with such a cargo the captain feared she would not sail as well as usual. However, she kept up with the Cecilia, a swift English bark, and not near so deeply laden. It was a lovely night, and everything looked so favourable that we were all in high spirits, and had great hopes of a speedy voyage. By daylight next morning* we were fifteen or twenty miles outside of Corregidor, which was much better success than we had allowed ourselves to anticipate.

It was quite calm during Monday morning: but in the afternoon a breeze sprang up. The Cecilia had gone ahead of us; but when this breeze fairly set in we caught up with her, and in three or four hours had left her five miles astern. This settled the point of the Harmony's sailing, and gave us great hopes of her future performances. The breeze gradually increased to a gale, and on Wednesday morning we were under double-reefed topsails, with a tremendous sea astern. I was strongly reminded of the waves in a gale off the Cape of Good Hope.

* We sailed on Sabbath, September 18th. It was *Manilla Saturday*, and I observed Monday, September 19th, as Sabbath. The day before had been observed as Sabbath by the men, who had nothing to do except to get the ship under weigh in the evening. As we sailed on Sabbath the "morning" above mentioned was Monday morning.

The vessel being very deeply laden, shipped a great deal of water: immense waves piled themselves up several feet above the bulwarks, and came tumbling in on deck, and the cabin was flooded with water several times. I was standing by the cabin door once, when a sea came over the ship's side, and before it was possible to escape, the water was up over my knees. The gale increased to a storm by noon, (Wednesday,) and though we were going right before it, its violence was so great that we were at last obliged to lie to, under a close-reefed main-top-sail, and foretopmast-staysail. Being from the east, it had helped us on wonderfully in our course.

The gale moderated during the night, and the sun shone out the next day, though the sea continued rough. Friday was a pleasant day; and my sea-sickness being now over, everything was agreeable. Being now pretty well acquainted with the ship, the comparisons I made between her and the Sea Queen, in which my last voyage was made, were by no means favourable to the latter. The Harmony was a superior vessel in every respect, except that her cabins, though all on deck, were not so well ventilated as those of the Sea Queen. But the masts, rigging, and sails of the Harmony were stronger and neater. She was a better sailer; her crew were Englishmen, and her steward, (an important consideration to a passenger,) though by no means a neat, driving fellow, was so far superior to the filthy butler of the Sea Queen, that the two should not be named on the same day. There were a few cock-roaches, but no ants or centipedes. Her captain was a stout, hearty, good-humoured Scotchman, with somewhat of the Scotch pronunciation and accent. He was an intelligent and independent man, a perfect sailor, full of sailor phrases, and as fond of his ship as if she were his wife. He was kind and yet strict with his men, and was therefore liked and obeyed by them. He used no profane language, (certainly never in my presence,) and was very attentive to the wants of his passengers.

Saturday, September 24, was a cloudy day, wind from the west, and our course nearly south. The captain could not get an observation of the sun, but, by his reckoning, we were at noon in lat. 11 deg. 53 min. N., and long. 114 deg. 20 min. E. This was a very unpleasant position, being but fifteen or twenty miles north of the North Danger—a small island, with not a tree on it, and a reef all around, which marks the north-western limit of the dangerous archipelago of shoals in the China Sea. Accordingly, every effort was made to get to the westward, but the wind now became unsteady, veering about so much, that it was hardly possible to keep the ship on any course, except to the north-east, which was directly contrary to the course we wished to go.

Sabbath morning (Sept. 25) was dark, cloudy, and squally: there was a heavy sea, and a rolling ship, with frequent showers, a hazy atmosphere, and exceedingly baffling winds. About ten o'clock A. M., the wind became steady at S. W.; ship went off W. N. W. five or six miles an hour, under double-reefed-topsails, and the weather began to look less threatening. At noon the captain came down and changed his wet clothes, being the third time that day, and said the prospects were more favourable. We had tiffin, and he remarked incidentally, that he had just been sending men aloft, but no dangers were to be seen, as the sea was clear on all sides. We were all in excellent spirits, and amused ourselves with conjectures as to the probable length of our voyage. After tiffin the captain took his segar and went on deck, and the passengers exchanged a few more sentences as to the time of arrival at Singapore, and were about quietly reclining on the sofas to read, when the ship struck against some obstacle with tremendous violence. It impeded her onward motion in a moment. We started to our feet; again she struck, and again she reeled like a drunken man. The deck quivered beneath our feet; and on going out we found the men running about, the officers giving their orders, and the terrified steward groaning and wringing his hands at the cabin door. So violent were the strokes, that I was apprehensive of the ship being broken to pieces, and ran to get my life-preserver. By the time I had it half inflated, the ship had beaten over the shoal, and I went up on the poop-deck. The captain had changed the ship's course, and I found him giving his orders, and pacing the deck in great agitation. The shock had been so sudden and unexpected, that he, as well as every one else, was taken completely by surprise. I had scarcely time to speak to him, or to reply to some observation that he made to me, when the vessel struck again with even greater violence. The sea was boiling in short uneasy waves on all sides, and we seemed to be above some deeply sunken rock, on which the ship's bottom was dashed every time she sunk in the hollow of the waves. Through the violence of the blows, large pieces of her keel were broken off, and rose to the surface; and the copper was torn off in masses from her bottom. At one time we could both *see and feel* the middle of the ship *rising up*, while her stem and stern *sank down*. In sailor's phrase, her "back was broken," and for a moment I fully expected she would break in two.

It was an awful time: a strong wind; a heavy rain falling, and an unquiet and restless sea; yet there were no breakers and no discoloured waters—the usual signs of a shoal,—and although in the intervals of rain we could see at least ten miles on every side, yet there was neither island, rock nor breakers in sight; nor any other sign of danger. Of this I am certain, for the captain requested me to look round and see; nay even when we were upon the shoal we could see nothing, for I looked over the ship's side when she was striking most heavily, and nothing was visible beneath the dark waters. Such shocks must be as dreadful as those of an earthquake, perhaps more so. They were the blows of an unseen enemy, and we could not tell at what moment we might receive another which should send us at once to the bottom.

The pumps were immediately manned, and the water that came up tasted sweet; it had already reached the sugar in the hold. On sounding the well, *three feet* of water was found. The four pumps were kept constantly going, the main hatchway opened and sugar thrown overboard to lighten the vessel, but this was soon abandoned. Some of the men were employed in getting the boats ready in case of emergency; we packed up a few clothes and valuables in as small a compass as possible, and waited in suspense for the result. As you may well imagine, I was on my knees more than once. It was a solemn time: but my mind was kept in a calm and composed frame.

We struck about half-past one, P. M. In less than an hour the vessel had three feet of water in the hold. In two hours more it had increased to six feet; in less than another hour there was seven, and in twenty minutes more *seven feet and six inches*; and this though the four pumps were kept constantly going, and all drawing well. It was now near five o'clock, P. M., and it being evident that the ship must sink, the pumps were abandoned and the boats got ready. It was very providentially ordered for us that the masts had not fallen when the ship struck so violently, as, in that case, it would have been difficult to get the long boat out. It was after dark, perhaps nearly seven o'clock, when the boats were ready, and we found it a work of difficulty and danger to get into them; for with the heavy sea running they rose and fell more than ten feet every minute. It was arranged that twenty-one, including the captain and passengers, should go in the long boat, and the mate and seven men in the jolly boat.

We managed to get in about seven o'clock, and pushed off from the ship. She was then settling fast in the water, which was already nearly on a level with her deck. The lights were left burning in her cabin, and the noble ship, which on that very day one year before commenced her first voyage, was left a shattered, sinking wreck. We wanted to see her go down, but as the sea was rolling heavily, wind high, and a drenching rain falling, it was neither comfortable nor safe to stay by her, and we kept the boats before the sea by means of small pieces of canvass. They had four oars in the jolly boat, and we had had as many, but three of them were broken in keeping the boat from dashing against the ship's side: thus we found ourselves in the open sea, four hundred miles from land, with only a single oar. A heavy rain fell almost constantly till midnight, from which we could have no protection, and in a few minutes we were drenched with the rain and the spray, which every now and then dashed over us. The boat, with so many persons in, was very deep in the water; and to add to our discomfort and apprehensions, leaked a good deal, so that one person was constantly employed in bailing her out. About midnight the wind and sea abated somewhat, the clouds dispersed a little, the moon dimly glimmered in the sky, and we kept on slowly to the north. Owing to the weather, I had slept almost none the night before, and exhausted with want of sleep, anxiety and fatigue, I managed to rest a little towards morning, though how or where it would be hard to say.

On Monday we rigged a couple of masts, and with a royal studding-sail, and main sky-sail, which had been thrown into the boat, we mustered a very respectable foresail and mainsail, using our whole oar, and one of the broken oars for yards. The boat was then lightened, by throwing overboard everything that could possibly be spared; the baggage and provisions were packed as neatly as possible, and a man and boy taken in from the jolly boat, which made our whole number nineteen men and four boys; a large number for a boat only twenty-one feet long, and eight feet broad. The provisions were then examined, and we found there was bread enough to last a week or ten days, but that we had a very small quantity of water. There could not have been more than eight or ten gallons. This was a cause of no little anxiety, for by our calculations we could not be less than four hundred miles from Manilla, (whither we now directed our course,) and at that season of the year, calms, and even head winds, which would make our passage long, were not unlikely to occur. Accordingly all hands were put on an allowance of *half a pint* of water daily, and bread in moderation. The water was served out twice a day in a cup which held a gill, and all drank out of the same cup. I had put a little keg of crackers on board, which kept dry when all the rest were wet with rain and salt water, and also a small box of raisins, which proved very acceptable. We had a few cheeses and some cocoa-nuts, the milk of which served us for two days, thus making a great saving in our little stock of water.

This (Monday) was a tolerably pleasant day. Pieces of canvass were nailed round the sides of the boat to keep out the spray, and having a fair light wind, we made some progress on our course. The sun shone out brightly in the afternoon, and dried our wet clothes, and most of us slept well that night. We began to cherish hopes of arriving at some land ere long.

Tuesday was a terrible day. Not a cloud in the sky; scarcely a breath of wind, and the hot sun of the torrid zone beating full upon us. There was but one umbrella in the boat, and we could not hoist an awning: but being sunburnt, and even blistered, was the least evil. Half a pint of water on such a day, when tantalized by the sight of an ocean of water, so clear but so salt, was a small allowance, and I almost prayed to be swallowed up in the raging sea, rather than be suffered to linger in so dreadful a condition. Yet there was no murmuring, and we all kept up our spirits.

As the jolly boat sailed much faster than ours, it was thought best she should go on ahead. She could be of no service to us, nor we to her, by keeping company, and by going on, she might escape danger, and even find means of assisting us. Accordingly she left us this afternoon, and we afterwards regretted deeply that she had not done so sooner. This night I slept badly; the baggage had been shifted to put the boat in better sailing trim, and there was not room to place one's self comfortably; lying down was at any time out of the question, for want of room. A fine favourable breeze sprang up soon after dark, and we made good progress.

On Wednesday the breeze became stronger, with a heavy sea. We went rapidly on, and in our lonely course found amusement in watching the large flocks of boobies that in some places almost covered the sea. They came around us in great numbers, and alighted on the yards, and even on the sides of the boat. In his eagerness to catch one the boatswain fell overboard, affording us all a hearty laugh at his expense. Several showers fell near us about dark, and we hoped to have caught some water, but could not. Slept miserably. In the part of the boat where I was, which was about six feet by eight in size, there were four persons to sleep, and one constantly employed in baling out the water.

Thursday morning commenced with rain, which soon wet us to the skin; but we did not mind that, for we caught several buckets-full of water, which, in the low ebb of our water-cask, gave us great joy; and we ate our breakfast in high spirits. For fear of suffering from thirst, I ate but little, seldom taking more than three small crackers a day, and a mouthful of cheese with a bunch of raisins.

From the progress we had made the night before, we had great hopes of seeing land either to-day, or early on the following, but we soon began to think of other things. About ten o'clock the wind rose, the sea ran very high, and frequent squalls of wind and rain darkened the heavens and drenched us to the skin. The captain sent the best helmsman to the tiller, and sat down himself by the compass, and for eight long hours he did not move from his seat. Conversation ceased; and scarcely a word was uttered in all that time, except the orders from the captain to the helmsman, "Port! Port your helm, quick! Hard a-port! Starboard now! Mind your port-helm," &c. Many a longing, anxious look did we cast before us to see if there were any signs of land; but still more to the west, to see if the gale gave signs of abating. But no! Darker and darker grew the heavens over us; higher and higher rose the sea; louder and louder still roared the waves as they rushed past our little boat, and faster fell the rain. If a single one of those waves had come over the boat's side, it would have overwhelmed and swallowed up the boat, and every one on board; and it was only by the utmost care and skill that she was kept before them.

Death never seemed so near before. An emotion of sorrow passed through my mind, as I thought of my friends at home who would, probably, be long in suspense in regard to my fate; and of regret, as I thought of the work for which I had come; but for myself, my mind was kept in peace. I knew in whom I had believed, and felt that He was able to save; and though solemn in the near prospect of eternity, I felt no fear, and had no regret that I had perilled my life in such a cause.

Thus the day wore away, and night approached without any signs of more moderate weather. The wind was now so strong, and the sea so high, that it was with the utmost danger that we could hold on our course. Everything was wet, and we tried in vain to get a light for the compass; besides, by our calculations, we could not be more than thirty or forty miles from land; and at the rate we were going, should reach it about midnight; but to attempt to land in such a sea, in the dark, would be madness itself. What could we do? Backwards, or sideways, we could not go, on account of the sea; to go forward was to throw our lives away; to remain where we were, *even if it were possible*, seemed to be remaining in the very jaws of death. It was, however, our only hope, if hope it could be called, and accordingly preparations were made for heaving the boat to. The foresail was taken down, and securely fastened to the yard; the largest cord we could muster (about thirty fathoms) attached to this and to the boat. The mainsail was then lowered, and watching our opportunity, the foresail was thrown overboard, cord paid out, and the boat's head turned to the wind. This last was a most perilous operation; for had a wave struck her while her broadside was exposed to it, all would have been over with us. The plan, however, succeeded admirably. The little foresail being between the wind and the boat, it served to break the force of the waves; and as it lay flat on the water, it was not acted on by the wind; and thus served also as an anchor to keep the boat's head to the wind. We then had the mainsail hoisted up in the form of a staysail, to keep the boat steady, and thus we were hove to.

For a while, the result was very uncertain. The wind howled past us with a force that made every plank in the boat quiver; the rain fell in torrents, with the violence of small hailstones, nearly all the night; and we could hear the great waves as they formed and rose away ahead of us, and then rushed toward us, with a sound like the whizzing of an immense rocket. Sometimes they would strike us as if with a heavy hammer, causing the boat to jump bodily away; and then again, their white, foaming, phosphorescent crests would be piled up by our sides, as if, the next moment, they would dash in and overwhelm us in an instant. There we lay, packed together so closely that we could scarcely move; while every now and then, a dash of spray came over us, covering us with pale phosphoric sparks that spread a dim and fearful light for a few inches around. Oh, it was a dreadful night! There was distress and perplexity, the sea and the waves roaring, and men's hearts failing them for fear.

Not one of our company, I will venture to say, had any expectation of seeing the light of another day. For myself, I thought deliberately of each and every member of our family, and breathed a silent farewell to each: of many of my friends by name, of former scenes and seasons: of various missionary fields, and offered prayers for each and all: of my own past life, and of the certainty, for so it then seemed to me, that in a few hours I should enter on the untried realities of which I had so often thought. I know not that my mind was ever in a calmer state, or that I could more deliberately reflect on what I wished to fix my thoughts upon: and though I could not feel those clear convictions of my safety I have sometimes felt, yet my faith was fixed on the Rock of Ages, and death seemed to have but few terrors for me. In such a night, and with such expectations, it was wrong to sleep; and though benumbed with the rain and cold, and almost exhausted for want of rest, I did not close my eyes during the whole time. Many precious Scripture truths passed through my mind; such as—"When thou passest through the waters I will be with thee, and through the rivers, they shall not overflow thee," which I applied to myself in a spiritual manner; for, situated as we were, I could scarcely expect to have them literally fulfilled. I know not when I felt more strongly the delightful sublimity of the expression, "He holdeth the waters in the hollow of his hand," or the feeling of security even for the body, which for a moment it gave me.

As you may suppose, there were few words spoken, and the only sound we heard, besides the wind and rain and the roaring sea, was that of the boys baling out the water. Towards two or three o'clock in the morning, (by our conjectures, for we had no light to see with,) the wind and sea seemed to abate, and finding we shipped very little water, we began to hope that our lives might yet be spared. The morning slowly dawned, but as it dawned the wind and sea increased. As soon as we could see, the foresail was hauled in and hoisted to the wind, and the mainsail spread, and we commenced again our perilous course. Soon the cry, "Land ho!" was raised, and when the morning had fairly dawned, we saw it stretching along right before us, about ten miles off. We must have been driven many miles during the night to be so near it. Soon our hopes were greatly excited, for the land had the appearance precisely of that about the entrance of Manilla Bay. We could see what we took to be Point Hornos, Mount Mariveles, the island Corregidor, and the Lora Mountains; and we were filled with joy at the prospect of so soon ending our voyage.

We steered directly for the land, meaning to get behind some projecting point, and wait till the sea became calm. Meanwhile, however, the wind and sea rose again; the heavens became black behind us, and there was a great rain. To our sorrow, also, we found that we had mistaken the land, for none of us had ever seen it before. But it was too late to go back, the squall was upon us; and though the rain fell so fast that we could not see more than twenty yards, yet on we must go. There was a little island on the right, and the captain was on the point of steering the boat so as to get round under its lee, when we saw heavy breakers right ahead. We turned off to the left, though at an imminent risk, for this brought our broadside to the sea, and several light waves dashed over us. There were breakers on the left too, but we were directed in a channel, between them, and rounding a projecting point of rocks, we saw a little cove sheltered from the wind, and as smooth as an inland lake. Soon our boat touched the bottom, only a few yards from the shore. We jumped overboard, secured her by ropes to two or three trees, and we were safe! It was a time of joy. With one consent, we gathered together under the trees, and offered up our thanksgiving and praises to God, with prayers for future assistance and protection. It was a scene worthy of a painter's skill,—our little boat fastened to the trees, our scanty baggage piled upon the shore, and ourselves under the custard-apple trees, standing with upturned faces, while the rain dropped upon our bare heads, as we lifted up our voices, and I trust our hearts also, to that God who had held the winds in his fist, and the waters in the hollow of his hand, and had brought us through dangers which we never expected to survive. It was well we came in when we did, for it was then high tide, and a few hours later the channel through which we had passed, was itself one mass of breakers. Our boat would inevitably have been dashed to pieces there, and some, if not all of us, would have perished among the waves.

After all due attention to our boat, and having refreshed ourselves with biscuit, raisins, cheese, and *plenty of water*, (for there were several streams only a few yards from our landing place,) our next care was to find where we were. We knew it to be an island, for as we came in we had seen land at a great distance eastward, which we supposed to be Luconia; but we were not certain whether we were north or south of the entrance of Manilla Bay. From a little point hard by the landing-place, we saw a telegraph station on a hill, and thus concluded that the island was inhabited, and probably by Spaniards. Accordingly, Captain Smith, Mr. G., (who spoke both Spanish and English,) and myself, started to discover what we might. Chun Sing brought me a cutlass that had been saved in the long boat; but being a man of peace, I told him to take it to the captain, and armed myself simply with a walking-stick. Thus accoutred, we set off; but Mr. G., weakened by exposure and want of food, broke down in less than three hundred yards, and declared he could go no further. He went back to the company we had left by the boat, and the captain and myself went on alone to the telegraph station. We found it deserted. Thence we kept on, and soon saw a bullock tied by the nose, a pile of boards and some paddy (rice) fields; sure signs that inhabitants were near. We were now joined by about a dozen of the sailors, two of whom had cutlasses, and the rest walking-sticks, and a Portuguese, who had been in the long boat, and spoke a little Spanish and English. Altogether we were a remarkable looking company, and being high in spirits from our late wonderful escape, we went on right merrily, save that our mirth was often checked by allusions to the other boat. We all thought she was lost, judging it impossible she could have weathered such a gale, and that all on board must have perished.

Finding a narrow path, we followed it over a hill and down a little valley, and presently came to a pumpkin field, in which was a little native house, and some Indians eating boiled pumpkins. They very kindly gave us some, and one of them who spoke Spanish told us there was a village about a mile off, where the Resguardo, (an officer under the Spaniards,) would receive and entertain us. He went along to show the road, and off we went, but instead of one mile it must have been three. We crossed hills, went through valleys, picked our way among bushes, through mud half-knee deep, and along the sea-shore, fording a great many small brooks, and being wet several times with rain; but we were used to the rain, and did not regard that. The sand got into my shoes, and I had to go barefoot most of the way. We passed several natives cutting wood; met several riding on bullocks, one of whom was so polite as to take off his hat when he saw us; and at length came to the village. It was a collection of some twenty or thirty huts by the sea-shore, and all the windows and doors of the houses were crowded with women and children, who gazed at us as if we had fallen from the skies.

Our guide led us to the house of the Resguardo, when who should come running to meet us but Mr. Fillin (the mate) and one of the men who had gone in the jolly boat. "Oh, captain," said the former, "is this you? How many of you are saved?" "Thank God, we are all safe, but I thought you were lost! Are you all alive?" "*I've lost four men, sir!*"

They had arrived in sight of land the previous afternoon about four o'clock, and when some four miles off, a tremendous sea came upon them, turned the boat clear end over end, and threw them all into the sea. Two or three clung to the boat, but were washed off by the waves; another (the best swimmer in the ship) tried to swim ashore, but must have been dashed against the rocks and carried out by a back current; while the mate and this other man, taking each an oar, had made for the land, and succeeded in getting ashore, through the surf, though with great difficulty and danger. Mr. F. was much bruised and cut about the feet by the coral rocks, and for two or three days was scarcely able to move. They had spent the night upon the rocks near the place where they landed. The next morning they found their boat and the oars, but saw no signs of their companions. They then started to find a house, and after several hours of very laborious walking, arrived at this village, only half an hour before we did, and were just telling the people they supposed all the rest of the ship's company were lost, when we came in sight. It was a joyful, yet a sorrowful meeting.

The people of the house received us kindly, and gave us hot coffee, eggs and sweet cakes, which, in our condition, dripping wet and cold, were very acceptable indeed. The house was crowded full of people, old and young, to gaze at us, and a big Manilla bloodhound in the corner gave us surly growls by way of music. It was Friday, Sept. 30, when we landed. We stopped in the village of Loc, island of Luban, at the house of Senor Nicolas Perralta, the chief man of the village, and an Indian, there being no Spaniards on the island. We stayed there two days, and were treated with much kindness by Senor Perralta, who gave us his own best room for our lodging. It was not furnished with beds, but we slept on the bare and not very even floor with much comfort, when we compared it with the crowded rough bottom of the long-boat. The inhabitants were poor, and we bought our own provisions, which our own cook and steward prepared for us.

But my story is growing too long, and I must draw it to a close. We remained in Luban two days; then hired a potine, or native schooner, with "mucho mulos velos!" amazingly torn and ragged sails, for $100, in which we left Luban on Sabbath morning, Oct. 2, for Manilla, (according to Manilla time, which we then used, it was Saturday.) We reached Manilla about two o'clock, P. M., the next day. The silly captain of the potine had almost wrecked us again in a squall off Corregidor at midnight, and had it not been for Captain Smith's presence of mind, who sent one of his own men to the helm, and took command himself, we should certainly have been cast away on the rocks of Point Limbones.

Mr. and Mrs. Moore and Mr. G. Sturgis were

seated at the fruit table when I re-entered their house. For a while they could scarce believe their eyes, and it was not till I spoke that they could believe it was the same person who had left them only two weeks before in full hope of a speedy voyage to Singapore. They received me most kindly. Great was the sympathy expressed by all classes in Manilla. The news of our shipwreck and wonderful escape spread like wildfire, for every one had seen and admired the Harmony, and every one knew and liked her captain. I received my full share of sympathy; but as an offset to this, had also the satisfaction of hearing that many of the sailors in the harbour attributed the loss of the vessel entirely to her having that —— clergyman on board! The long-boat was visited and inspected by many in Manilla, who could scarce believe it possible that twenty-three persons had been stowed away in so small a space; and how we weathered such a gale, which was severely felt in the roads at Manilla, where many ships had dragged their anchors, was a wonder to all. Captain Cole, of the Delhi, a large American vessel, which had been obliged to lie to in the same gale, told me he considered our escape little less than miraculous. Indeed the more I have heard of the ravages of that gale, the more I am astonished at our escape. During the very time we were most exposed to its fury in the long-boat, a Spanish vessel, was driven ashore on Luconia and lost, and the Conrade, an English vessel, was thrown on her beam ends, dismasted and finally foundered, while one-half of her crew were drowned.

When I look back and consider how many wonderful circumstances conspired to secure our safety in the midst of most imminent danger, it is hard to believe that it has been a reality. It seems, even now, like some terrible dream from which I have hardly yet awaked.

It was most providential for us that the ship struck by day, and not by night; that her masts did not go overboard when she struck, as they certainly would have done, had she not been a new and strong vessel; that we got safely into the boats in the dark with that heavy sea running; that we had provisions enough, and sails when our oars were broken; that we weathered that severe gale; that by daylight we were so near the land; that we escaped the breakers by coming in at high tide; that we found that little sheltered cove; that we met such kind treatment at Luban; that we arrived safely at Manilla, notwithstanding the dangers of Corregidor, and that none of us (so far as I know) have suffered any serious inconvenience from so much exposure to sea, and sun, and wind, and rain. All that I experienced was a soreness in my limbs and a slight fever for several hours after we landed on Luban. I cut a walking-stick the day we left that island, which has been mounted and sent to my father as a memento of that wonderful deliverance, and I am sure that all our family will join me in the prayer, that the life thus spared may be devoted to Him who first gave it to me, and now has rescued it from the engulfing sea; that though I shall not attain to the eminence of that Moses who was drawn out of the waters, I may yet, in some humble degree, be like him—a leader to rescue God's chosen people in China, and lead them like a flock in the green pastures of his holy word.

I must not omit to mention two other items of great importance, in which the hand of God was manifested for our preservation; the first was that the cord, which, by means of the foresail, held the boat's head to the wind, did not chafe or give way, notwithstanding the constant strain upon it. We were very apprehensive of this, for it was not as thick as a man's thumb, and our lives seemed to depend upon that little cord. The second was that the heavy gale we had on Thursday and Thursday night was *from the west*. Had it been an easterly gale, like the one we experienced in the same place only nine days before, it would either have entirely overwhelmed us, or else have sent us half way to Cochin China. Even the heavy rain, uncomfortable as it was, tended to our safety, for it kept the sea from raging as it would otherwise have done. A heavy rain has something of the effect of oil on the waters. It keeps the waves down.

As so many persons were to go in the long boat it was impossible to save anything, except absolute necessaries and valuables of small size. All I saved, therefore, was my watch, my pencil case given by Mr. B., what little specie I had in the vessel, (about $100 in gold,) the clothes on my back, and a few other articles of dress, my Bible, and my cloak. Everything was wet through by the rain and salt water, except my Bible, which I had taken the precaution to envelope in the thick fold of the cloak, and which was thus only slightly damp. Everything else was abandoned. Fortunately I had but a small part of my books with me, perhaps one-fifth. Among these were all my Chinese books; a volume of Flavel, which I prize above its weight in gold; a number of valuable papers, and all my written sermons. With my clothes and other articles thus abandoned, were some parcels sent from the missionaries in China to their friends in Singapore, Bangkok and Malacca.

Arrived at Manilla, it was with some difficulty I could muster a suit of clothes to "go ashore." I had my coat and pantaloons, a pair of slippers, a shirt without bosom and collar, a pair of woollen stockings, and a cap that barely covered my head. I had no vest, but that was concealed by buttoning the coat; collars are not indispensable, and I borrowed a rusty black cravat from Capt. Smith, who happened to have two or three. In such a suit, with my sunburnt face, (from which the skin all peeled off in a few days,) my Luban walking-stick, and my cloak on my arm, I set foot in Manilla again. But I was among kind friends. Mr. and Mrs. Moore supplied every want.

I was at some loss, then, what course to take, but finally thought it best to return to China. Mr. Elgar, the brother of Mrs. Moore, gave me a free passage to Hong Kong, in a vessel of which he was part owner, and for that place I embarked October 10th, with several fellow-passengers. When we left Manilla, in the Harmony, the port-captain, who came off to give the ship her clearance, was very merry, and said to me, "Ah, senor padre, vengas casar senor Moore!" (Ah, sir priest, you only came here to marry Mr. Moore.) But when he came to give the Diana her clearance, his manner was quite altered, and almost melancholy, as he said, "Ah, senor padre, no otro matrimonio! no otro matrimonio!"

We reached Hong Kong safely, though after a rather rough passage, on the 17th of October; just four months after I had left Macao for Singapore. Through what varied scenes I had passed, yet out of them all the Lord delivered me. In the Sea Queen I had an opportunity of studying the first part of Acts xxvii. From my experience on board the Harmony, I have come to a better understanding of the latter part of the same chapter.

"Oh, that men would praise the Lord for his goodness, and for his wonderful works to the children of men. And let them sacrifice the sacrifices of thanksgivings, and declare his works with rejoicing. They that go down to the sea in ships, that do business in the great waters, *these see the works of the Lord*, and his wonders in the deep. For he commandeth, and raiseth the stormy wind, which lifteth up the waves thereof. They mount up to the heavens, they go down again to the depths; their soul is melted because of trouble. They reel to and fro, and stagger like a drunken man, and are at their wits' end. Then they cry unto the Lord, and he bringeth them out of their distresses. He maketh the storm a calm, so that the waves thereof are still. Then they are glad, because they be quiet. *So he bringeth them to their desired haven.*"

W. M. Lowrie.

Macao, December 17th, 1842.

My Dear Father—The Bazaar arrived here today from Singapore, of which I was informed by having a packet of letters sent to me. Opening it, I found letters for Mr. Buell, Mr. McBryde, Dr. Hepburn, and to my great satisfaction, two for myself, one of which was from you, dated May 12th. I read it very speedily, and could hardly refrain from tears as I did so. Had you known precisely my feelings at the present time, you could hardly have written anything more appropriate than its conclusion. It was written to encourage me in trials, and to point me to the sure source of consolation. Trials have come upon me within the last twelve months, wave after wave, and each one, like Job's messengers, more severe than the preceding, and for awhile I thought I could hardly sustain them. My leaving home was a trial, but for that I was prepared by long expectation, and sustained by special communications of grace. My delays in the Sea Queen, and the exceedingly unpleasant accommodations there tried me much more severely; but it was profitable, and taught me many useful lessons, the benefit of which I experienced when shipwrecked in the Harmony. Besides these outward trials, I have experienced much anxiety in deciding on the best course to be pursued in relation to the China mission. In these circumstances you can scarcely understand how much I was encouraged by that train of thought which connects our tribulations here, and our poor weak services, with the glory of the Saviour, and the inconceivable displays of his wisdom, justice, love, and mercy, as manifested to the universe on the judgment day!

Affectionately your son,

W. M. Lowrie.

Macao, December 24th, 1842.

My Dear Mother—Yesterday was a happy day for me. You know how I have been disappointed hitherto about getting my letters. They had all gone on to Singapore, and when the Bazaar came up, and did not bring them, I was afraid that I might have a long time to wait yet, before they came to hand. Yesterday morning Mr. Bridgman's servant came over from Hong Kong, and brought me a packet that had been sent there by mistake. I opened it, and behold, one, two, three, four, yes, fourteen letters, from father and mother, and John C., and Elizabeth, and John M. I put up my Chinese books in all haste, and sent off to tell my teacher he "need not come to-day," and then—did not I have a feast? You do not know in the United States what a letter is worth. When you are separated only a few hundred miles, and have regular mails, it is nothing very special to have a letter once a month or so. But when the sun is shining on you, while your friends are sleeping on the other side of the world, ah, that is a different thing. My first emotion was one of sincere gratitude for such a favour; and my second, perplexity which to open first; and you would have been amused could you have seen me, while I was reading. Sometimes I laughed till the tears came into my eyes; sometimes a sentence brought *other* tears, and yet not tears of sorrow these; and sometimes a sigh escaped me, as I thought of the blasted hopes and disappointments implied in some of the various items of news that met my eye. I seemed to be among you again, and lived over the day of parting, and the few preceding weeks. And yet, eleven months and more have passed since then! and what remarkable things have happened in that time! at least to myself, for as far as I can gather, you have had but few important changes since I left.

. . . . I am well, and contented, and happy, though still sometimes lonely, and occasionally perplexed. My future movements are still uncertain.

With much affection, and many fond remembrances,

I remain truly yours,

W. M. LOWRIE.

Macao, December 27th, 1842.

JAMES LENOX, ESQ.—MY DEAR SIR:—I have lately received, by the Bazaar, a volume of the British Reformers, which my father informs me is from yourself. The receipt of it gave me much pleasure, not merely on account of the intrinsic worth of the book, but principally because it assured me I was still kindly remembered in a family, with which my intercourse, though short, was very pleasant.

A missionary to China, I find, has need of a good many qualifications; and at present it seems probable that one qualification of which he will find peculiar need, is a thorough acquaintance with the writings and spirit of the ancient Reformers from Popery. One of the very greatest difficulties with which we shall have to contend, will arise from the opposition of the Roman Catholics. It is impossible to say how many native Roman Catholics there are in China. Probably the accounts their priests give of their numbers are exaggerated; but it is certain there are many. Their priests, too, are far more numerous than the Protestant missionaries; and being all unmarried, and many of them zealous and active, and enterprising, they bid fair to go far ahead of Protestant missions. I do not think that their celibacy is any advantage in the long run, nor would I wish to see many unmarried Protestant missionaries here; but a few of the right spirit are greatly needed. If we had some twenty or thirty single men, of thoroughly cultivated minds, and prepared to submit to trials and privations to which a lady ought not to be exposed, I should not, humanly speaking, be much afraid of the contest with Popery in China. At present, however, there is no prospect whatever of such a band coming out to join us; and the few who are here are scarcely able,—indeed we are not able,—to occupy the ports already thrown open, but must stand still and see the Popish priests go, not two and two, but by sixes and tens, and establish themselves in every place where a foothold can be gained. Already they have erected a bishoprick at Shanghai, though I have not heard that a single Protestant missionary is going there. I do not think that many of the priests in China, or in that swarming Romish hive, Luconia, are men of much ability, or of extensive acquirements. Some of them, however, are; and they will easily make up in numbers what they lack in mental culture, while the perfect subordination of their system gives them advantages which we look at, but cannot hope to equal. There is, indeed, scarcely anything in reference to China that gives me so many distressing apprehensions as the activity of the Romish priests, contrasted as it is with the apathy of Protestant churches in England and America. England has only three, and America only thirteen missionaries actually in China; and if the whole number labouring for China were collected, they would not amount to thirty, of whom not more than one-half are qualified by acquaintance with the language for efficient labour. It is true that the

God we serve is able abundantly to produce the greatest effects by the fewest and simplest means, but the time does not seem yet to have come when a nation shall be born in a day; and till that time comes, perhaps I should say, in order that it may come, we must use means in some degree proportioned to the results we hope for. But I have filled up my sheet with what, perhaps, will not be very interesting to you. I had no intention of writing at all on this subject when I took up my pen, but the mention of the British Reformers led my mind to a subject that often has a painful interest to me. I cannot see through it, but I feel that we who labour in China will have great need of the "faith and patience of the saints" of olden times, if we expect to maintain our standing here against the last efforts and long-protracted dying agonies, for such I believe they will be, of the man of sin.

I often think of you, and of the pleasant Sabbath I spent at New Hamburgh. It would give me great pleasure to hear from you at any time; a *letter*, in these ends of the earth, is an object of great value.

I am, with much respect and esteem, truly yours,

W. M. Lowrie.

Macao, December 29th, 1842.

My Dear Father—Since my letter of December 17, sent by the Delhi, I have received yours of February 22 and March 12, May 3 and June 4, for all of which I am under very great obligations to you. It is a little remarkable, that though you have probably less time for writing than any of the family, yet you have written more than all the rest of them put together, and given me more news. Many particulars in your letters have interested me very deeply, particularly those concerning the funds, and your efforts to increase them, and your accounts of Princeton students, and the prospect of more missionaries. As to the former subject, I fear it will be many years before the Church comes up even in a moderate degree to her duty. Indeed, I have long thought, that the present generation of Christians will never do all that may be expected. As long as a Christian man is allowed to give five dollars for his annual subscription to the missionary work, and the next day buy fifty dollars' worth of tulips, and yet retain his standing in the Church, I have little hopes of seeing the right spirit prevail. I have thought, therefore, for years, that our hopes are in the Sabbath-schools. None are so easily interested in missions as children, and none may be so easily trained to proper principles as they. I have sent by the Akbar four letters to Sabbath-school children. They are just such as I used to speak to the children of my Sabbath-schools, and nothing that ever I said interested them so much. They are intended for the "Foreign Missionary," and I shall probably send some more soon. If they are judged suitable, I can furnish a good number of them gradually. Of course originality is not the main thing in such articles, although I know that to four-fifths of the Sunday-school children, in our churches, even to those at your very doors, the facts I have stated, and may yet state, will possess all the freshness of some new discovery. I have seen a whole school staring with eyes and mouth open, at the narration of the commonest facts in regard to the heathen; and it is mainly for want of early instruction and training in regard to the facts and principles of missions, that you find it so difficult to bring the churches to give freely of their substance to further them. This opinion is formed on a more thorough knowledge of the real state of the case, than is generally possessed. I hope to send soon some thoughts on this subject, founded mainly on facts that I have seen, and inferences that seem to me to be justly drawn from them.

. . . . I propose to study Chinese pretty diligently for the next three months; by that time I hope to hear from you, and to know definitely who is coming, if anybody, and when. After that I may have to go to Hong Kong, as all the missionaries will probably leave this place in March.

With much love for yourself and all the family,

I remain your affectionate son,

W. M. Lowrie.

Macao, December 29th, 1842.

Mr. John Lloyd—My Dear John:—Though I have several friends, who, if they knew I was writing to you, might think they had a prior claim to yours just now, yet the associations and recollections of this day lead my mind most strongly to yourself; and though I have written one letter of some length to you since I came out, yet I feel as if I wanted to send another. . . .

This day is the anniversary of my spiritual birth; eight years ago to-day! What would I not have given eight years ago, to have been assured that I should persevere thus long in the Christian course? If any one had shown me all the temptations and trials I was to experience in that time, and then assured me that I should survive them all, and be the better for them, I could scarcely have believed him. Yet it has been so, and having obtained help of God, I continue to this day, and humbly hope, that through him I shall persevere even to the end. I trust he has taught me to look upward both for strength and for happiness, and more so lately than ever before. My soul doth, therefore, magnify the Lord.

I spent the greater part of this afternoon in reading over your letters. I wish I had yourself here to talk to, for I sometimes feel a little lonely; especially as both my colleagues are at present at other stations, and it will be some little time before we can get together.

So many things crowd upon me, that I hardly know what to write about. I could easily tell you a long story of adventures and perils, and strange sights and scenes, and wonderful deliverances, but I have not time for that, and you will probably see some of them in the Chronicle. Many of them I must reserve for your private ear, "when we meet in Pèkin, China," as you said in one of the letters I read this afternoon. I am now devoting some five or six hours daily to Chinese; and though as yet I have made little progress, (it is only a month since I commenced it regularly,) yet I feel somewhat encouraged. It will be long, however, I fear, before I can speak it at all; and I fear that at best, I shall have to speak "with stammering lips and another tongue, to this people." Owing to uncertainty as to my future location, I have thought it best to commence the Court dialect, (commonly called the Mandarin,) which is not spoken, except by the literati and public officers. My progress will, on this account, be slower at first, but I think more rapid, steady, and successful in the end.

I know you are anxious to know how I feel about matters and things in general, and though it is yet too soon to speak definitely, yet to you I can speak freely; for you will know how to account for it, if I should afterwards change my opinions. So far, my fears have been mostly disappointed, and my expectations more than realized. I think that for two or three years before leaving the United States, I had as little romance in regard to missions, as any one could have, who had never been actually on heathen ground. Consequently I have not been disappointed. Parting with friends was a sore trial, but I had so long expected it, and prayed for sustaining grace, that I found it far less difficult to bear than I had anticipated. It was a great relief to me that it was quickly over. The ship left the wharf at half-past twelve, and I was truly glad that none of my friends came with me to the Hook. I have at present no wish to return. Since I landed in China I have, as you are aware, had a pretty full share of trials. Now no chastisement for the present is joyous but grievous. So I found them. Nevertheless, although the remembrance of them is yet fresh, and the unpleasant effects of them still continue to a degree, yet from what I have already felt, I am fully assured that afterwards they shall yield to me the peaceable fruits of righteousness. In general the year, (it is nearly a year,) which has past since I left New York, *has been one of the happiest I have ever spent;* and I now look back on it with as much satisfaction as any other equal portion of my life, perhaps I should say with more satisfaction. I came out almost unwillingly. I felt loath to leave a field I had long desired to occupy: I have not found everything here arranged as I desired, nor have I been able to accomplish all that I wished. I have been in unpleasant society: I have suffered in body: I have hung in the jaws of death for hours together, not expecting to live from one moment to another: I have been obliged to wait for months and months for letters from home, and I am now in a station where I have no colleagues in the same mission, and do not expect to have for some months; and yet with all these adverse circumstances, I am glad I came, and pray that I may be suffered to remain. The work is great; there is plenty of it. A wide and effectual door is opened, there are few to enter, while the enemy is very busy sowing tares. I do not think there is that promise of immediate usefulness here that there is in many other places. I hardly hope to see such churches formed here soon as have been formed in Africa, and in India, and in the islands of the sea. Indeed, I may never have the privilege of seeing any Christian church formed here; yet, notwithstanding all this, I think the prospect of usefulness is very great indeed; and for men of the right spirit and qualifications, who are willing to wait for the fruit of their labours till they enter heaven, if it be their Master's will that they wait thus long, I know of few fields so inviting. At present, I think the great difficulty is the language; but every year this difficulty is becoming less, as new facilities in the way of books for its acquisition are being prepared, and places are opened where free intercourse with persons who speak it in its purity is allowed. In a few years I think it will not be considered a very difficult task for persons of good common sense, perseverance, and ordinary abilities to acquire it. At present, however, let nobody who cannot study Latin and Greek, and who is subject to the dyspepsia, come out to China. They had better go elsewhere. Such being my views, dear brother, I have some commands to lay upon you,—the first and chief of which is, get ready to come out here as quick as you can. I am going to write to father, and tell him to catch you by the back of the neck and put you down in the hold of one of Mr. Olyphant's ships, if you ever talk of going to any other part of the world. I'll take charge of you out here. Seriously, though, I want you and——to come out to China; and if either of you do not come, I shall expect a very satisfactory and lengthened communication from you, showing good reasons for not doing it. I speak of you two in particular, because I think you as well qualified as any of the missionary students I know in the Seminary, for this field. The second command is, to pay considerable attention to the Roman Catholic controversy; you may find need for it here. Thirdly, in regard to wives; if you can get good ones, get them by all means; but I beg you not to delay coming for want of them. Shall the heathen perish, and your period of active labour, short at best, be rendered still shorter, because you cannot come alone to labour, where merchants spend their ten, twenty, and thirty years in celibacy, for the sake of gain? . . . Spend your vacations in looking for wives, (Dr. ——'s advice to the contrary, notwithstanding,) but do not keep the ship in waiting. I do not know how I shall get along without one. There is at present no prospect of my getting one, but I am not sorry that I took the course I did in this matter. My opinions may change hereafter; when they do, perhaps I'll tell you.

I could write much more—indeed, I feel loath to stop, but I must write another letter or two to-night, as the vessel goes soon. Dear brother, how often I think of you, and long to see you! The memory of joys that are past is sweet to my soul.

That the richest of heavens blessings may ever rest upon you is the prayer of

Your brother in Christ,

W. M. Lowrie.

CHAPTER IV.

1843.

Residence in Macao—Voyage up the Coast—Description of Amoy and Chang Chow—Return to Macao.

In the early part of the year, Mr. McBryde and his wife were obliged to leave China on account of the failure of his health; and in the summer, Dr. Hepburn and his family arrived at Macao, from Singapore. Mr. Lowrie spent his time chiefly at Macao, engaged in the study of the Chinese language, and preaching on the Sabbath to the American and European residents of that place. In August he commenced a voyage to the north, with the intention of visiting all the newly-opened cities, to make inquiries as to their relative advantages for missionary labour. His description of Amoy and Chang Chow, will be found in the following journals. Proceeding from Amoy to the north, owing to contrary winds, the voyage was slow, and they were several times driven to seek for shelter on the coast, by stress of weather. After almost reaching Chusan, the vessel was driven back by the north-east monsoon, and the voyage was then relinquished.

In the meantime the Executive Committee had decided to occupy three stations in China,—one in the Canton province, one at Amoy, and the other at Ningpo or Shanghai, as might be found most eligible. Dr. Hepburn was assigned to Amoy, and after being once driven back by a severe gale, he reached his field of labour in October.

During his residence at Macao, the correspondence of Mr. Lowrie with the Executive Committee at home was very full, and contained much information of great service to them in deciding on the various questions relating to the missionary work in this great field of labour. Active preparations were made by them during this year to send out a large missionary force, which will be noticed in the proper place.

At the close of this chapter will be found a proclamation of Sir Henry Pottinger, "Her Britannic Majesty's plenipotentiary, &c. &c.," censuring the visit of Messrs. Abeel and Lowrie, to the city of Chang Chow. This proclamation, and the letter to the Chinese authorities, are extraordinary papers, in more respects than one. They were uncalled for,—no complaint had been made, and Sir Henry himself became the informer. They were insulting and arrogant, for he censures American citizens, who were in no respect amenable to him, or subject to his jurisdiction. They were based on a false assumption, for the supplementary treaty had not then been published, and no law or regulation had been infringed. The inference that they passed themselves for Englishmen was equally gratuitous, and was contradicted in the very account that drew forth his impotent rebuke. There is something ludicrous, moreover, in the charge that two unarmed and peaceable men had forced their way among fifty thousand men, and there bearded their highest officers. Mr. Abeel was absent, and the duty devolved on his associate in the alleged trespass, to assert their rights as American citizens, and to decline the jurisdiction so arrogantly assumed. Had he used much stronger language, few of his countrymen would have been displeased.

Macao, February 24th, 1843.

My Dear Mother—. . . . I have just heard that Mr. Canfield [of the African mission,] is dead. This was unexpected and most distressing news, though I never thought that either he or Mr. Alward would endure that climate as well as I probably would have done. If the hand of God's providence had not so remarkably brought me here in spite of myself; and preserved me through dangers, when time and again it seemed as though I should be overwhelmed in the waves, I should almost wish that I had gone to Africa. The curse seems still to rest on Africa. Ethiopia stretches out her hand, but her teachers are removed far off. She still sits in darkness. Oh that light may speedily arise upon her! At times I can hardly help wishing myself there, if it were only to escape the drudgery of this terrible language. Yet I do not see much reason for discouragement so far; counting up the other day, I found myself master of more than *six hundred characters*, which, for only three months of uninterrupted attention, is pretty good progress; better than I expected. By the time the Chinese tailor "rubs a crowbar down to a needle," I hope to understand the language pretty well. But when will that be?

February 25th. Saturday night! How many, many thoughts of former days and former joys crowd around me, as I lay by my books and papers, to prepare for the coming Sabbath! How the time rolls on! It seems but a day since the ship left the wharf, in my own native land; yet more than a year has flown away, and I have passed through scenes that make me feel as if many years had been crowded into one. I have seen joy and sorrow since that time. I have felt my heart uplifted as on eagles' wings, and again it has sunk to the earth. I have looked upon the ocean when calm as a sleeping infant's slumbers. I have laid my hand upon its foam-crested waves, and felt that a half-inch plank and a slender cord alone preserved me from going down like lead in the mighty waters. I have seen plan after plan fail, and hope after hope disappointed. I have stood a solitary stranger amidst thousands who spoke a different language, without being able to utter a word that they could understand. Again and again have I been taught to say, "I am a stranger in the earth." Yet, withal, light has arisen to me in darkness, joy has come to me in sorrow, and hope has sprung up after disappointments; for "tribulation worketh patience, and patience experience, and experience hope, and hope maketh not ashamed." The love of God is shed abroad upon me, by the Holy Ghost, and the grace of Christ is sufficient for me. Would I go back? no! Do I regret that I came? no! Lonely I am at times; sorrowful often; perplexed, but not in despair; cast down, but not destroyed. The past is gone, but its pleasant remembrances and painful lessons remain; and deeply as some of them have been felt, already I can say,

"The sunshine to the flower may give
The tints that charm the sight,
But scentless would that flow'ret live
If skies were always bright.
Dark clouds and showers its scent bestow,
And purest joy is born of woe."

The future is still future, long or short, happy or mournful, "all to me unknown;" but I know what is far better, "The Lord reigneth, let the earth rejoice." . . . .

Yours affectionately,
W. M. Lowrie.

Macao, May 14th, 1843.

My Dear Mother— . . . It is Sabbath night, and though I do not often write letters on this day, yet occasionally I feel it a privilege to spend a part of this day in epistolary correspondence of a particular kind. I do not do it for the sake of saving time, but on the same principle that would induce me, if in America, to diversify the exercises of the day by Christian conversation with those around me. Before breakfast this morning, a Chinaman came to my door with a couple of letters, sent to me from Hong Kong. They were from father, dated Aug. 30th and December 13th, 1842, both overland, but delayed a good deal in arriving. After breakfast, I spent some time in preparing for preaching. I preach now every Sabbath in the chapel here, being the only clergyman in Macao except Mr. McBryde, who is not able to preach. Just as I was about to go to the chapel, a bundle of letters and papers from the "Paul Jones," came in. I had a week ago received half a dozen letters, and supposed there were no more; these had gone to Canton by mistake, and now were returned. It was quite a temptation, but I left them unopened till I returned from church, and then found one from brother John, one from father, and one from yourself, dated December 28th and 30th. Dear mother, I cannot express my thanks to you sufficiently for that letter. You seemed to fear that it would afford me little gratification, but it has been the most interesting letter I have yet received from you. I like "news" very well, but I like kind words and warm expressions of affection a great deal better, when I *know* that they come unstudied from the heart. I cannot describe to you how much I value such a sentence as "It is past nine o'clock, and all are waiting for me for prayers, where we always remember 'him in a *foreign* land.'" It brought the warm tears to my eyes, (I can hardly see now,) pictured before me—oh, how distinctly! the scenes of other days, when I too knelt with you, and when my voice was heard among you. I could see again the quiet room with its cheerful fire, and the table with its well-remembered cover and lamp, and the family Bible with its broken binding, and each familiar face, aye, and the accustomed seat in which each one sat. I could hear the voice that read; I almost fancied I could join in the familiar tune that was sung—*and so I can*, though separated from you by half the circumference of the world. The praises we sing, though sung on opposite sides of the globe, ascend to the same gracious God, and the prayers we offer reach the same mercy-seat, and the same grace that sustains you is sufficient, more than sufficient, for me. Tell Mrs. C., if you see her, that it has greatly cheered me to hear that her prayers have been offered for me, for I have learned to place a high value on the prayers of others, however unknown they may be to the world. How do we know but that in the world to come, we shall find much of our usefulness attributable to the prayers of those who remembered us, when we knew not that they ever thought of us?

"Little Sam is gone, and you are gone, and soon

it will be said, they are all gone;" and if *soon*, why regret that one has finished his journey a few hours sooner than the rest, and another gone by a different route? Are we not strangers here, and do not strangers sojourn but a short time in the land of their pilgrimage, and are not pleasant companions often obliged in their voyages to pursue different roads? When the journey is over, we will recount our toils, and how we have been led by ways we knew not. Oh, how true is that! I have been led like a blind man, by a way I knew not, but already, if I am not mistaken, I see it was the best way.

My journal has afforded you pleasure, more than I thought it would; but in heaven we shall need no journals, and shall then rightly estimate the importance of every step we took. We shall then see through what dangers we have passed, when we least suspected they were so near; we shall see how an angel was sent in this place to sustain us, and in that an evil spirit was driven away. We shall see how influences that we did not dream of were directing our course, and as we contemplate the wonderful network of our history, we shall more and more admire the wisdom and goodness of Him by whom our bodies were so "curiously wrought," and our actions so carefully ordered. We shall be at home then, and shall "go no more out."

How pleasant is the Sabbath! It comes to me in this heathen land, to tell me that even here God is gracious; but there, where one unending Sabbath prevails, there shall be no painful sights of unhallowed desecration, no strivings with inbred sin, no weariness; we shall go no more out, nor wish to go, for there is fulness of joy in the presence of God, and at his right hand are pleasures for evermore. I sometimes feel as if I did not want to live any longer; surely "I would not live always;" but when I look round and see these poor heathen, I think that perhaps I may do something. I am willing to stay, and when I think of Him who hath done so much for me, I am dumb. Here am I, Lord; do with me as thou wilt.

But I must close for the present.

Affectionately yours,

W. M. Lowrie.

Macao, May 17th, 1843.

Mr. John Lloyd—My Dear John:—Your long, long expected letter reached me eight or nine days ago. I was very glad indeed to hear from you, for I had not expected to be sixteen months without a letter from my old crony. But no matter, I'll pay you for it when you come out here. I shall expect to see you in China before the end of next year, without fail. The various items of your letter were very satisfactory to me, as they recalled many old associations. I proceed to answer some inquiries you have made. . . . As to the Chinese climate, I have not as yet sufficient experience to speak fully about it. I have been nearly a year here, and during that time have not had one day's sickness, and have taken only one dose of medicine. I think it probable, however, that new comers will be liable to fever and ague in most of the new ports, until they become acclimated. The heat of summer is great; the thermometer now ranges above 80°; but it is not as bad as that of India, and we have cool and bracing winters. There is not commonly any frost or snow in this latitude, or at Amoy, but ice and snow are both found at Chusan, Ningpo, and Shanghae, where I think we shall have our principal stations.

As to the language, I suppose it pretty certain that the Chinese is the hardest language in the world, except the Japanese; which is harder, because one must learn Chinese in order to learn Japanese. But then a good many considerations remove the terror that some of the Singapore missionaries were so anxious to excite on this subject. 1. The language has been learned, and spoken fluently and intelligibly, though not of course perfectly, by a number of persons within the last forty years; and I have yet to learn that any one of those persons possessed any remarkable talent for learning languages. My impression is, that not one of them possessed such a talent to any great degree. 2. The facilities for learning the language, in the way of elementary books and free access to the people, are vastly better than they were twenty years ago; and every year they are getting better. 3. The dialects spoken in the north, are said to be easier, decidedly, than those spoken in Canton and Fokeen provinces; and it has been with the dialects of the two latter, that foreigners have been most conversant. Several of those who have learned Chinese, were over thirty years of age before they commenced it; two, I believe, were over forty; yet they are making progress. I have not made any "considerable attainments" yet. Owing to my various wanderings, of which you have heard somewhat, it was six months after I got here, before I began to study regularly. I have now been studying regularly for about six months. I can read easy sentences; can talk a very little with my teacher; and I look forward with hope to the future. Yesterday I told my teacher that the Chinese was a hard language to learn, and I feared it would take me four or five years to talk it well. He said, no, it was not hard; and that in one year I should be able to converse satisfactorily. I told him he was flattering me; but he said, "No, I am a very old man, why should I flatter you?" So I said no more. I only believe the half of what he says; but even that is better than I expected. At first the study was *prodigiously* dry—worse than anything I ever undertook; but now I begin to feel a good deal of interest in it. Come out and study with me, and I can give you a good deal of assistance. I am obliged to study with almost no assistance from others, as the Pekin dialect, to which my attention is now directed, is not attended to by any of the missionaries whom I have access to. With your talents, I know you need not be afraid to commence the language. Tell Hugh Brown I expect *him* to come here also; and I wish you would turn the attention of Dr. Culbertson to this field. A person, however, who does not make pretty reasonable progress in Latin, Greek, and Hebrew, had better not come to China for the present. The case may be different a few years hence, when a greater variety of missionary labour can be employed than is at present practicable.

I am serious when I say that I wish you and Brown and Culbertson to regard this letter as a direct call to each of you to take China into careful consideration before you conclude to go elsewhere; and I trust you will be well satisfied that it is your duty to do so, if you decline coming here. I would not speak so decidedly if I did not think I had grounds for my opinion; but knowing you three, and this field as well as I do, I think it has very strong claims upon you.

I recommend you to learn the radicals immediately, so as to be able to write the whole of them off, and give the name and meaning of each, without once looking on the book. You will find it of incalculable advantage. I speak from experience. I also advise that by all means you learn to speak in the way that —— recommends, i. e., by using the abdominal and intercostal muscles. I am convinced that if you do so, it will facilitate your progress in the most difficult part of the spoken language, the tones. The reason why we find it so hard to use the Chinese tones easily, is because of our habit of using the lungs instead of the abdominal and intercostal muscles. I wish I had known this in America. The time you spend in learning this will be by no means lost, while, if you neglect it, I fear you will always regret it.

But it is past ten o'clock, and I must close for the night. Would that I could see you. Pray for me; but I know you do so, and I thank you for it. It does not surprise me to hear that I have fallen into the general mass, and only come in under the general prayer of "Lord, bless the missionary." It was to be expected. But there are a few who, I trust, will not so soon forget me. The Lord ever be with you, and keep you, is the prayer of your friend and brother in Christ,

W. M. Lowrie.

Macao, July 20th, 1843.

My Dear Father— . . . . I find myself obliged to confess that the warm weather has its effects upon me. For a month after it commenced I felt as strong and as much disposed to study as ever; but, for the last two weeks, I do not feel able to sit at my books nearly so constantly as before, nor to take such long walks as usual. I have lost a good deal of my appetite, and they all tell me I look pale, and thinner than usual. Such is the worst side of the picture; on the other hand, I am not sick, not low spirited, suffer no manner of pain, can read and write, and laugh and talk as usual, and do anything that does not require long and close mental effort. I sleep soundly, and the time passes away rapidly. I don't expect to do much studying for a couple of months to come. I had hoped to be on my way to visit Amoy and Chusan ere this, but have not yet found a suitable vessel, nor do I know of any. If one does not offer soon, I shall be obliged to postpone it till some time in September or October. . . .

Your journal of a day interested me very much. I would give you something of the kind in return, but am really so ashamed of each day's work for the present week, that I would rather not. I manage to keep up what little I know of Chinese, and to add a little to my stock; to read some; and write some; to take a walk every day; and to preach once a week to the English and American residents. As I have not yet brought myself to read other men's sermons, I have commonly to prepare one every week. This takes a good deal of time and thought, and I sometimes feel as if I ought not to do it, as the strength thus employed could be used in fitting myself for my missionary life. Yet as there are some who seem to feel an interest in attending, and as I am the only minister here, it does not seem right to neglect them altogether. I should like to be among the Chinese.

Your suggestions about a Chinese dictionary are important, but I hardly know what to say in regard to them; it will be time enough for me to think of such a thing, when I can call myself a Chinese scholar. I make no pretensions to that name now, nor can I even guess when I shall deserve it; and if I ever do deserve it, I may prefer some other kind of labour, besides dry dictionary-making. Still, I consider it a duty to keep something of the kind in view. You of course will not mention that I do so, as I do not wish it to be known. The thought that I may perhaps be of some assistance in that way, is one thing which, with others, induces me to study the Mandarin, and to prefer one of the northern ports.

I cannot tell you, my dear father, how much I value your letters. The spirit of kindness and affection they breathe, is to me most truly refreshing and delightful, and I sometimes almost feel as if it was worth while to be separated from you in order to enjoy them. But I do not altogether give up the hope of seeing you again, though I have little expectation of seeing you in the United States. When I get into my own house at Ningpo, or some other regular Chinese place, I mean to send you and mother a special invitation to come and see me. I rather think, too, that you will find it hard to refuse my invitation. With many affectionate thoughts of you, and of all the members of our beloved family, I remain as ever,

Your affectionate son,

W. M. Lowrie.

JOURNAL TO AMOY AND CHUSAN.

August 31st. Got under way from Hong Kong about nine o'clock, A. M., but having light and unfavourable winds made very slow progress. Obliged to come to anchor at night opposite Chek Chu, on the southern side of the island.

During the voyage from Hong Kong to Amoy we passed in sight of three of the great opium depots along the coast. These three were Tong-san, How-tow-san, and Namoa. At these three places, the opium dealers in Canton and Macao, have ships constantly stationed to keep supplies of opium, and to them the smaller vessels, or "opium clippers," as they are called, resort for cargoes, which they carry to different parts of the coast and dispose of always for silver. The number of vessels employed in this traffic is very great. A single mercantile house in Canton and Macao, employs about fifty vessels, ships, barks, brigs, and schooners, while another house has thirty or more.* These vessels carry

* The amount of capital embarked in the opium trade is enormous, as may be judged of from the number of vessels employed. The smallest of these vessels probably costs the owners upwards of $5,000 annually. A schooner like the ——— or ——— costs from 800 to 1200 dollars a month merely for her sailing, i. e. wages, wear and tear; so that the annual expense of one of the least of these messengers of evil, is greater than the whole expenses of our mission in any year since its commencement; while the brigs, barks, and ships cost still more. This

almost nothing but opium, and receive almost nothing in return but silver. The laws of the Chinese against the introduction of opium are very severe, but at present they are a mere dead letter; the opium smugglers laugh at them, and carry their vile drug recklessly to all parts of the coast, where it is purchased by the Chinese, and carried into different parts of the country. The Chinese officers themselves, instead of striving to prevent its introduction, connive at it, being frequently bribed for that purpose by the smugglers. One of the very greatest difficulties in the way of Christian missions in China, arises from the prevalence of the use of opium; and it is to be feared that it will long continue in the way. When a man acquires a taste for opium, there is nothing he will not do to gratify it; and its use is most deleterious. It injures his bodily health, it stupefies his mental powers, and it deadens his moral feelings, and when the habit of using it is once confirmed, it is almost impossible to abandon it. The fondness for opium is one of the strong chains in which Satan has bound this great people, and it is a heart-sickening reflection, that this evil luxury is supplied to them by the merchants of the two nations which profess to be actuated by the purest Christianity. It is almost impossible to find a vessel going up the coast which does not carry it.

September 5th. Reached Amoy, and was received with a hearty welcome by the Rev. Mr. Abeel and Dr. Cumming. They were the only missionaries then residing at Amoy, or rather at Kulangsu, which is a beautiful little island not more than one-fourth of a mile from Amoy.

In the evening after reaching Kulangsu, Dr. Cumming and myself went over to Amoy, to see the place. We crossed from Kulangsu to Amoy

is merely for wages of the men and officers, and the wear and tear of the vessel, and is exclusive of all the money expended in purchasing the opium, storing it, and packing and repacking.

for ten cash a-piece, (it takes eleven or twelve cash to make a cent.)

"Multitudes, multitudes," was the impression that forced itself upon me in walking through the crowded streets, and looking out over the close-built environs of this great city. The suburbs are much larger than the city itself, and most of the merchants' shops are there. Each street, both within the city and in the suburbs, is closed at each end by gates every night; all are narrow, and all are dirty. It is hardly possible for foreigners to live in the close filthy quarters generally occupied by the Chinese. We can live in houses like theirs with but little difficulty, but their position is generally low and damp, and their being so dirty and so closely crowded together, combines to render them unhealthy.

Nine opium ships were anchored close alongside of Amoy, and also *two* vessels that had no opium on board. I was told, on good authority, that every man in Amoy who could afford to buy opium was in the habit of smoking it. The Chinese officers make no effort whatever to prevent its introduction, and I saw opium pipes openly exposed for sale in the streets. A few years ago it would have been almost as much as a Chinaman's life was worth, to have been detected in the sale of anything used in consuming the prohibited article.

Infanticide is very common in this province; very many inquiries have been made by the missionaries, and all the testimony goes to prove that it prevails to a fearful extent. It is not saying too much to affirm, that in the districts around Amoy, one-fifth, or one-sixth of the children perish by the hands, or with the consent of their parents. One poor man said to Mr. Abeel with an air of the greatest simplicity and sincerity, "Teacher, before you came, I killed five of my children; I would not do it now, for you have showed me that it is wrong, but before you came I did not know that—who was there to tell me?" Alas! who was there to tell him? The opium smugglers are dealing their poison all around, but very rarely does a missionary appear amongst them, and those who do come, have difficulties to contend with as they sit upon the damp tiled floors of the native houses, and breathe the unwholesome air of the swampy fields, such as rarely enter into the minds of those who dwell in their ceiled houses, and talk in their own native language.

I visited the grave of Mrs. Boone. It is in a beautiful quiet garden, a little tree stands at the foot, and an immense banian spreads its shade over the whole. She died August 30, 1842. It was a time of sadness and sorrow when that first member of the missionary band here fell; but I could not regard her lonely grave in any other light than as a pledge that the kingdom shall yet be the Lord's. For not alone shall that Christian wife and mother sleep here; others of the missionary circle shall also toil, and lie down here, and around them shall sleep those saved by their means, and sooner or later we shall look upon graves, even in this heathen land, with the same feelings of calm and joyful hope with which we behold them in Christian lands. May the Lord hasten that time! for it is a sorrowful thought as we look upon the countless graves that throng every hill-side around us, "Not one of all these myriads ever heard the name of Christ—where now are their souls?" It was a pleasant thing in my native land to go to the grave-yard on Saturday evenings, or the Sabbath morning, and sit upon the tombs, and think of heaven; but I cannot do that in China.

We left Amoy on Thursday, September 7. I could scarcely take my eyes away from the first of the gently rising hills that was seen. It was so different from all that I had witnessed for nearly twenty months, and reminded me so strongly of objects seen in my own native land, that it required but little stretch of fancy to cover the scene with the peaceful homes, and smiling villages, and solemn churches of America. But, alas, how different the reality! Multitudes, multitudes of immortal beings, but all ignorant of the truth! An opium clipper followed us out of Amoy, and being a faster sailer than we, soon passed us on her way to Chimmoo Bay, another great opium depot. It reminded me sadly of the truth that the men of this world are wiser in their generation than the children of light. But I found consolation where I had not looked for it. We were sailing on the wide sea. The whole expanse of the Pacific Ocean, with its unfathomed depths and uncounted waves, was rolling on our right, and its waters washed the shores of the most populous empire on the earth. Behold! "The earth shall be filled with the knowledge of the glory of the Lord *as the waters cover the seas*," Hab. ii. 14. What though men, for the sake of gain, follow practices that injure their fellow-men, and impede the progress of the Gospel, it shall not always be so; for thus saith the Lord, "They shall not hurt nor destroy in all my holy mountain; for the earth shall be full of the knowledge of the Lord, as the waters cover the sea," Isaiah ix. 11. With such an assurance from such a source, what more do we want to confirm our faith and encourage our hope?

Friday, September 15. When within one hundred and twenty miles of Chusan the monsoon changed, and after beating about for several days, and making no progress, we anchored at the Island of San-pan-shan, in order to replenish our water-casks, and wait, if perhaps the weather might become more moderate. The island of San-pan-shan is in north lat. 28 deg. 5 min., and east long. 122 deg.

Just above our landing place, and near the principal collection of huts, was an idol temple, dedicated to Ma-tsoo-po, a favourite Chinese goddess. There was nothing remarkable about it, except its filthiness, and two figures about two-thirds the size of men, standing on a block of wood near the door.

They were painted black, with red and glaring eyes, and horribly-distorted mouths, all begrimed with smoke of incense-sticks, and dirt; they were fit representations of the horrid character of him whom this deluded people worship. There were several brazen incense-stands on the altar, one of which I wished to take away, but the people would not allow of it. "No, it was Ma-tsoo-po's." I would give a good deal to be able to transport the two black images as they are, to the Mission House in New York.

Wednesday, September 27th. Finding that our vessel was in no condition to beat against the monsoon, and that our prospect of reaching Chusan in her was very poor, we reluctantly turned about, and arrived at Amoy yesterday. It is a mysterious dispensation of providence, but doubtless He who holds the winds in his fist has wise ends in view, in disappointing my hopes: "What I do thou knowest not now, but thou shalt know hereafter."

Took a boat and went to see a Budhist temple about two or three miles south-east of Amoy. It stands at the foot of the high ridge of hills running from the city of Amoy into the interior of Amoy island, and is about half a mile from the shores of the bay. In front of the temple is an enclosure containing four open buildings, in each of which are two gigantic stone tortoises six feet long and four feet broad. Each tortoise supports a white stone tablet, ten feet high and four feet broad, and covered one with Chinese and the other with Tartar inscriptions; the Chinese characters are certainly very well adapted for inscriptions, and I have rarely seen any specimens of cutting in stone so beautifully executed as these are. The purport of the inscriptions seemed to be maxims and moral sentences: but as to their particular meaning, I forbear to interpret it. Directly behind these tablets was the entrance of the temple, with all its array of dingy paintings, grotesque carving and queer dragons above the door. On entering, the first object seen was a gilt statue of Budh, of gigantic size, with a green veil over the window of the inclosure where he was seated. Behind him was another gigantic image, and on either side were two other giants; on one side a male and a female with a guitar in her hand, and on the other side a female, and a black and horrid-looking male attendant. Each statue is said to be eighteen feet high, and of one solid stone. Here we were met by two of the priests, pale in countenance, dressed in white, and of rather pleasing manners. Only one of them said anything, but he was quite talkative. They gave us tea without sugar or milk, and promised to call at the mission house in Amoy, after which we left them.

Near this temple, I saw what is rather uncommon in China, regularly-inclosed graveyards. There were a great many uninclosed tombs all around, but here were three graveyards; each of them had a large tomb in the centre, and a great many of common appearance regularly arranged around, completely filling up the inclosed spaces. The burying-grounds were all small, but extremely full. The largest was only one hundred feet square, and yet it had three hundred and fifty graves in it, all of which seemed to be of about the same age. It is not known to foreigners, and not to any Chinese of whom we made inquiries, who are buried there. The inscriptions at the entrance of each would perhaps tell, but it requires time and patience to copy and translate them. Just within the entrance of each was a stone with the inscription *fuh shin*, happy spirits! Alas! are they happy? None were children's graves.

October 1, Sabbath. In the morning attended Mr. Abeel's Chinese service; about twenty were present, which is a smaller number than usual. Among them was a Budhist priest, and several very respectably-dressed gentlemen. Most of them attended well. In the evening preached to the soldiers; owing to the sickness prevailing at present, the congregation was small; only about seventy were present, yet it was the largest number I have preached to at one time since leaving New York.

October 2, Monday. Monthly Concert to-night. I conducted the services and made the first prayer, then read Psalm lxviii., and made some remarks on the frequency with which the promises of the conversion of the world are followed by glorious ascriptions of praise to God, as shown:—Ps. lxviii. 31, 32, Is. xliv. 23, and xlix. 12, 13. Mr. Roberts then prayed, and made some remarks on the necessity of faith in Christ, and of entire dependence on his grace, rather than trusting in feelings and frames of mind. We sang a hymn, and Mr. Abeel prayed. It was a pleasant time.

JOURNAL TO CHANG-CHOW.

October 3. Mr. Abeel and I have been talking for some days of making an excursion into the interior, some thirty or forty miles, and to-day we went off to engage a boat. There are so many rivers and streams along the coast of China, and the Chinese so commonly live near the water, that almost all travelling is in boats. Hence the expression, Haou fung shwuy, literally meaning a fair wind and tide, is equivalent to saying, "Good luck go with you," or "May you have a prosperous time." After a deal of chaffering and bargaining, and being almost deafened by the noisy Chinese we had to talk with, (when talking earnestly, the common people actually *shout* their words,) we arranged with an old man to be taken to Chang-Chow, a city of the second order, and said to be twice as large as Amoy, for three dollars and a half. One of our Chinese friends promises to accompany us.

On the 4th about one o'clock, P. M., we arrived at the city. It was soon evident that we were something "uncommon." Numbers of people came in with us, and as we passed through the streets and were discovered by those ahead of us, the wonder and the crowd increased. Our complexions and dress, our stature, and my spectacles, at once drew the attention of everybody. The shopkeeper turned away from his customer, the carpenter dropped his plane, and the shoemaker his last, the tailor his needle, and the apothecary his pill-box, and even the beggar forgot his vocation; the women peeped out from the doors, and the children ran on before and stopped to have a good look at us; old and young, high and low, were filled with one common feeling of surprise, and gazed at us as if we had fallen from the clouds.

Thursday, Oct. 5. The morning being bright and pleasant, we started for a walk before breakfast, and the lower bridge being hard-by the place where our boat was anchored, we went there first. It is built on twenty-five piles of stone about thirty feet apart, and perhaps twenty feet in height, above the surface of the water. Large round beams are laid from pile to pile, and smaller ones across in the simplest and rudest manner: these are then covered with earth, and the upper part is paved with bricks or stone. One would suppose that the work had been assigned to a number of different persons, and that each had executed his part in such manner as best suited his own fancy, there being no regularity in the paving; bricks and stone were intermingled in the most confused manner, and the railing was sometimes of wood, and sometimes of stone. The length of some of the stones used in paving the bridge was very remarkable; some of them were eight, others eleven, others fourteen, and three of them eighteen paces each, in length, so that these last must have been about forty-five feet long, and two or three broad. They were of unhewn granite, but from the constant crowd of passengers for a hundred years or more, were worn quite smooth.

The bridge averages eight or ten feet in width, and about one-half its length on either side was occupied by shops in which various articles, principally eatables, were exposed for sale. I may remark here that the short account of this city contained in the work of Abbe Grosier, on China, which is compiled from the memoirs of the Jesuit missionaries, contains several mistakes. The work referred to speaks of but one bridge, whereas, there are two; it gives that one bridge thirty-six arches, whereas, there are but twenty-five, and they are not, in any sense of the word, arches, being simply timbers laid from pier to pier. It also speaks of the "two ranges of shops furnished with the most precious things of China, and the rarest merchandises of foreign lands." If this account were true in the days when the Jesuits went through the land with the utmost freedom, it is not so now, for the articles we saw in these shops were of the commonest and coarsest kind. It also says, that since "the tides reach regularly to Chang-Chow, this place has become the resort of a multitude of vessels, by means of which a commerce is held with Amoy, Pow-hou, and Formosa, and from hence depart all the Chinese who go to traffic at the Philippine islands;"—all this is to be taken with large allowance. The tide does reach Chang-Chow, but even at high tide, only the smallest vessels can come up so far—and when the tide is out, a common whale-boat is in danger of grounding. I take it for granted, therefore, that no vessels go from this city either to Formosa or the Philippine islands; and certainly, though there are a goodly number of small boats in the river, there are no vessels there fitted to encounter a sea-voyage. From Amoy vessels do go to all the parts mentioned above, and to many others, and the goods they bring back are conveyed in smaller vessels to the city of Chang-Chow; but the statements just referred to (see Grosier's "La Chine," vol. 1, p. 96) are not sanctioned by what we saw. If the accounts

16 *

the Jesuits have given of other cities of the empire, are equally defective and erroneous, we have small reason to thank them for their contributions to our stock of knowledge of China. The reader of Abbe Grosier will not find one of the particulars of the following account in his work.

There were many persons passing and repassing, as we crossed the bridge, and the various odours that filled the air were not the most agreeable. Having crossed the bridge, and passed through a village at the end of it, we went along the southern bank of the river to the second bridge, which is about a mile from the first, and similarly constructed. On coming to it, our guides pointed a little further, and told us there was a temple there worth seeing. We accordingly kept on, and were soon well repaid for our additional walk, by a sight of one of the oldest buildings I have ever seen. It was a temple said to have been built in the Suy dynasty, about twelve hundred years ago. The various gateways and small buildings usually found in front of Chinese temples, were decayed and in ruins. Two pools on either side of the main entrance, were covered with the broad-leaved water-lily. The main building, which is of wood, is very high, and every pillar, board, stone, and tile, bore the marks of extreme age. On going in, we were utterly astonished. Seven gigantic images, in sitting or standing postures, gilded and painted, but faded and dusty, and tarnished with age, were arranged across the middle of the temple; while on either side was a row of fifteen Chinese worthies, either sitting or standing, and as large as life. Behind the seven first images were three others: the very smallest of the ten was at least eight feet in height, while the largest, if they had been standing, would have been fifteen or eighteen. An immense drum occupied one corner of the room, and a bell another. The roof was most curiously composed of carved wood, and inscriptions in various styles of Chinese writing were painted, and gilded, and carved on the pillars, walls, ceiling, and tablets of the temple. It had been repaired in Kang-he's time, though it was now in a sad state from age and neglect. It was sickening to look on the gloomy monsters whom this people worship as their gods, and to witness the ingenuity and expense lavished on these dumb idols, and to think of the dreadful degradation of the people that can worship such works of their own hands. Yet it is also cheering to think that their superstitions are old, and many of them seem almost ready to vanish away. Not a great many new temples are built, and those already existing are often in very poor repair. The people appear to have little reverence for their idols, and their worship consists of little else than a heartless round of unmeaning ceremonies. Oh, for that time when idols shall be utterly abolished!

From the main temple, we went to a small side building, which contained a single idol, standing, with one hand folded on the breast, and the other hanging open by the side. I got up on the pedestal, which was three feet high, and reaching with my umbrella, could barely touch the hand that was laid across the breast. The open hand was two feet long, and the whole image could have been little less than twenty feet high. It was cut out of one solid rock, which formerly occupied this spot; without removing it, they hewed out the image and erected the house over it.

Breakfast being over, we entered the chairs provided for us, and being escorted by the interpreter, and two or three of the officers, proceeded through the city. We were carried through several streets, some of which were narrow and offensively filthy, but many of them were wide, i. e. for a Chinese city, say eight, ten, and even twelve feet, and lined with pretty good-looking houses.

We were carried to the north-west corner of the city, and presently found ourselves in an open space with rising ground beyond, and a very large temple directly in front. It was built in the Tang dynasty, from nine hundred to twelve hundred years ago, and bore the marks of age, though in much better repair than the one we had previously visited. The scene presented when the doors were thrown open and we entered, was quite unexpected. Eight gigantic figures, even larger than those we had previously seen, were arranged across the temple. Some of them seemed almost to support its high roof on their heads: thirty-six Chinese sages occupied either side, in rows of eighteen each. The roof of the temple was constructed in the most elaborate manner, and was supported by several noble wooden pillars. The most curious things we saw, were a couple of large lockers or cupboards, closed and locked. They were about eight feet square and two feet deep, and their contents were unknown. The people all declared most seriously that they had not been opened for years, and if they should be opened, death would surely come out in some terrible form, or some dreadful plague would visit the people.

Behind the temple the ground rose steeply, and three of its summits were crowned with little open towers. We climbed up in the hot sun, expecting to obtain an extended prospect, but the scene that met our eyes greatly transcended our expectations. Fancy an amphitheatre thirty miles in length by twenty in breadth, hemmed in on all sides by steep, bare, pointed hills, a river running through the plain, an immense city at our feet, with fields of rice and sugar-cane, noble trees and numerous villages stretching away in every direction. It was grand and beautiful above every conception I had ever formed of Chinese scenery. The eye wandered over that immense plain, and returned again and again to the contemplation of particular points, till we were almost wearied by the sight of so much magnificence: and when we came to particulars, the wonder was increased rather than diminished. Beneath us lay the city. We could trace its walls in nearly every direction. It would have been nearly square, had not the southern wall curved outwards from following the course of the river. It was very closely built, as almost all Chinese cities are, and had a vast number of large trees in every part, within and around. On inquiring the number of inhabitants, our guide answered, that in the last dynasty it had numbered seven hundred thousand souls, and now there were more. He thought there were a million of people within the walls. This is probably a large estimate, though it is the one commonly given by the Chinese:—yet allowing only half their estimate, how large a number is even that! The villages around also attracted our attention, and I tried to count them, but after enumerating thirty-nine of large size, distinctly visible, in less than half the field before us, I gave over the attempt. It is certainly not going too far to say, that in that plain, there are at least one hundred villages; some of them may be small, but many of them would number their hundreds and even thousands of inhabitants. Oh, what a field for missions is here, if the country were but open, and the churches ready to enter it! How many, many souls there were beneath our eyes, all ignorant of the true God, and of the way of life! The prospect before us was surprisingly beautiful, but alas, for those who dwell amidst those fair scenes, where

"Every prospect pleases, and only man is vile!"

Oh, how often does the thought come across the missionary's mind in China, "multitudes, multitudes!" but alas, they are scattered, as sheep having no shepherd. Oh, that Christians could but see them, and have compassion upon them! Then would they pray the Lord of the harvest to send forth more labourers into his harvest, for the harvest truly is plenteous, but the labourers are few. This country will yet be opened. The doors have already begun to unclose, and no human power is able to shut them again. What though they move but slowly, and grate harshly as they turn on their rusty hinges, they move none the less surely for all that; and the field that is opened to us, by the first unclosing, is so vast that our numbers are quite insufficient to occupy it. What then will be the case when the whole country is thrown open? When we have properly occupied the five ports now open, and are ready to extend our efforts beyond, it will be time enough to wish for a larger field. Doubtless God will give us a larger field before we are ready to enter on it.

After dinner we went up in a boat some distance above the city, and walked among the rice-grounds and sugar-canes. How much the latter reminded me of the luxuriant corn-fields of Maryland! We saw several men watering the rice-grounds by means of the chain pump, which is worked by the foot, and is described in Davis's China, ch. 19. This may be the same contrivance that was used in Egypt, and is referred to in the Scriptures: "thou sowedst thy seed, and wateredst it with thy foot as a garden of herbs;" Deut. xi. 10. The people gathered around us, and Mr. A. addressed them in two different places. Some of them attended carefully, but most of them seemed more disposed to examine our dress than to listen to religious discourse.

Friday, October 6. Arrived at Cho-bey before daylight, and soon after sunrise went ashore to see the place. It is a walled town, but the part within the walls is by no means so extensive as that without. Here, as elsewhere, crowds followed us, noisier too, and ruder than those of Chang-Chow, though they offered us no manner of insult, and most readily allowed us to pass wherever we chose. We found it quite a large and populous place, stretching at least a mile along the shore, and I know not how far back from the river. It is a busy, bustling place of trade; the shops were crowded with goods, commonly of a very coarse quality, and the streets thronged with people. For dirt and filth, it excels every other place I have seen, and some of the streets were actually sickening. Several persons who had been to Amoy, recognized Mr. A., and one of them, who had been a patient of Dr. Cumming's at Ku-lang-su, volunteered to guide us through the streets, which are so narrow, from three to twelve feet wide, and so crooked, that we should have found it difficult to proceed alone. The number of fresh fish in the markets was really surprising. The river is here not one-fourth of a mile wide, and hardly six feet deep, and yet as far as we could learn, it supplies the whole of the teeming population of both its banks, including those of the cities of Chang-Chow, Cho-bey, and Haeteng. Here we saw immense numbers of fine large fish, fresh from the water, and excellent in flavour, as we proved by experiment. After walking till we were tired, we stopped in front of an idol temple, and Mr. A. addressed the crowd that gathered around us. They were quite attentive, and the questions asked by several of them, showed that they understood what was spoken to them.

It was now noon, the sun was hot, we had been wearied at Cho-bey in the morning, besides being almost overpowered by the excitement of the two previous days, and the wind being ahead, it was important to secure the favourable tide, which was now making for Amoy. Accordingly we turned our faces homeward, and at sunset re-entered our houses in Ku-lang-su; glad and thankful for the wonderful things we had seen, the favours received, and the mercies enjoyed during our three days' excursion.

In looking back over this excursion, and over the whole of my voyage, there are several points that deserve to be prominently brought forward; and though my journal is already long, a few remarks on each will not be out of place.

The attentive reader of this journal will have been struck with the frequent reference to the amazing populousness of the country; but it is impossible to convey any adequate idea of the real state of the case. If the cities of Boston, New York, Philadelphia, and Baltimore were situated in a valley forty miles long, and ten or fifteen broad, and the whole intervening country were so thickly covered with villages that a man should never be out of sight of one or more of them, still the population of that valley would not be as great as is the population of that part of China, of which the preceding pages speak. At seven o'clock in the morning, we were at Amoy; by two o'clock P. M. we had passed Haeteng and Cho-bey, and were anchored at Chang-Chow. Here were four cities, any one of which would be a city of the first size in the United States, and around these four cities, there must be at least two hundred villages and towns; and this is not all, for within thirty miles of Amoy, in another direction, is the city of Tung-an, said to be twice as large as Amoy, with, I know not how many towns and villages in its neighbourhood. The mind is overwhelmed to think of this immense population, numerous as the sand on the sea-shore, and all so closely crowded together, and so easily reached, by water communication, for in a boat you may go to any one of those places in less than a single day. If the country around each of the other ports is as populous, as we now know that around Amoy to be, and the probability, from all I can learn, is that it is quite as populous, then what fields are here for Christian effort! I am astonished and confounded, and even, after what I have seen, can scarcely believe the half of what must be true respecting the multitudes of people who live in

China, and the multitudes who are perfectly accessible to the efforts of the missionary.

It has been strongly and repeatedly impressed upon my mind, from what I have lately seen, that to no country in the world will our Saviour's words, "to *the poor* the Gospel is preached," be found so applicable as to China. Many people look on China as it were some great mine of gold and jewels, where every man is clothed in silks and faring sumptuously every day; but nothing can be further from the true state of the case. There are many wealthy men in China, and wherever the missionary goes, he will meet them, and associate with them. But the great mass of the people are poor, in the strictest sense of the term. It cannot but be so, where a country is so crowded with inhabitants, that there is sometimes hardly room to bury their dead out of their sight, the great majority of the people must be poor. You see it here, in the coarse clothing they wear, the food they eat, the homes they inhabit, the furniture they use, and the wages they receive. You see it in the fact that their only coined money is so small that it requires twelve hundred to make a dollar, and happy is he who receives two hundred of these for his day's labour. Let the missionary who comes to China, bear this in mind. The brightest talents are needed in preaching to the poor, but especially will he need the graces of humility and self-denial, of faith and of patience, in his intercourse with this people, and his efforts to instruct them. This is a point that admits of much enlargement, both in proving the poverty of the people, if that be necessary, and in speaking of the qualifications necessary to one who labours among them. But a word to the wise and the *thoughtful*, is sufficient.

It is a sad and melancholy thing to be obliged to refer so often as I have done to the prevalence of the use of opium in China. The number of vessels employed, and the amount of capital embarked in the opium trade, have been slightly referred to in the preceding pages. At some other time I may give fuller statements on this subject; but at present, all that need be added, is, that the half has not been told. The connivance of the Chinese officers at the traffic, and the eagerness of the Chinese people to procure the drug, have also been referred to. I have only further to say, that wherever I have been in China, I have seen it used. In all the opium depots along the coast, it is of course freely used. At Amoy, "every man who can afford to buy it, uses it." In the little island of San-pan-shan, the only question the people asked of the Christian missionary, was, whether he had opium to sell, and there he saw the floor of the idol temple covered with the half-stupefied smokers of opium. While at Chang-Chow, one of the officers came on board the boat where we lodged, and while he was on board, I perceived the peculiar smell of opium, and looking down, saw two men smoking it in the hold beneath my feet. I have been made sick by the smell of it, in an opium house at Canton, and have held my breath as I passed the opium dens in Macao. I have walked on the steep hill-sides of Hong Kong, and there have seen *common beggars*, who dwelt "in cliffs of the valleys, in caves of the earth, and in rocks"—and who were too poor to buy an opium pipe, smoking opium out of a little earthen vessel in which they had drilled a hole, that it might serve as a substitute for a pipe! And what hope can there be for such a people? Men of the world, honourable and upright men too, will sell them opium for money. The Chinese will buy it, let the emperor thunder against it as long as he chooses, and the smoker will use it, though it weakens his body, impairs his mind, stupefies his conscience, and renders him miserable when not under its influence. There is no help for them but in God. The use of opium in China will never be abolished, until a reformation, similar to the temperance reformation of America, commence among the people themselves. And that reformation I fear will not commence, and certainly will not be completed, till the religion of Christ takes deep root, and becomes the predominant power in China. Let Christians, then, cry mightily unto God, in behalf of this ancient people. His hand is not shortened that it cannot save, nor his ear heavy that it cannot hear.

Hong Kong, October 16th, 1843.

After getting back to Amoy on Friday, I spent part of that night and the next day in writing. A little vessel of some thirty tons burden, here called a lorcha, being about to sail for Macao and Hong Kong, I found Mr. Roberts had taken passage in her. As there was no prospect of a vessel soon for Hong Kong from Amoy, and as I was anxious to reach home soon, I concluded to take a passage in her too. Mr. Abeel did not want me to go so soon; and certainly, although she promised a safe and quick passage, there was every prospect of its being an uncomfortable one, the vessel being so small, and likely to roll so much. No danger, however, was apprehended, and the price of passage, only twenty dollars, was an inducement. I should probably have had to pay forty or fifty dollars, besides waiting some time, if I went in a ship. The lorcha was manned by three Englishmen and four Chinese, had mat sails, and had recently come up from Macao against the monsoon.

Monday at noon, though the wind was very high, we started. Soon got to the mouth of the harbour; but there we found the wind so strong, and the sea so high, we were afraid to go out, and therefore put back to wait for better weather. The wind abated during the night, and the next day, we started again, got to sea, and were fairly on our course. The wind was still strong, and the sea rough, but we went on finely, and in six hours were a long way off from Amoy. Soon after dark, however, our rudder was broken by the violence of a wave that struck it. The rudders of all the Chinese built vessels are very large awkward things, and very apt to be broken. We found ourselves quite helpless, as we could not direct the vessel's course at all. Being quite dark, there was nothing we could do but heave the vessel to and let her drift till daylight. In so small a vessel, and in such a situation, I considered it a little unsafe, and kept awake nearly all night, to see how she would behave. But though the wind and sea were strong and rough, she rode like a duck, and though rolling very much, took in little water. Mr. Roberts was very seasick.

Wednesday morning, the weather continued clear but rough, and we found ourselves drifting along the coast. The men tried to make a new rudder with two bamboo poles, but it would not work. They then slept several hours, and tried to repair the broken rudder; but did it so awkwardly that it also was useless. They seemed disposed then to do nothing but wait for calmer weather. At this season of the year there was no prospect of the weather growing worse than it then was. I knew, also, that the course of the wind and current would cause us to drift down along the coast in sight of land as far as Pedro Branca, a rock forty-five miles from Hong Kong. After reaching that rock, there would be danger of being driven out into the open China Sea; but at the rate we supposed we were going, we did not expect to see Pedro Branca for five or six days, and we were pretty sure in that time that the weather would moderate. I concluded, therefore, that there was no immediate cause of apprehension, but it was very unpleasant to think of spending so many days in that little rolling damp place. Yet there seemed to be no help for it, and I tried to nerve my mind to bear it. A little spray occasionally dashed over us, and sometimes a few drops forced themselves through the windows, and made our sleeping place wet, but altogether, it was very far superior to the long-boat. During Wednesday night I found Mr. Roberts was a great deal alarmed. However, I was an older sailor than he, and my former "experience" now wrought "hope," so that I had little fear.

Thursday we drifted on, gradually however edging off further from the land. One of the men had been along the coast frequently, and said he knew where we were, all the time. According to his account, we were drifting at about thirty miles a day.

Thursday night also Mr. Roberts was much alarmed, and I confess I did not myself like the idea of our getting out so far from land as we evidently were. However, I slept well, as I had done the night before. The weather too seemed to be a little better; wind abating some, though the sea was still rough.

Friday morning at daylight we could scarcely see the land, and by nine o'clock, we were out of sight of it. Finding the men were disposed to do very little, I took the matter in hand, and representing the danger of being out at sea, urged the propriety of running the boat on shore if possible; and if nothing better offered, of trying to go to Hong Kong by land. This stirred them up, and they agreed to try and repair the rudder a little better, and do something in that way if possible. We saw several fishing-boats going out to fish, a pretty sure sign that the fishermen anticipated a calm time. After a little while the men got their rudder repaired. She worked admirably, and we went on our course finely. "Thank God," said one of the men, "we shall see Pedro Branca to-night." This was before eleven o'clock A. M. In half an hour or so, I said to the captain, "Is that an English or a Chinese vessel, away off there?"—"Well, I was just a lookin'; oh, I 'spose it's a Chinese vessel." The mate looked at it steadfastly, "That! that's Pedro Branca! forty-five miles from Hong Kong!" So it was, we had drifted a hundred miles further than we thought, and had come altogether one hundred and sixty miles in less than three days! How providential it was we got the rudder repaired at the time we did! If we had not, the probability is we should on that day (Friday) have been in the China Sea; and then almost our only hope would have been to have been picked up by some vessel. Truly goodness and mercy have followed me hitherto.

Saturday morning at daylight we were within ten miles of Hong Kong. An American vessel was just before us. As soon as the men saw her, they said, "That's an American ship." "How do you know?" said I. "Oh, any one who's accustomed to vessels can almost always tell an American vessel, they always look so clean." The remark is one often made.

We anchored at nine o'clock A. M. in Hong Kong harbour, and having breakfasted, and called the men into the cabin to render thanks to God for the goodness and mercy received on our voyage, we went ashore; we were only one day longer in coming than we had expected to be, notwithstanding the loss of our rudder.

Most of my friends in Hong Kong declared they never would go to sea with me, as the elements were leagued against me, and that I must consider myself as settled in Macao or Hong Kong. The ship we saw, which got in just before us, was the Zenobia. I did not get my letters till evening, and it kept me till bed-time to get through with all,—but oh, what news! a beloved brother hopefully pious; a donation of ten thousand dollars for China; five new missionaries preparing for the same great field! My heart was full. For hours after I went to bed I could not sleep. Oh how I thought of the past, the present and the future! I got up and walked about the room; being "merry," I sang a hymn; and knelt down to pray. Oh, it is worth a great deal to get such news, and so delightful after the unpleasant contrast of the week previous.

Found the Hepburns had started about ten days before in a very fine vessel for Amoy; was very glad to hear it, though I knew that with the winds they had had they could make little progress, and would have a dreadfully rough time.

Sabbath (yesterday) I preached in the chapel here in the morning, and talked to the boys in Mr. Brown's school in the evening.

To-day I meant to have gone to Macao, but not being able to get the specie on board the Zenobia safely deposited, I found it necessary to remain another day. Just about four o'clock, who should come in but Dr. and Mrs. Hepburn, driven back by the bad weather? They were far more surprised to see me than I to see them. They have had dreadful weather, and a rough time. Poor Mrs. H. was very sea-sick, but looks quite as well as when I left Macao. They will probably start in a few days to make a second effort.

Macao, October 22d, 1843. The gale in which we lost our rudder in the lorcha, and drifted so far, was quite terrific further south. The vessel in which the Hepburns were, had to put back with the loss of spars, sails, &c.; several other vessels had also to put back, and this last week in Hong Kong, we heard that the vessel in which Mr. Medhurst and Mr. Milne were proceeding to Chusan, had lost her top-masts, had her captain swept overboard and drowned, and was finally obliged to put into Manilla in distress. Mr. Milne, describing the gale, said that "for ten hours they expected nothing but death."

This week I have had a regular attack of chill and fever, the first for thirteen years. It was brought on, I have no doubt, by the exposure of the last six weeks. Last Thursday was the first day I have spent in bed from sickness, for more than eight years.

October 24th. How sad and mysterious oftentimes are the dispensations of Providence! I must close my journal with the death of the Rev. Mr. Dyer, who has been so long engaged in preparing Chinese metal type. He came up here in July with the other missionaries of the London Missionary Society, to attend a missionary meeting ordered by their society in Hong Kong. After transacting all the business required, he went to Canton to see the place, and was there taken with the disease that has prevailed so fearfully in Hong Kong this year. He began to recover, took his passage in a vessel going to Singapore, and came down to Hong Kong; I saw him there on board his ship, the day I got back from Amoy. He was recovering rapidly. The vessel came over here, and was unexpectedly detained several days; he had a relapse, was brought ashore to our house, and died this morning at ten o'clock. Yesterday his mind was wandering all day, but this morning he was sensible, knew us all, knew he was dying, said he felt "very happy," and often repeated "sweet Jesus, sweet Jesus." I was with him when he died. His spirit seemed to depart with scarcely a struggle. He had been out in this region seventeen years, and there is no one who can take the place he occupied. He has left a wife and four children. Humanly speaking, his death is a very great loss. He was a man of piety and prayer, and of a most catholic spirit.

Thus we go: one after another is called to his long home. In one respect, the death of these servants of God is even cheering. Their work is finished, and thus another part of the great work God has to do on earth is accomplished. It will not have to be done again. . . .

Macao, November 4th, 1843.

TO THE SOCIETY OF INQUIRY IN THE WESTERN THEOLOGICAL SEMINARY.

DEAR BRETHREN:—On the 27th of July, this year, a letter was put into my hands, addresed to my colleague in this mission, the Rev. T. L. McBryde. As you will have learned before now, he sailed for the United States, early in the month preceding its arrival. He left with me, however, a discretionary power to open his letters, and suspecting from the postmark that it was from your society, I opened and read it. I suppose that a letter from myself in reply, will be nearly equally acceptable, especially as I was brought up almost in sight of your Seminary, and have spent more than half of my life within thirty miles of it.

I can assure you, that it will ever afford me great pleasure to correspond with you. I have been a theological student myself, and know the interest that such students feel in letters from missionaries; and I can speak from experience too, when I say that a missionary is glad to receive letters from a society like yours. It was interesting to me to read your accounts of the revivals of religion in the West, for it recalled the memory of other days, when I also shared in such precious seasons. Dear brethren, you cannot too highly value, nor too sedulously improve, the opportunities you now have of intercourse in Christian society,—of labouring for the good of souls, and especially of being present where the Spirit of the Lord is poured out. Should you ever become missionaries to the heathen, there is nothing that, in the review, will give you more real delight than to recall such times. I have in my native land mingled in various scenes; I have gone to the literary feast, the crowded assembly, and the cheerful social circle, and found pleasure in all; but I now recall, with far more satisfaction, the solitary walk over the hills with a single Christian brother, the visit to the poor old Christian negro's cottage, the little prayer-meeting in the house where the lame mother in Israel joined in the song of praise, and the country Sabbath school. I have forgotten many other things, but I have not forgotten the Brainerd meetings of Jefferson College, nor the time when, in one of the rooms in your seminary, a classmate and myself bowed the knee in prayer to our common Father. Lay up a store of such things for recollection, and they will cheer many a lonely hour in your future course.

Your letter asks several questions, which I will answer, and also, if you permit, will add some other items. You ask what special preparation is necessary for the field of labour? I think, *principally* those of a spiritual nature. I mean, strong faith to believe God's promises that the world shall be converted, for you will find little in the outward aspect of things to make you think so; patience and perseverance, for both are needed. You may have to labour here for many years, and see little apparent fruit of your labour. Above all, put on charity, which is the bond of perfectness. Cultivate the spirit of love and forbearance, for you will find abundant occasion for its exercise. I trust you have none of those romantic notions that will induce you to think a missionary a superior being. We are men of like passions with others. We come from different parts of the world with different views, from the influences of very different states of public feeling. We come to a country where there is no public feeling, where each man must judge for himself, where there is no standard of public opinion such as you have at home. In such circumstances, it is natural to expect great diversity of views, and nothing but the spirit of meekness, and forbearance, and love will enable you to live happily with your fellow-labourers. The longer I live, the more I am struck with the expressiveness of those reiterated commands of our Saviour in his last address to his disciples, to love one another. Brethren, study and practise the thirteenth chapter of first Corinthians, and it will do you good wherever you are.

As to other preparations, the more you know on all subjects, provided you know it well, the better. There is hardly an item of general knowledge of any kind that I ever acquired, which I have not already found occasion to bring into use. On subjects of general knowledge, it is important, if you come to this field, to know pretty well the histories of England, France, and India. I take for granted that you know the history of our own country thoroughly, and can tell why the American flag has thirteen stripes, and twenty-six stars. Study Geology and Botany by all means. These two sciences are of prime importance, and you will almost daily find the benefit of an acquaintance with them. I do not think a knowledge of medicine necessary to a missionary to China. If you have an opportunity of learning something about it, very well; but you will not, I think, find it advantageous to unite an extensive medical practice with the preaching of the Gospel. The two should go together, but it seems better that they should be performed by different persons.

I think the climate of the ports of Ningpo and Shanghae will be found most suitable for persons from the United States. Persons disposed to bilious complaints and dyspeptics will suffer a good deal in the Canton and Fuhkeen provinces. I think a confirmed dyspeptic might almost as well not come here. Persons liable to consumption would find the Canton and Fuhkeen provinces delightful residences, and I think that even those of bilious habits would be nearly as safe in Ningpo and Chusan, as in the United States. They have ice and snow there in winter. The Chinese language is very difficult, and I am disposed to say, that one who cannot make some tolerable progress in Latin, Greek, or Hebrew, may as well not come here. The language is *the* difficulty in China. I do not think it unattainable. I think its difficulties have been exaggerated. I think that every year its acquisition will be found easier, because more facilities in the way of elementary books, and access to the people, are being afforded. In other respects, I do not consider the field as "peculiarly arduous." On the contrary, it is a peculiarly inviting one. I came here almost unwillingly, for I wanted to go to Africa, but what I have seen has made me glad I came; and if I know my own heart, its desire is to live and die among this people. One thing is very certain, missionaries who come to this people will find them in general poor and ignorant. Here, emphatically, "to the poor the gospel will be preached." You must therefore make up your minds to become teachers of babes when you come to this people. There are, I admit, many exceptions, and you will often meet men of considerable learning and tact, but the mass of the people are as above described. Your own experience has probably already taught you, that it is more difficult for an educated man to come down and instruct the ignorant, than it is to instruct those who already know something. This suggestion, therefore, may assist you somewhat in judging of the qualities a missionary needs, in instructing this people: they are patience, a facility in finding comparisons, a talent for simplifying, an engaging address, &c. &c.

. . . . There are many items of intelligence I might communicate to you; but you will see in the pages of the Chronicle and Foreign Missionary, much more than I can possibly write at this time, and therefore I shall refer you to them. I do so the more readily, because I have nothing of especial interest to communicate to you, except what this letter contains, which will not appear in one or other of those publications. My own progress in the language has been but small. Nearly one-half of the time, since my arrival in China, has been spent in voyages, and other engagements connected with the mission; so that altogether I have given but eight or nine months' close attention to it. Still I am encouraged, and hope ere long to have a tolerably good acquaintance with it.

Allow me, in conclusion, to make some remarks on your own duty in reference to the heathen, and these I trust you will receive not as coming from a superior, but from one himself recently a theological student, and still remembering the feelings of such. Your letter speaks with just severity of the inconsistency of those who pass resolutions to do something special for the cause of foreign missions, and yet make no special efforts to accomplish their resolutions. You speak too of the apathy of the churches on this subject, and, as I think, partly lay the blame at the door of the pastors of the churches. I am convinced from what I have seen, and I saw a good deal before leaving the United States, that the fault is with the ministry. "Like priest, like people," is an ancient and true proverb. But I do not mean to blame the ministry in general, nor to pass an indiscriminate censure even on those of them who have done little or nothing. My object rather is to forget the things that are behind, and to press forward to those that are before. Hence it has ever appeared exceedingly important, that the students in our theological seminaries should have the right spirit in the matter. Could I but see the right spirit prevailing in our theological seminaries, I am almost certain that in ten years our whole church would assume an entirely different appearance, as it regards the cause of foreign and domestic missions. Why? Because in that time I suppose our seminaries would have supplied five hundred pastors of churches at least, and they would be settled in all parts of the country. Suppose now that those five hundred pastors had the right spirit, and joined their influence heartily with the ministers already earnestly engaged, and what would be the effect? Their influence would be felt in all our Presbyteries and Synods. When the Assembly passed resolutions, there would be men enough to respond to them. We should no more hear that more than half our churches give nothing at all to the cause of Christ. The whole appearance of things would be entirely altered. Now, brethren, you form a part of those five hundred ministers. The most of you, I suppose, will become pastors in different parts of the country. What is your spirit now in regard to the benevolent operations of the day? What do you intend to do when you are settled over your several charges? Shall the theological students of 1853 make the same complaints of you, that you make of your predecessors?

I have no doubt that many of you, I trust all of you, intend to do something at least for foreign missions. Your own personal duty as to becoming missionaries, is a subject I shall not now touch upon. I wish to refer to the influence on behalf of foreign missions, which you may exert on the people. Your intentions are doubtless good, but what preparations are you now making? What do you know of missions? Do you think you will be able to keep up the interest of your people in the Monthly Concert? Do you think you will be able to teach them the true principles of missions; not romantic views, but sober, common-sense, Christian principles? Do you think you will be able to sustain the interest of your people from year to year, and not merely to sustain it, but to cause it to grow; to take deeper root; to become more and more a matter of principle, and less and less one of mere impulse? Do you think you will be able to do without the visits of agents? I trust you will pardon me if I say, I fear that some of you cannot answer these questions in the affirmative. I do not know any of you personally, and therefore you will not of course consider my remarks as personal. I only speak from my knowledge of theological students in general, and that has been pretty extensive, and sufficiently accurate to justify me in making the above remarks. It is no easy thing to bring the church up to the mark, and to keep her there, and you will find this very soon after you are settled in the ministry. You will find that without a tolerably thorough and extensive acquaintance with the history and principles of missions, you cannot do it.

Do you ask me, then, what you are to do? I say, first *learn*. Now is your time, while you are in the seminary. Lay a deep and broad foundation of missionary knowledge; study the prophecies of the Bible in reference to this point, and study them specially. See what prophecies relate to Africa; what to the Jews; whether there are any for China. Learn the history of the progress of the gospel in all ages and countries, but particularly within the last fifty years. Study the history of particular missions. I take it for granted you will study the history of our own Board and its missions, but I hope you will not confine yourself to them. God has blessed other societies, both in America and England, abundantly; and now, when the means of information are so accessible, why should you not avail yourselves of them? Study the Bible with reference to this point. Why is it that some men at Monthly Concerts read only the seventy-second Psalm, and the sixtieth chapter of Isaiah? They really seem to think that there are no other parts of the Bible that speak of missions. Having learned these things—and you see from this hasty outline that there is not a little to be learned, and that you can best commence learning it while in the seminary—the next thing will be to *teach*. This will be your duty in the public services of the sanctuary, in the Monthly Concert, in friendly visits among your people, and, above all, in the Sabbath-school. Let it be a special object with you to interest the young, and you will certainly succeed. But I have written till my hand is wearied, and perhaps have wearied your patience. What I have written, however, though hastily penned, has not been hastily gathered. I trust it will not be hastily passed over by you. I shall be most happy to hear from you as soon as you wish to write, and shall prefer that you ask me questions, which I shall answer as I can. I have some questions to ask you in return, to which I shall be glad to receive answers. What is the order and nature of your exercises in the Society of Inquiry, and the Monthly Concert? Do your students make it a point of conscience to inquire into their own personal duty to the heathen? And is this done in the early part of your theological course? Do your students generally *read* the missionary publications, particularly the Chronicle and Herald? I don't mean, do you *take* them? for I have known many students to take, who scarcely ever read them. Is your Monthly Concert well attended? Do you have any missionary exercises in your Sabbath-schools? And if so, what and how frequently? Have any of your students ever written one or more missionary sermons *before* leaving the Seminary?

If you publish a catalogue, I shall be glad to receive a copy. And now, dear brethren, I must close. I make no apology for the plainness of my remarks and questions, and trust you will receive them in the same frank and Christian spirit with which they are made. Pray for me. That the choicest blessings of God may ever rest upon you, is the prayer of

Your brother in Christ,

W. M. LOWRIE.

Macao, December 15th, 1843.

MY DEAR MOTHER—. . . It has become so cold within a day or two past that I have to think of old times. . . . My teacher comes in with half a dozen jackets on, and draws his hands into the long-lined sleeves of the third of them, sitting as snug and cosy, as if he had a little fireplace under his elbows. By the way, it is extremely common for Chinese of any wealth to carry a small metal vessel, as large as a man's fist, with live coals in it. It is used to warm their fingers with, and when covered up in the long sleeve must diffuse a very grateful warmth up the arm. Frost and snow are so seldom met with here, that neither the Chinese nor the Portuguese ever build fireplaces in their houses. If necessary they use a brazier with charcoal, but commonly adopt the expedient of heaping on additional clothes. Did I ever describe to you the winter dress of the generality of the Chinese about here? You would laugh if you saw them. I do not know what they have next to the skin, but from the waist to the ankle the outside dress is a pair of very closely fitting drawers, which show exactly the form of the whole of the lower extremities. Then the upper part of the body is covered with the loose jacket, of which they wear as many as the weather requires, or their means permit. Their appearance is consequently next thing to ridiculous. The whole of the upper part of the body looks like a barrel with a head on the top of it, while the legs stick out beneath like a pair of compasses. What adds to the effect of the whole, is, that the drawers are of various colours blue, green, yellow, black and white. Many a time I have laughed at the comical appearance of a young dandy, who thought he was making a grand display in his new clothes and well-turned limbs. I should like to see one of them in Broadway, with his thick soled shoes and green tights, his wadded vests, and round cap and long tail behind. Yet, after all, I am a great admirer of the Chinese modes of dress. Their drawers, and the thick-soled shoes, and the tails are the worst parts; but the better classes do not wear the drawers, or at least they wear another garment over them. . . . . It would amuse you to see how universal the use of the fan is. I have seen a coolie or common labourer, sweating along the streets under a heavy burden, and fanning himself all the time. It is funny to see some of the mechanics, and others a grade or two above the coolies, fanning themselves in summer. Their dress then consists of a pair of very loose trowsers fastened round the waist by a string, and an upper garment reaching a little lower than the top of the trowsers, and hanging loose over them. You will see them every now and then putting their hands behind them, and fanning up their backs, under this jacket.

My teacher is quite intelligent for a Chinese, though he knows almost nothing of anything beyond China. He thinks it very strange that we say north, east, south, and west, for the Chinese say east, west, south and north. It is also very strange to him that we say north-east, south-east, &c., for the Chinese say east-north, east-south, west-north, &c. I was amused at a talk we had yesterday about the Chinese queue, or tail, as we commonly call it. He said that formerly it was not worn, but that the present fashion of shaving all the front of the head and leaving it to grow long and braiding it behind was introduced about two hundred years ago, by the present Tartar dynasty.

I told him about the death and resurrection of Christ, at which he seemed much surprised. He asked if Christ was not a man like Confucius. I told him no, but the Son of God. As his curiosity seemed to be somewhat excited, I told him I had a biography of Christ which I would lend him, if he wished to read it. He said he would, so I gave him a New Testament, which he took away with him.

Oh that the Spirit of God may make it a blessing to him. . .

With love to all the family, I remain,

Yours affectionately,

W. M. Lowrie.

Macao, November 20th, 1843.

To the Society of Inquiry of Princeton Theological Seminary.

Dear Brethren:—It is now rather more than two years since I finally left your institution. I did not intend that so long a time should elapse without writing to you, for both my own inclinations, and a kind request from your corresponding secretary, have made me wish to hold a correspondence with you. Circumstances, however, over which I have had little control, have induced me to defer writing till the present period. You may be sure it has not been for want of interest in your institution that I have so long delayed. On the contrary, the thoughts of hallowed seasons in the old Oratory where you meet, have been among the most pleasant of the many pleasant recollections I have brought from the land of my birth.

You have doubtless heard marvellous accounts of the difficulty of the Chinese language, and the time necessary to gain even a 'smattering' in it. Ten, fifteen, twenty, and even twenty-five years have I heard assigned as the time in which a person may hope to gain some little acquaintance with it. Now all this is certainly incorrect. There is no doubt it is a very hard language. If any of you come here, you will need a great deal more resolution and spirit than you found needed for Hebrew. It is, I suppose, the hardest language in the world, and perhaps no foreigner will ever acquire it *perfectly;* certainly no foreigner ever has acquired it perfectly. But I have seen several men who have been here much less than ten years who do speak it with great fluency, and are quite intelligible, not merely to the teacher who has become accustomed to their pronunciation and modes of thought, but to the people in general, and that too in the most difficult of all the dialects. Nor are those who have made such acquirements men of the most splendid talents, and wonderful facilities in learning languages. They are little, if anything, superior to the most of those who become missionaries. It is also a most important consideration that the facilities for learning the language are now vastly greater than they have ever before been, so that at the northern ports especially, a person may hope to learn the language in two-thirds of the time that was formerly requisite. By *facilities* I mean, books, teachers, and especially opportunities of access to the people. I do not wish to give you the impression that it is a light work to learn it. If any of you come here with that impression, you will be sadly disappointed. But if you come, and sit down manfully to the task, determined from the outset to be satisfied with nothing less than an accurate acquaintance with the *tones*, and with the *sounds*, and with the *idioms*, you will find yourselves in two years' time proceeding with profit and pleasure. By that time you will have gained much acquaintance with the character of the people; you will be astonished at the vastness of the field open before you, and you will thank God that he has sent you to labour for this great and ancient race.

If you come here as missionaries, you must expect many trials. They will come upon you in unthought-of ways, and where you looked for most joy, you may perhaps find most sorrow. I am led to make this remark for two reasons. It is a fact that Chinese missionaries have been remarkably tried, some by sickness, some by loss of relatives, some by personal inconveniences and disappointments. There are some twenty or more missionaries to China, not including females; of these twenty, there are scarcely three who have not met some sore trial within the last fifteen months. I do not know whether missionaries to other countries have been so generally afflicted; but very many of them have, and you may be called to experience the same. There is also another reason that induces me to think that missionaries to China must expect trials. We have a very great work to perform. If China contain, as it probably does, one-third of the population of the globe, and if this people is to be converted to God, then no words of mine are needed, as no human words are able to express the greatness of the work before us. But when was it ever known that any great work was accomplished without labour and toil, self-denial, sacrifice, and oftentimes the acutest mental anguish? Has not every great work that ever has been performed for God in the world been watered by the sweat, and the tears, and the blood of his servants? And can we expect that the conversion of the most populous nation of the globe shall be accomplished with ordinary efforts and ordinary sorrows? General experience is against it. The experience of missionaries to China is against it. And the example of God our Saviour, who, to accomplish the world's redemption, became "sorrowful even unto death," should teach us, who are to be "partakers of his sufferings," not to expect it. We need to be humbled in the dust before we can be trusted with success, where success is to be so glorious. We need to be purified in the furnace before we can labour with acceptance, where our acceptable labours are to redound so much to the glory of God; yet do not think that these trials will make you unhappy. For a time they will be hard to bear; but "He giveth more grace." And great as have been the trials of the missionaries here, I have seldom associated with persons who seemed so truly happy as do most of my fellow-labourers in China. These trials are necessary for us here, and it was well remarked to me by one who was herself called to bear the yoke, "Trials are one of our most precious means of grace."

If I may judge from what I have seen in the papers, the impression is gaining ground, that missionaries should be unmarried men: and some of the principal reasons adduced for this opinion are, that it will cost much less to sustain them; they will be much more free to move about and embrace favourable opportunities of doing good; they will be less likely to go home; and after all, the wives of missionaries do not do so very much, in the way of direct labour, and would not be very much missed. Those who are in favour of the marriage of missionaries insist very much on the direct usefulness of the wives of missionaries, and there are many who seem to think this is the chief reason for sending them. Now, with all due deference to the advocates of both sides, it strikes me that these arguments place the subject on the wrong ground, and present it in a false light.

Missionaries are men of like passions with others, and in the present day, when miraculous influences have ceased, I know not why they should be judged of in a different way from other men; or why the broad principles of the Bible are not as applicable to them as to other men. Now one of the first principles of the Bible on this subject is, "It is not good that the man should be alone." This principle, I conceive, was recognized by our Saviour when the disciples said, "It is not good to marry." He who knew what was in man, said, "All men cannot receive this saying—he that is able to receive it, let him receive it." This is the rule by which this question must be decided. It is not good for the great majority of men to be alone; first, because, if alone they are exposed to temptations, which sad experience proves that most men cannot withstand; secondly, because, though they may by grace withstand the temptations to actual sin, yet they are not contented; and they want those solaces of affection which the human heart craves, and those counsels of intimate friendship that are so grateful to him that is separated from the influences of Christian society. If, then, you can live sinlessly in the unmarried state; if you can be contented; if you can be satisfied without the kindly influences of female society; then I say, it is probably your duty to be an unmarried missionary, but not otherwise.

The expense is not the question; and as long as the Church is so abundantly able to bear it as she now is, it is a shame to mention such a consideration, or to ask, why does not the missionary live as the whalers and fur-hunters do?

There is force in the consideration, that an unmarried missionary is more free to move about, and at times to occupy stations where married men cannot easily go, and the consideration should have its own weight with those who think of this subject. But there is equal force in the consideration, that permanent good, and visible effects have most commonly followed where the married missionary has settled, and by his settlement concentrated his efforts. The direct usefulness of the missionary's wife, is by no means the main point in deciding this question. Her first duty in all cases is to attend to her husband and children; and if she have time and strength for more than this, then that is all clear gain. Let her preserve her husband from those temptations to which unmarried men are exposed; let her soothe him in his hours of despondency; let her relieve him from the household cares that must interrupt him if unmarried; let her soften the disposition that without her influence would become rough and rude; (for as Bacon says, "Certainly wife and children are a kind of discipline of humanity;")

let her show by her silent example what a Christian wife and mother is, and how she should be treated; and if she never learns a syllable of the native language, or teaches a single heathen child a letter, she has accomplished a work worth ten times more than the expense of her outfit and support. These observations may excite a smile, but they are not written in levity. They may appear strange, and half-romantic, but only to those who have romantic views of missions. Much thought and the acquaintance of several missionaries, convince me that they are the words of truth and soberness. As to the question whether it is the wife who causes the return of the missionary, although the general opinion seems to be that it is, yet I have my doubts. Certainly the experience of the Presbyterian Board does not say so; for of all their missionaries who have returned on account of ill health, Mr. Rogers of North India is the only one who has yet been taken back by his wife's ill health; in every other case it is the husband's ill health that has taken the wife back. The experience of the American Board seems to be different; but I should be glad to see a fuller array of facts, than the celebrated paper of Dr. Anderson presents. It does not strike me that the whole of the facts, in regard to the return of *all* who do return, is there presented. If I remember rightly, that paper speaks of the return of so many married missionaries, but does not say anything about the return of unmarried missionaries.

I have been exceedingly pained by some articles I have seen lately in the papers, in reference to the claims of the domestic and foreign fields. The spirit of the articles referred to has not been of the right kind. I have no doubt their authors meant well, but it appears to me to be an exceedingly erroneous course, to attempt to set the claims of foreign and domestic missions in array and in opposition against each other, or to say that too much attention has been given to the one, to the neglect of the other.

The attempts I have seen in some of the papers to show that literally more has been done for foreign than for domestic missions, I pass by, as unworthy of an answer: you can count every cent that is expended for the foreign field, but you have not the statistics for one-half the expenses of the domestic field; and yet it is easily shown that even the half of those expenses is much greater than all that is expended abroad. These men talk of the vastness of the domestic field, of the favourable openings, of the need of labourers; and they tell us that these men are our brethren, and have special claims upon us. I admit it all, and if I could add anything to the force of what they say, I would beseech you, by the mercies of Christ, and by your love for the souls of your brethren, to do with your might what your hands find to do for them. But why should this be done by disparaging the claims of the foreign field? O brethren, if I could show you what I have lately seen,—the numerous openings where the gospel may be preached, the unnumbered thousands who are accessible with far more ease than the scattered inhabitants of the West, the fewness and feebleness of the labourers sent by the Church,—and if we could all feel that these, too, are our brethren, seeing God hath made us all of one blood to dwell on all the face of the earth, you would give little heed to such unworthy comparisons. If the church were now doing all in her power; if every nerve were strained as much as the gospel requires, then there might be occasion to pause, and ask, Are we not doing too much here, or too much there? But as long as more than half the Church is doing nothing, absolutely nothing, let there be no more complaints that too much is done for the heathen. I object to the papers referred to, because they give countenance to the idea, that the interests of the foreign and domestic fields are not the same. If there is any man who renounces such an idea, it is the missionary to the heathen. Our hearts rejoice within us when we hear of the extension of the cause of Christ at home, and that the gospel is preached to the poor and the destitute. Why? Not only because of the amount of actual good accomplished, but because we know that thus new funds, and new men, are raised up for the foreign field, and additional prayers ascend on our behalf. Every conquest at home increases our strength abroad. But if we are told that these conquests are to be gained henceforth by diminishing the efforts abroad, and disparaging the importance of the work in which we are engaged, then we have small reason to rejoice. But I will not believe that such one-sided views shall ever gain general currency among those who see and know, that one of the surest ways to promote vital piety at home, is to make it active and expansive; so that, while it rejoices to do good to those around, it embraces the world in the wide arms of charity.

I observe that one of the "standing requests" you propose to your foreign correspondents is, "Can you send us any curiosities?" To this I answer, "Yes, plenty; if I had the money to buy them with." Such things are not easily to be procured without paying for them; and as a missionary's salary does not commonly give him a great deal of spending money besides his necessary expenses, he cannot easily send many curiosities to all who would like to have them. I will, however, keep my eyes open, and endeavour to make some addition to your cabinet. Allow me to suggest whether it would not be better for you to make an annual appropriation of ten, twenty, or thirty dollars, and request some of the missionaries to procure articles for your cabinet? I will most cheerfully undertake any such commission for you, and will procure either such articles as you may specify, or myself select such as may be interesting. There will be no difficulty in remitting the money, for all that is necessary is to pay it at the Mission Rooms in New York, stating that it is "for curiosities, &c., for the Seminary at Princeton." Have you a set of the Chinese Repository? I know you have one or two of the volumes; but it is very desirable that you have the whole set, for there is no work, ancient or modern, that gives so much information concerning China. If you will give me instructions to that effect, and tell me what volumes you have, I can easily procure you the others. There are now twelve volumes; the first and second are six dollars each, and the other ten three dollars each, being forty-two dollars for the set. It is continued yearly at three dollars a year.

I must now bring this long epistle to a close. That every blessing from above may rest upon you, may direct your future course, and crown your labours with success, is the prayer of your friend and brother in the gospel,

W. M. Lowrie.

Macao, December 30th, 1843.

My Dear Father.—. . . . The principal occurrence of interest during the month has been some rather public discussions of the visit paid by Mr. Abeel and myself to Chang-Chowfoo. After my return, Mr. Bridgman and others importuned me to write an account of it for the Chinese Repository. I declined at first, from a dislike to make myself so prominent as such an account would necessarily make me. Being still urged I consented, and Mr. Bridgman and myself looked over it carefully to see that there were no incorrect statements; and, not to offend our English friends, omitted all reference to the manner in which the officers at Chang-Chow spoke of Americans. The article was read with interest, and among others an English officer of some influence in Hong Kong spoke of it quite favourably. Judge, then, of my surprise, when a few days afterwards Sir Henry Pottinger published a proclamation expressly referring to it, pointedly condemning our conduct, and informing the Chinese authorities of the Provinces of Canton and Fuhkeen, that the "party, &c., were Americans!" This excited no little talk, and I heard many persons condemn Sir Henry's course as impertinent and uncalled for, though I found that the insinuations of the proclamation were leaving unfavourable impressions as to my conduct. I accordingly prepared a reply, and sent it to the "Friend of China." A *cautious* friend in Hong Kong, without my leave, withdrew the article. When he gave me his reasons, I did not deem them sufficient. I could not see how a plain and manly defence of one's course against uncalled for and injurious charges was improper. I considered too that our American citizenship and freedom from the surveillance of English authorities, were important circumstances in our favor in carrying on the work of missions here, and were to be defended and maintained. Accordingly I wrote another article, which appeared this week in the Friend of China.

In consequence of Sir Henry's letter to the governor of Canton, the latter addressed a letter to the American consul, informing him of the affair, and urging him to enforce on his countrymen the necessity of obedience to the treaty. Mr. Forbes wrote back that his countrymen would always obey the laws when made known; but that when we went to Chang-Chow, the supplementary treaty was not known to us. He also wrote me a very gentlemanly letter, more, I suppose, as a matter of form than anything else, informing me of the communication of the governor of Canton.

The notoriety attending this affair has been not a little unpleasant and annoying to me, but I do not feel that I have done anything to be ashamed of. I suppose it is to be considered as one of the necessary trials of this state of warfare, and a wholesome discipline to prepare me for future trials. Pray for me that I may have wisdom and prudence to guide me in all my ways.....

Your affectionate son,

W. M. LOWRIE.

CHAPTER V.

1844.

Residence in Macao—Letters—Chinese Printing with Metal Type—Arrival of New Missionaries—Their Fields of Labour.

DURING the year 1844, the missionary force in China was much enlarged. In February, D. B. McCartee, M.D., and Mr. R. Cole, printer, and his wife, reached China. The Rev. R. Q. Way and his wife arrived in July, and the Rev. Messrs. J. Lloyd, A. P. Happer, M.D., A. W. Loomis, and M. S. Culbertson, with Mrs. Loomis and Mrs. Culbertson, in October.

The location of these brethren at the different missions, was a subject of much importance, and of some delicacy. In relation to it, the officers of the Board had conversed freely with the new missionaries, after which, with some general suggestions from the Executive Committee, the matter was left to their own decision. Though younger than some of his colleagues, yet as the missionary longest in China, much of the responsibility rested on Mr. Lowrie; and until their respective missions were fixed, it was to him a time of much anxiety and care. After a season of prayer for Divine direction, with much harmony they arranged their places at the different missions. At Canton were settled Mr. Happer, and for the present, Mr. Cole, with the press; at Amoy, Mr. Lloyd and Dr. Hepburn, who were to be joined by the Rev. H. A. Brown, when he should arrive; at Ningpo, Mr. Lowrie, Mr. Way. Mr. Culbertson, Mr. Loomis, and Dr. McCartee. This arrangement involved the separation of two friends, Messrs. Lloyd and Lowrie, and most deeply was it felt by both. Both were convinced, however, that the interests of the Master's cause required this trial, keen as it was, and after a short interview of two weeks, they parted to meet no more on earth.

The printing press and the Chinese matrices were received in February, when Mr. Cole arrived. The theory of printing the Chinese language with metal type—a large portion of them being divisible characters—was to be reduced to practice, and tested by actual experiment. The type were to be cast, and four thousand different characters were to be arranged in cases for the compositor. To be convenient, the characters most frequently used required to be placed together, whilst regard was to be had to the principles of the language, as arranged under the different radicals or keys. Mr. Cole was experienced in English printing, but he had no knowledge of Chinese, and the entire arrangement of the Chinese characters devolved on Mr. Lowrie. Everything was new. Some of the characters occur very rarely, others occur repeatedly on every page; hence some approximation of the relative number of each had to be made, before the type could be cast, and the difficulty of this work was increased by a large part of them being divisible. After months of labour, these difficult matters were accomplished, and the press went into successful operation in June.

Besides attention to the press, much of his time was required on behalf of the other missionaries. He was their general treasurer. He was in a measure at home; they were in a strange place; their business affairs necessarily fell to his share, and his services were of much benefit to them. His correspondence with the Mission House was also very full.

Much to his regret, these various items greatly interfered with his Chinese studies.

During this year, Mr. Lowrie prepared a series of articles on the history of the missionary work in China, with a brief account of the Jews and Christians in China, which were published in the Chinese Repository. They were afterwards reprinted in the United States, under the title of the Land of Sinim, or an exposition of Isaiah xlix. 12.

Dr. McCartee left Macao for Ningpo in June, and Mr. Way and his wife in August. Mr. Lloyd left for Amoy in November. Owing to the north-east monsoon, the other missionaries for Ningpo did not set out till the February following.

Macao, January 18th, 1844.

My Dear Mother—This day finishes two years since I left the United States. I know not how the time has seemed to you, but to me it appears under a very singular aspect. It has gone so rapidly that I can scarce conceive so much has really elapsed; and yet it has led me through so many strange scenes, that I can scarcely crowd them all into it. I like to look back occasionally, for the immediate effects of all I have seen have passed away, and they come up before me quietly and calmly to be thought about. I try to look forward, but in vain, for I know not what a day may bring forth. I am just as uncertain as I was two years ago, where my lot shall yet be cast, or whether I shall ever find a "place of rest." It is not an easy thing to learn to live by the day, or in "patience to possess one's soul." I want to be moving, to be doing something, to see results; but my mouth is closed, and at present my feet are bound. Sometimes it is, "Oh, that I had wings like a dove, for then would I fly away;" but then again the word comes, "The husbandman hath long patience." This is a trial of missionary life that did not at first enter much into my thoughts, its comparative inaction. I am busy as I can well be, yet my life is as quiet as it was in the Seminary, and I see even less of company. It is nearly three weeks since I have spoken to a lady, and it is three months since I have spent a day in a house with one. So we pass away. We are strangers here, at one time walking in the crowded streets, and at another threading the wilderness path alone, but ever pressing on to the end of our course. Shall it be long or short? painful or pleasant? But these are not the questions for us to ask. It is ours to take no thought for the morrow.

January 19. As clear and bright a day as it was two years ago, but a good deal warmer. After reading a page or so in the *San Ko Che*, or History of the Three States, I started off about eleven o'clock, with my teacher, to visit the temple of Wa-kok. (I wrote a description of it some time ago for the Foreign Missionary.) I had been there often, but wanted my teacher to explain some things which I did not understand. As you may suppose, I talk with him in very broken language, and can understand only a part of what he says, but we make out to talk a good deal together. I think I can see his respect for the superstitions of his own country perceptibly decreasing, though I fear that it is only to make way for an indifference to religion that is even worse. A couple of well-dressed and respectable-looking men were bowing and kneeling, lighting incense-sticks, and burning paper before the images. He said they were praying for wealth; but he acknowledged that the images could not hear them. They went to several of the images, and as they went to each one, an attendant struck the bell and the drum several times. I asked him what that was for? He said, to "rouse the attention of the idol, and make her hear!" I asked him what sort of gods these were, when it was necessary to awaken them to make them listen to their worshippers? He said, with a good deal of earnestness, "I don't worship these; I worship only the spirit that is represented by them." However, he acknowledged that most of the people worshipped the idol. He then asked me, if we used no images of Jesus Christ. I said, no; that the Roman Catholics used a crucifix, but that I thought this wrong, and that it was folly to worship any image. "It had eyes, but could not see; ears, but could not hear; nose, but could not smell; feet, but could not walk." It is just so here. O that he were a Christian! He is a very amiable man, a man of some learning, and simple-minded, and might do great good if converted. I like him far better than any teacher I have yet had, and he seems very well satisfied to stay with me; though he does get tired sometimes, when I ply him with questions, and keep him sitting by me for three or four hours together. I told him the other day, that in the United States we elected our own *Hwang Shang* and *Tsung Tuk*, "Emperor and Viceroys." (The Chinese have no word corresponding to President and Governors.) I think I never saw a man so astonished. He held up both hands, and stared at me, and at last exclaimed, "Hi yah! Astonishing! I never heard of such a thing!" He said at first it was a very bad plan, for the people would be always fighting. But after I had shown him that in this way we secured the election of just officers, and men who would not oppress us, while their officers, according to his own acknowledgment, were extremely venal and extortionate, he said, "Well, perhaps it may be good for you, but I am sure it would not be possible to do so here;" which is very true. It is wonderful how ignorant the Chinese learned men are. I believe he looks on me as a sort of Baron Munchausen, though I have told him very little that is not known to every school-boy in the United States. . . . .

Hoping to hear from you soon, I remain, as ever,

Yours affectionately, W. M. Lowrie.

Macao, February 1st, 1844.

My Dear Father—It seems to me, the more I think about the matter, that there must be a radical change in the literature and literary style of China, before it can be made the vehicle of permanent and extensive usefulness. A great deal is said of the fact, that so many in China can read, but it is to be feared that a great deal too much is expected from this. Their literature at present, and the style in which it is written, reminds me very much of the state of Europe before the Reformation. There were learned men then, and they had a learned language, different from that of every-day life, which the common people did not understand. This learned language was known to the learned all over Europe, and even some of the poorer class could read it, for the alphabet was the same in most places; but *they* did not understand what they read, and of those who did understand, and wrote in the learned language, the less that is said the better. Who reads their writings now, or cares for their opinions? A new mode of thinking, and speaking, and writing was introduced after the Reformation, and the old has disappeared. Very much the same revolution, in my humble judgment, must occur in China. They have a learned language here, and unless a book be written in that language, it has little favour. That language may be learned by many years of study, but it is not the language of the people, nor of nature. Many who can pronounce the characters do not understand them; and the world will be never the worse, if nine-tenths of the books at present in circulation here be lost for ever. Some Chinese Bacon must arise, and do for China what Lord Verulam did for Europe.

I speak with a good deal of diffidence on these points, for I am only forming my own opinion about them, and others who ought to know more think differently. I am, however, very far from supposing that the Chinese styles, either of printing, or speaking, or writing, or acting, are always the most tasteful, or the most convenient, or the most practically useful. In general I think them very much like their thick-soled shoes, which my teacher says "are very good-looking, but not so good to walk with." There can be no doubt of the truth of the latter part of this remark, while each one must judge for himself of the *good looks.*

. . . . I send you my *Luban walking-stick*, which you must take good care of, though I hope it will be long before you need to use it. I do not want to use it myself, for it might get broken or be lost, and therefore, for safe-keeping, I will put it in your hands.

That every blessing may ever rest upon you is the prayer of

Your affectionate son,

W. M. LOWRIE.

Macao, February 10th, 1844.

REV. JOHN LLOYD—MY DEAR JOHN:— . . . How it made my heart beat to think that *this year* I may see you here! I fell into a reverie just now, and thought I was walking along the beach and you landed. What a shaking of hands and an embracing there was! Then I began to ask you questions; but though you talked fast, you did not talk half fast enough to satisfy me. . . .

Many thanks for your long, kind letter. It is the second I have received, and I hope I may have another soon. I am glad my journal gave you so much pleasure.

How many things we shall have to say to each other when you come. Yet sometimes I fear we shall not be allowed to meet; or if we meet, shall have to part again; and I feel as though I ought not to hope for too much. How often we are disappointed in the very place where we expected most! I have learned some deeply painful lessons since I came here, though not more painful than needed.

Why do you give way so much to melancholy forebodings?

> "Why should the children of a king
> Go mourning all their days?"

Our gracious Father has now led you along for more than nine years, and are you still afraid to trust him? How much would you and I have given, nine years ago, to be told we should persevere till now! yet here we are. Thus far the Lord hath led us on, and will not he whose hand has ever been around us still lead us? Can he not take as much care of us hereafter, as he has hitherto done? I know, would that I felt it more, that at best we are very unprofitable servants; but can we ever repay God for his mercies? must we not at last enter heaven in the righteousness of another? Oh, let us look to Christ, in whom is all our strength and hope; and while we labour, never forget that we are accepted, not in our own works, but in the Beloved.

I am very well, very busy, and commonly very happy. Chinese is beginning to look inviting, and many a hearty laugh I have with my Chinese teacher. He does not speak a word of English, and my Chinese is broken enough; but we make out pretty well on a good many points. Do not be afraid of this language. It is hard enough, *but can be learned.*

Give my kindest regards to Brown and Culbertson, whom I expect to see with you before this year rolls away. The sooner you come the better, for I suppose I must be unsettled till you all come out, and I am getting tired of that; so be in a hurry.

It is nearly ten o'clock. My hand is so tired,

that I can scarcely write legibly, and if I had five hundred things to say, they would have to stay unsaid....

Commending you to God and the word of his grace, which is able to build you up and keep you until the appearing of our Lord, I am as ever your brother in Christ,

W. M. Lowrie.

Macao, May 14th, 1844.

My Dear Father— .... My letters to the committee will have shown you how often I am embarrassed and at a loss how to decide the various important questions occurring here. *I wish you would come out here;* you will find enough to call into exercise all your experience. You may lay the foundations of this mission on a better basis than we who are here can do. My wish is to be prudent and thoughtful, and to do all for the best; but I am young and inexperienced, yet I have more experience of the Chinese than any of my colleagues. I have no disposition to decline responsibility, and have frequently to take more than my share. What can we do? There are things which must be done, and our fears are that they may not be done in the best way. You are not yet sixty years old, yet *Ricci* was fifty when he came to China; and you have had ten years of thought about this country, and are younger in constitution than most men of the same age. Your coming might do more good than for twenty boys to go abroad before their constitutions are settled, and who may die before they come to their prime. It often seems to me that we are commencing at the top instead of the bottom, when we lay light and untried materials in the foundation. If you can come for life so much the better, but at any rate come for *five years*. Live here and spy out the land. I have not made this request in a spirit of levity, but after a good deal of thought and prayer. I know how important your presence is at head-quarters, and I know you will consider the matter calmly. God will direct you; and for myself, I will remember what the old farmer said, "I can't go with you, but God Almighty will."

My teacher was reading the New Testament to-day, when he observed, "This Jesus must have been a very benevolent man. How kind it was in him to heal those sick people, and to provide them food when they were hungry! Truly he was a good man." "Yes," I observed, "he was all you say, and far more, for he was God as well as man, and came from heaven to save sinful men, and without him no man in the world can be saved." "What!" said he, "can none be saved in China without him?" "No, not one." "Do you believe this?" he asked. "Yes, most certainly; and I have left my father and mother, to come to China to tell you of this blessed Saviour." "And how long has this been known to the Western nations?" "O, a great many hundred years." "Why, then," said he, "was not this knowledge sent sooner to China?" . . . . —A solemn question for every Christian. . . .

I am your affectionate son,

W. M. Lowrie.

RECOLLECTIONS OF A MISSIONARY.—NO. I.

—It was a very hot day in August, 184–, and I was lying on a couch, suffering from debility induced by the heat of a tropical summer. While thus reclining, the physician of the place, a serious and moral man, but at that time making no profession of piety, called to see me. He said he had a patient recently brought from a neighbouring city, and dangerously ill of a disease at that time prevailing, who expressed a wish to see an evangelical clergyman; and that he, (the physician,) would be much pleased if I would call on him. I went immediately, and on being shown into the sick room, found a young looking man, who held out his hand and expressed much gratification that I had called. His Bible was lying on a chair at his bedside, and it was not many minutes before he had told me fully and frankly his state and feelings. He was the son of a pious man, who had done much for the cause of missions in his own land. He himself had united with the Church in his youth, and for several years maintained a fair character, and thought himself a Christian. Of late, however, and especially since coming to this heathen land, he had greatly backslidden, and as he said, had so far forgotten his profession as to fall into open sin. While in this state he was attacked with a disease which had already proved fatal to several persons; and though there was at first nothing very alarming in his own case, yet it had aroused him to think on his ways, and the Spirit of God seemed to have brought his sins strongly to his remembrance.

When I saw him he was in great distress, fearing lest he had committed the unpardonable sin, and that there could be no hope for him. A few minutes' conversation showed that the instructions of his excellent father had sunk deep into his heart, and that he was tolerably well acquainted with the doctrines of religion, so that it was an easy and a pleasant duty to give him the instructions his case required. Doubtless there are those in our days who commit a sin for which there is no repentance, and for which we are not commanded to pray; but there was no evidence that such was his case, and on this point his mind was relieved. He feared, however, that he was not one of the elect;—could there be hope for him? I told him my belief in the doctrine of election was as firm as my belief in my own existence, but God's secret decrees were not the rule of our faith and practice. Repent and believe, and be saved; let him make his calling sure, and the question of his election need not trouble his mind. To this he freely assented, and then with tears in his eyes, and the utmost earnestness, asked if I thought it possible God could or would forgive so vile a backslider as himself. Taking up his Bible, I opened it at the beautiful passage in the fourteenth chapter of Hosea: "Take with you words and turn unto the Lord: say unto him, Take away all iniquity, and receive us graciously, &c.," and read and explained the whole chapter. Never did it appear so rich and precious to my own soul, and the sick man heard it with entranced attention. When it was finished, he exclaimed, "What precious words those are! Will you not pray with me?" After prayer, and a little further conversation, I left him, promising to see him again in the evening.

About sunset I called again, and found his disorder making rapid progress, so that occasionally he seemed to be wandering in mind. But his thoughts were on his soul's concerns, and towards Christ; his mind was calmer than when I first saw him, and though he expressed much fear of death, yet he seemed to apprehend fully that the grace of Christ was his only refuge, and I could not but hope that his faith was fixed on the Saviour; and with a mind much lightened in regard to him, I returned to my room. The exposure and exertions of the day in my weak state were too much for me, and a sleepless night left me with but little strength in the morning. As the day proved stormy, it seemed imprudent to venture out, and accordingly I wrote a note to the physician, requesting him to inform me if his patient should wish for me, as otherwise I could scarcely leave the house. The kind-hearted physician himself had some conversation with him, and finding him in the intervals of his delirium, to be much more peaceful, and apparently hopeful, did not send for me. He died in the night, and when I called early the next morning I found him laid out, with an expression of countenance like one who had gone in peace.

Among strangers, we buried him in a stranger's grave; for excepting the physician and myself, there were none in the place who knew him. He had but recently arrived in this country, and as we found in a day or two after, his partner died of the same disease on the same day.

Soon after his death I wrote to his mother, his father being dead, an account of his last moments, and of the hope I had that "the root of the matter was found in him." Several months passed away, and amidst other events the above was almost forgotten, when one day a small package from a distant land came into my hands. It contained a beautiful copy of the Memoir of McCheyne, and a note breathing "the most heartfelt gratitude," and the assurance of "earnest and constant prayer for my welfare." For some reason unknown to me, the writer wished to be unknown; but I could not avoid associating her, (for it was a lady's hand,) with the person spoken of above. Is it not true that bread cast upon the waters is found after many days—and that often in a way not anticipated? The parents of that young man "bestowed much labour" in forwarding the cause of missions, and the dying hours of their son were cheered and consoled in a strange land by a missionary of a different country, and a different denomination. I went in weakness to visit him, without a thought of reward, but how often has the thought cheered me since, that in a distant land there is one or more whom I have never seen, whose fervent prayers are offered up on my behalf!

RECOLLECTIONS OF A MISSIONARY.—NO. II.

In December, 184–, I was requested to visit a dying ship captain. This was Saturday evening. I went immediately, and on entering the house where he lay, found an elderly man in the last stages of consumption. He was a pious man, and amidst all the temptations and annoyances to which such persons in his situation are exposed, had in good measure kept himself free from reproach, and had made his ship a house of God upon the sea. Of late he had been quite unwell, and was brought ashore to the house of the consignee of his ship, where it is to be feared there was little care or respect for religion. Being a stranger, he did not know there were any missionaries in the place, and it was not till this day that he was informed that there were. One of the boys from his ship was attending him with the faithfulness of a son; and finding that he was drawing near his end, informed him that I was residing not far off, and had me sent for.

He was not able to bear much conversation: but the little I had was satisfactory, and he appeared exceedingly grateful to have met a fellow-believer to speak with him in his last hours. After prayer I left him, promising to call again. The next afternoon, while administering the Lord's Supper to the little band of fellow-labourers, and fellow-Christians in that place, I received a hasty summons to see him. On going to the house, I found the yard just before his window filled with native workmen, in the employ of the *Christian* owner of the house, busily packing and nailing boxes for a ship's cargo! Passing through the crowd, so unseemly on such a day, and in such a place, I went to the sick man's room, but found him nearly speechless. He knew me, grasped me by the hand, and to my inquiries as to the state of his soul, gave me to understand, though more by looks than by words, that all was well within. After a short prayer he fell into a doze, from which he did not again return to consciousness, and in a few hours his spirit departed. To him I have no reason to doubt heaven was as near even in that land of strangers and heathenism, as though he had died among his friends. The next day he was buried. A part of the ship's crew, one or two of the merchants of the place, and myself, were the only spectators; and few or none of those who now read the inscription over his tomb, in the field that was "bought to bury strangers in," have any knowledge of the person who sleeps beneath. Many such graves are there, for many have come from far distant lands to rest there.

"He that watereth others shall be watered himself;" and in the pleasure that this event afforded me, I found the first mitigation of one of the greatest sorrows that a gracious God has ever been pleased to lay upon me.

At another time I was called to visit another ship captain, but my memory recalls few of the circumstances connected with the occasion, except the following: After his decease, at his request, a sum of money, amounting to about twenty dollars, was put into my hands for any charitable purpose to which I might choose to apply it. On the very day it was received, a poor heathen woman, one of whose sons had been of some service to a fellow-missionary, came to me to beg for assistance in the case of another son, who was afflicted with the leprosy. She was in great distress: for the neighbours, apprehensive of catching the disease, had told her she must either place him in the hospital for such cases, or else leave her house, and seek another abode. She was poor, and knew not where else to find a house, and to place him in the hospital required an admission fee of twenty dollars, a sum she could not hope to borrow, nor to earn for many months. It seemed a providence: the money just sent was at once placed at her disposal, and with a light heart she went on her way rejoicing.

But a few weeks before leaving the place where I had been residing for more than two years, I was requested to visit another ship captain, who had been brought ashore with a dangerous illness, and was supposed to be near his end. Unlike the one mentioned in the first part of this paper, the owner of this house was seriously disposed, and had not only spoken faithfully to the sick man himself, but induced him to send for a clergyman. On being shown into his room, he seemed very glad to see me; but I was painfully impressed with the eagerness he expressed for "comfort." He was a well-educated, intelligent man, and had thought some for himself; but I was sorry to find, was quite skeptically disposed. He could not believe that mankind were so bad as clergymen commonly thought they were. He could scarcely believe that the Son of God had come down to suffer for the inhabitants of this petty world, which was, in the greatness of the universe, "but as a single leaf in the forest." Surprised at these remarks, I asked if he was not a believer in revelation. "Oh yes," said he; "yes, but sometimes these thoughts will come into my mind." I besought him to exchange these thoughts for others better suited to his situation, and after some further conversation and prayer, left him with my mind ill at ease; for all his anxieties seemed to be for comfort, and none for pardon and reconciliation with God. Yet he professed much gratitude, and begged me to call again. I did so in a day or two, and found his disorder had taken a favourable turn, and with it his seriousness had nearly gone. It was difficult to induce him to speak of his soul; but having no reason to hope that he would recover, as his physician thought the disease would soon return, I endeavoured as faithfully as possible to warn him of his state and prospects. He listened politely, but with little interest, until a fit of coughing seized him, and I thought it best not to say more. I called once or twice after, but he declined seeing me, and the gentleman of the house with whom he was staying, told me that as soon as he began to think himself getting better, his thoughts returned to earthly things. Poor man! A few days after this, he embarked in a vessel for his native land, and the next notice I had of him was, that he died soon after getting out to sea, and was buried in the ocean.

Macao, December 27th, 1844.

REV. JOHN M. LOWRIE—MY DEAR COUSIN:—Since April, 1843, I have preached in English, once a week, to a small congregation of English and Americans, some of whom are pious. It is the custom of most of the missionaries just to take printed sermons and read them off, which is well known by the people. I have done so myself several times, but never liked the plan, nor felt comfortable in adopting it. As the people who attend are very intelligent, I found it required a good deal of care to prepare sermons that would be profitable; and that I could give most instruction in the fewest words, and with least labour to myself, by writing out my sermons. I have done this commonly, and have now nearly fifty written discourses, besides several skeletons. As I lost all my written sermons when shipwrecked, the preparation of these has been attended with some degree of labour, and takes as much time as I can at present afford to give. I felt, indeed, some scruple about giving so much time to a work not directly the one for which I came here, but felt satisfied about it on considering that I am still young, and the labour and study of preparing sermons would be of essential benefit to me; and I have found it so. Preaching is a very delightful work, and I have only regretted that I could not give more time to it. . . .

It was a great disappointment to Lloyd and myself not to be together, but it seemed to be clearly the will of Providence that we should deny ourselves that gratification, and it is quite uncertain whether we shall ever see each other again. As it was, we could be together less than two weeks, and in that time I did not learn half as much as I wanted. Hugh Brown, too, will go to the same station with Lloyd, and as Happer will be at Hong Kong, I shall be "a stranger in the earth." So be it! It is good to feel that this is not our home, nor our rest.....

I am your affectionate cousin,

W. M. Lowrie.

Macao, December 28th, 1844.

Rev. James Montgomery—My Dear Brother:—Your letter of January 15th, which came to hand August 6th, gave me great pleasure, for it told me that though you had not written, your heart was still unchanged. I observed one thing in it, which has struck me in a number of other letters I have received. Speaking of my shipwreck, you remark, that you could scarce help thinking that I was preserved for some great end in this part of the world. The same idea has been expressed to me by several other of my correspondents, and I can sometimes scarcely avoid thinking it may be so; and yet the thought of it almost makes me tremble, for what a responsibility does it throw upon me, and what a foreshadowing, so to speak, is there in such an expectation of great trials and conflicts? It is through much tribulation we must enter into the kingdom of heaven. It is in the way of "much tribulation," that great good is commonly effected; and if I am to be the instrument of good here, I cannot expect to avoid trials and sorrows, greater perhaps by far than any that have yet come upon me. I do not murmur at this. If I know my own heart, I do not wish to shrink from any cross or any burden God sees good or needful to lay upon me; but oh! how much do I need grace, yea, "more grace," to fit me for the trials of my work here. Pray for me, that having done all and suffered all, I may stand accepted in the merits of Jesus Christ. I have had some little experience of tribulation since leaving the United States. I have known what it is to bear with long delays and hopes deferred, making the heart sick. I have gone through perils on the deep, and have been tried with the perversities and waywardness of some who had made the warmest professions of attachment.

Whither do all these things tend? Is the trial over yet, or am I to go through the furnace again? Dear brother, I confess my heart sometimes trembles when I ask myself these questions. For after all this sifting and searching, and refining, I still find so much of dross and impurity, that I sometimes think the furnace must be made "one seven times hotter," before I am fit for my work. If I have a work to do here, God will certainly prepare me for it. I do not wish to shrink from the preparation, but I do feel that without more grace I cannot endure it. Yet I dare not give way to fear. Hitherto the Lord hath helped me. In every trial hitherto, grace has been sufficient, and shall I not trust him for the future? And when I look back I am obliged to say, that notwithstanding all the sorrows I have felt since leaving the United States, no period of my life has been so happy as the last three years. As the sufferings have abounded, so have the consolations; and were it not for some undefined anticipations of the future, I should be ashamed to speak of my sorrows that are past at all. . . . Surely it is a wonder of sovereign grace, that God saves any of such a sinful race as ours is! We fight against him, and provoke him, even when he has shown us his love.

We have now a pretty large mission here, and I trust will soon be settled and all at work. *Cannot you come?* I should rejoice to have you with me; and I can assure you that I do not think your age a sufficient reason for not coming, if you have no other. Farewell, pray for me, and believe me,

Ever yours, in Christian bonds,

W. M. Lowrie.

CHAPTER VI.

1845.

Different Missions Established—Leaves Macao—Voyage up the Coast—Ningpo—Letters and Journals.

During this year the missions of the Presbyterian Church in China began to assume a more settled form. In the first part of the year, the missionaries had all reached their respective stations, and commenced their work under favourable and encouraging circumstances. In April, Messrs. Culbertson and Lowrie arrived at Ningpo, and Mr. Loomis at Ting-hai, on the island of Chusan; and in July the printing-press was removed to Ningpo. In May, the Rev. H. A. Brown reached Amoy. During the year, a boys' boarding-school was commenced at Macao, and another at Ningpo, under circumstances of much promise. During the summer, their number was lessened by the return home of Dr. Hepburn and his wife, on account of the failure of Mrs. Hepburn's health. This was a great trial to the mission at Amoy. Dr. Hepburn had acquired a knowledge of the Chinese language, and was greatly esteemed both by the native population and foreign residents.

The missionary labours of the year at Ningpo, the description of the country, and the general aspects of this new field of labour are so fully related in the letters and journals of this period, that nothing further need be added here.

In connection with the account of the missions in China, it is proper to notice the Edict of the Emperor, dated 28th December, 1844, giving full toleration for the exercise of the Christian religion. This remarkable document is one of the great events of the age. It was granted at the request of M. Lagrene, the French ambassador, on a memorial to the Emperor, from Keying, the Imperial Commissioner. It gives full toleration to all who profess the religion of *Tien Chu*, or the Lord of Heaven. This is the term used by the Roman Catholic missionaries to denote the Christian religion, and when the edict was issued, it was considered sufficiently comprehensive to embrace the Christian religion as professed by Protestants.

By later proceedings of the civil authorities, this construction appeared to be erroneous. On the 2d of November, 1845, proclamations were issued by the authority of the Imperial Commissioner, and the Lieutenant Governor of Canton, stating "that the religion of the Lord of Heaven consists in periodically assembling for unitedly worshipping the Lord of Heaven, in respecting and venerating the cross, with pictures and images, as well as in reading aloud the works of said religion."

By this explanation Protestants were excluded from the benefits of the edict of toleration, and much dissatisfaction was felt and expressed at this restriction. But this feeling was of short duration. On the 22d of December, 1845, Keying, the Imperial Commissioner, in a letter to the Consul of the United States, at Canton, states, "that some local magistrates had made improper seizures, taking and destroying crosses, pictures, and images, and after deliberation it was agreed that these might be reverenced. Originally, I did not know that there were among the nations these differences in their religious practices. Now, with regard to the religion of the Lord of Heaven, no matter whether the crosses, pictures, and images, be reverenced or not reverenced, all who, acting well, practise it, ought to be held blameless. All the great western nations being placed on an equal footing, only let them acting well practise their religion, and China will in no way prohibit or impede their so doing. Whether their customs be alike or unlike, certainly it is right that there should be no distinction, and no obstruction."

Thus did this subject come three times before the civil authorities of China, and the important distinction between Protestants and Roman Catholics was thus brought to their notice; and much to the credit of the Chinese government, all are equally protected.

Hong Kong, February 12th, 1845.

My Dear Father—Your very welcome letter of August 30th, came to hand last Sabbath, being the first I have received from you for four months, the longest period of not hearing, since my first letters reached me. It does begin to appear as if years had elapsed since I saw you. Letters written home and answers received, answers written back, and replies to those answers received, and soon I shall have replies to these last.

Having finished all I had to do in Macao, I left that place January 21st, and came here to take passage for Chusan. I expect to have as a fellow-passenger, the Rev. T. McClatchie, missionary of the Church Missionary Society, of whom I have formed a very good opinion. The Rev. George Smith, his colleague, is in very poor health, and I fear can do no more than visit the different ports, and then return to England. I shall regret this exceedingly, for I have conceived a very high opinion of him. The connection of these excellent men with the Established Church of England, gives them much influence with the people from England in China; but at the same time it requires them to be doubly cautious not to give any ground of complaint against themselves. On this subject, however, I feel daily that we have reason for gratitude in our American citizenship, and the perfect freedom of the Church from all connection with the State. It is not by might nor by power, but by God's Spirit that our work is to be done. May God grant the time soon to come when the kingdoms of this world shall become the kingdoms of our Lord Jesus Christ!

Your affectionate son,

W. M. Lowrie.

THE VOYAGE UP THE COAST.

Macao, January 19th, 1845.

It is three years to day since I left my father's house. Many changes have come over me since then; trials and afflictions have befallen me, but out of them all the Lord hath delivered me, and having obtained help of Him I continue to this day. For nearly two years I have been preaching to a small congregation of English and Americans, once every Sabbath. To-day I preached my last sermon to them, and bade them farewell. How many of them shall I meet in peace at the great day of reckoning? As far as they are concerned at least, I feel myself pure from their blood. I have not shunned to declare unto them the whole counsel of God. And to some at least it has been a blessing; would that the same could be said of all!

January 21st, 1845. I bade farewell to Macao, and turned my face to the north. It was not without apprehensions that I contemplated another voyage, and that against the strong north-east monsoon; for nearly every voyage I have made since arriving in China has been attended with disaster, and not a few of my friends shook their heads ominously when I spoke of tempting the sea again. Yet the path of duty seemed clear. Nothing further of any consequence remained for me to do in Macao, and it was desirable, on several accounts, that I should as speedily as possible proceed to Ningpo. Committing my way, therefore, to that God who had heretofore led me, even through the deep waters, and preserved me in the most imminent perils, and led me by paths that I knew not, I left Macao, a place that had become endeared to me by many associations and recollections.

It was far from my intention to have spent so long a time in Macao; but various intimations of Providence had kept me there nearly two years and a half. How many events have occurred in that time! When I arrived, there was war between England and China, and most men thought it would be of long continuance. Yet in a few months the war was ended, a treaty of peace was negotiated, and five ports in China were thrown open to foreigners. Extravagant hopes began to fill men's minds, and many expectations were indulged, which have not been realized. When the supplementary treaty was signed, (Oct. 8th, 1843,) boasts long and loud were uttered, and hopes rose yet higher. But had men been wise and studied God's law and providence, they must have seen there was reason to fear that treaty could not prosper. The *Christian* Plenipotentiary who negotiated it, agreed to the proposal of a heathen statesman, and signed it on the Lord's day! There was all the parade and circumstance of military pomp, and men in their joy forgot that there is a God who will not suffer his law to be violated with impunity. This treaty, far less than the treaty of Nanking, has satisfied the expectations at first formed. Rather it has bitterly disappointed them, for some of its clauses have nearly crushed the commercial importance of Hong Kong.

What changes and accessions in our own mission! I have seen McBryde go home, and have welcomed here, Hepburn and Cole, and McCartee and Way, and Loomis and Lloyd, and Culbertson and Happer. Several of them are already settled in their appointed stations, and now our Chinese mission, after various fluctuations, wears a more settled and promising aspect, than at any former time.

What changes in the other missions! Mrs. Boone and Mrs. Dean, Mr. Dyer, Mr. Morrison,* Mrs. Ball and Mrs. Shuck, have gone to their reward. Some have gone home on visits, one no more to return. Others have come in their places. More than half the missionaries now in China have arrived within the last three years, though of these several had been labouring in other parts for the Chinese. It has been a time of breaking up and settling down again; but like the sea whose waters heave, even when the storm has died away, there is a heaving and a motion yet. What shall the end of these things be? Little do we know, and still less can we foresee, but "the Lord reigneth, let the earth rejoice." Whatever changes may occur, all shall accomplish good. "I will overturn and overturn and overturn, until he come, whose right it is: and I will give it him."—Ezek. xxi. 27.

Comparatively few vessels sail for the northern ports of China during the N. E. monsoon, and I was detained nearly a month in Hong Kong. Yet the delay, though tedious, was not unpleasant, for there

* Although Mr. Morrison was not a missionary himself, he was one of our warmest friends, and his death was as much a loss to the missionaries, as to any other class in China.

were many friends there, and letters from home brought me cheering news. At length I succeeded in getting a berth on board the Rob Roy. She is a clipper bark, built in Calcutta, to trade between India and China. The captain and mates are English, and her crew a motley mixture of Bengalis, Malays, Manilla men, with one or two Arabs, two Chinese, and a Portuguese from Goa, who is the blackest man on board.

I regretted much that the vessel sailed to-day, which is the Sabbath, but this I could not prevent; all my baggage of course was put on board yesterday, and had she sailed early in the morning, I should have slept on board. But knowing that there would be much bustle and confusion, I thought I could spend the Sabbath morning more profitably on shore. Got a note from the captain, saying she would leave anchorage at eleven, A. M.; so about ten I bade my kind friends farewell, and came on board. It looks but little like the Sabbath here. The men were washing the decks, officers busy, merchants and clerks from the town on board, and altogether it was far, far from pleasant. Shortly after eleven we started, but were detained nearly two hours in getting out of the harbour, by the consignees not having all the papers ready. How little of the Sabbath was kept by the consignees, officers, and sixty-three Lascars and other persons concerned in the sailing of this single vessel!

We left Hong Kong on the 16th of February, with a fair wind, which carried us out of the harbour, but it soon fell calm, and then we had the N. E. monsoon directly in our teeth. Our vessel is a very fast sailer, and consequently in "beating passages," very wet, and her deck was seldom dry. On the 18th we passed immense numbers of fishing-boats; I counted one hundred and ninety-five at one time in sight, and that was not nearly all. We kept close along the Chinese coast for several days, beating against the wind, and making tolerably good progress. After reaching Breaker Point, we stretched across the Formosa Channel. The wind was strong, and the sea high, and for two or three days we were uncomfortable enough. In eight days after leaving the port, we saw the high land on the southern end of Formosa. This large and populous island, which may be called the granary of some of the eastern provinces of China, is as yet without the presence of any missionary, either Protestant or Roman Catholic. The western part is under the dominion of the Emperor of China, but the inhabitants of the mountains in the centre have not been subdued, and the eastern shore is almost unknown.

We were so much favoured in the first part of our voyage that we reached the latitude of the Chusan islands in sixteen days, which at this season of the year is a very quick run; but the remainder of our voyage was not so speedy. We had then less than two hundred miles further to go, but a succession of baffling head winds caused us to spend a whole week in going that short distance. It was not till Tuesday, March 11, that we cast anchor at Woosung, twenty-three days after leaving Hong Kong. In the favourable monsoon the voyage is made with ease in less than ten days. It was a very rough voyage, and except in urgent cases should not be attempted, especially by females. The roughness of the passage renders it nearly impossible to spend one's time profitably, and three or four weeks, or even five, for the voyage is often that long, is too much time to be thrown away. There is also all the risk, which is not small, and the exposure, which, coming from the warm latitude of Canton, to the colder climate of the north, is not a little disagreeable. Yet men of the world submit to all this, and much more, for the sake of earthly riches, and the missionary should not hesitate to do the same, when the great object of his life can be gained by the sacrifice of some personal ease or comfort.

Most persons dislike the sea, and it is common to speak of the monotony and tedium of long voyages. There is little to be seen that is new after the first few days, and without caution and watchfulness, one is apt to become impatient and fretful. Yet with due care, it need not be so. The best of all expedients to make the time pass pleasantly, is to have something to do, and to do it. It requires some resolution to keep one's self constantly employed, but the exertion is amply repaid. And there is much, even amidst the sameness of sea life, that is deeply instructive. God has so ordered all things in nature, that they form a constant commentary and illustration of invisible and eternal things. That more of such analogies can be traced in the sailor's life than in any other I will not presume to say, but I have often been surprised, and oftener still instructed as well as gratified, with the illustrations of the Christian's course which the voyage of a ship affords. The various changes of the weather, now calm and sun-shiny; now stormy and dark; now rapidly speeding on with prosperous breezes, and anon, painfully labouring against the wind; who has not felt such changes as these in his Christian course?—The unceasing diligence of all concerned, especially the captain and officers, their constant study of the charts and books of directions, and their anxiety to secure observations of the sun and stars, that they may know their daily progress and position; who does not recognize in this the duty of the Christian to study carefully the great chart and book which God has given to direct us on our way, and by earnest *looking upward*, to gain wisdom from on high to lead our steps?—The constant look-out for danger, and the anxiety to avoid hidden shoals, to mark the progress and direction of the currents, and to take advantage of every wind that blows; how often have they reproved me for being so careless of danger, and so negligent where Christ said, "Watch!" and so indifferent to the

Spirit's influences, which, "like the wind," must waft the soul to heaven. When the ship has dropped her anchor in the port, universal joy possesses every heart. The dangers and watchings and fatigues of the voyage are over, the rewards of labour are now to be enjoyed, and the quietness and peace of home to repay the toils and perils that are past. "They are glad because they are quiet, and because they are brought to their desired haven," but how much more real and satisfying is the Christian's joy, when he enters the haven of rest, his home in the skies! *There* "there is no more sea."

The entrance of the great river Yang-tsze Keang (*child of the ocean*) is rather difficult, especially to vessels drawing much water. So much earth is brought down by this immense stream, and deposited in the sea, that the water is quite shallow for many miles, and a vessel is in danger of running aground long before the land is seen. The coasts of China in this latitude are low, and perfectly level, and the land can scarcely be seen more than ten miles off. The strength of the tides is also very great, and several vessels have already been lost on the sands and rocks off the entrance of the river. Until light-houses are erected, and buoys properly placed, more than ordinary caution will be required of the officers of vessels visiting Shanghai.

After entering the river, the course is north-west, to Woosung. Entering the Woosung river, the course is south-west, about fourteen miles to Shanghai.

The whole country for many miles around the city is a perfect plain, having only sufficient elevation and depression to carry off the water. There is not a single hill within twenty miles of Shanghai, which of course, renders the appearance of the country uninteresting. The soil, however, is rich and productive, and excepting the space occupied by the graves, is in a high state of cultivation. There are no stones, nor even small pebbles, for in a trip of some twenty miles along the Woosung river, not a stone was to be seen, except such as had been brought from a distance. Farm houses and small villages dot the country in every direction, and clumps of bamboos, with orchards of peaches and plum trees, and willows by the water-courses, relieve the sameness of the ground. Two crops, one of wheat, and the other of cotton, are raised every year, and in some parts a third crop of rice is also procured. Rice, however, is not so much cultivated here as in the more southern parts of China, and as there are few paddy fields near the city, the ground is not so marshy as to render it unhealthy.

The city of Shanghai is pleasantly situated at the junction of the Woosung and Hwangpoo rivers. It is of a circular form, surrounded by walls, about fifteen feet high, and nearly four miles in circumference. The suburbs near the rivers are thickly inhabited, and the population is estimated at about two hundred thousand inhabitants. By the Woosung river it is connected with the city of Soochow, the capital of the province, and one of the most luxurious and wealthy in the empire, and also with the Grand Canal which reaches to Peking. Hence its situation is one of great importance, and its trade is immense. Rows of junks are moored for nearly two miles along the bank of the Hwangpoo, on the east of the city, and vessels are constantly arriving and departing. Already it is attracting a large share of foreign commerce, and many suppose that it will soon rival, if not surpass Canton, as a place for foreign trade. Sixty-five foreign vessels have already entered the port, though it is but a year and a half since business commenced to be done there. The great tea and silk districts of China are nearer to Shanghai than to Canton, and if proper encouragement be held out, a large part of those articles which were formerly carried at great expense to the latter place, will find their way either to Shanghai or Ningpo.

Every foreigner who has visited this place, gives the inhabitants a much better character than those of Canton. They are rather taller, of a more ruddy complexion, and much more civil and well-disposed than their southern countrymen. In passing through the streets one is rarely insulted, and the opprobrious epithets so common in Canton and Macao are scarcely ever heard here.

The Roman Catholics once had a strong footing in Shanghai. Paul Siu, an officer of the highest rank, and his daughter Candida, who were the two most powerful and liberal friends the Jesuits ever possessed in China, were natives of this city, and several monuments to his memory are still found within the walls. In one place, the heathen descendants of Siu offer incense to his image. One of the idol temples in the city was formerly a chapel of the Roman Catholics, and is even now commonly called the "Teen-choo-tang," or "Hall of the Lord of Heaven," the name they give their places of worship in China. There are many Roman Catholic converts in the province of Keang-su, and several foreign priests, who dress in Chinese clothes, and live as the Chinese do. The R. C. Bishop of Keang-nan and Shantung, an Italian, and a nephew of the Pope, by the way, resides within five miles of Shanghai.

Saturday, 30th March, 1845. Left Shanghai on yesterday, and reached Woosung to-day about eleven o'clock. I went ashore, and strolled up the banks of the Yang-tsze Keang about three miles. The river is so wide, you cannot see the other bank. The country being very low, high embankments are raised to protect the land from the high tides. The embankment along the Yang-tsze Keang, is faced with solid masonry four feet thick and about fifteen feet high, for several miles—how far exactly I cannot say, but as far as I went or could see, it was so. The termination of my walk was the little city of

Paouhau, which is walled and has four gates. The city is square, the circuit of the walls very little more than a mile, and nearly all the houses are ranged along the two streets that extend from the gates and intersect in the centre of the town. The rest of the space within the walls is occupied by gardens. I should not think the population was more than two thousand. The houses outside the walls were larger and more numerous than those within. I went right through the town, then out at the same gate, a crowd of boys at my heels, then half round the walls, and then back to the ship.

Tuesday, April 1st. About eleven o'clock in the morning, cast anchor in Chusan harbour, and my joy at finding myself safe at my journey's end, was only equalled by that of finding the Isabella Ann with Loomis and Culbertson safe on board. She arrived on Saturday, after a thirty-eight days' passage, which, from the accounts they have given me, was not only very unpleasant, but even dangerous; but we are all safe here. Thanks to God, who holds the winds and directs the storms.

In the day-time went through the city of Tinghai. Loomis and his wife remain here for the present. The Culbertsons go to Ningpo to-morrow. I shall remain several days and go to Ningpo early next week.

Tinghai is in the centre of a large valley, with high hills on three sides. At this time the valley is all green and yellow with crops of beans, barley, and cabbage in flower, and looks very well. The streets are, I think, cleaner than is usual in Chinese towns. In the evening I walked with Loomis and Culbertson over the little island just opposite Tinghai; a splendid view from the top; quite delighted to find some blue and white violets growing on the hill.

Wednesday, April 2d. Went to the Isabella Ann to see about my freight. Found my mattress was missing, and several boxes of my books wet. Had not time to open them, but shall doubtless find them much spoiled. The Rob Roy being so full, I could not bring them in her, and had to send them by the other. Mr. Bates, an American merchant, the only American here, has very kindly offered me a room while I stay here.

Thursday, April 3d. I had my boxes from the Isabella Ann taken to Mr. Loomis's house, and as they had got wet on board the ship, I had serious misgivings about their condition. I opened them to-day; but, oh, what a mess! My books, my noble books, on which I prided myself so much; some were utterly ruined, more than half are seriously injured, three-fourths are greatly defaced, and not one-fourth have escaped without some damage. Five hundred dollars would not replace the injury they have suffered.

The mate of the vessel who stowed them away, "thought they were spirits of wine," and put them in the part of the vessel where such articles are kept, where, if water should come, no harm is done! I fancy he had some *spirits* in his head when he thought so. Well, there was no use of crying, or scolding, or fretting; so I did not lose my temper. I only wished I had not brought so many; but as wishing was of no avail, I commenced to rub and air them. I got two Chinese to help me. They will be a pitiable sight when all is done.

Friday, April 4th. A wet, rainy forenoon. Went to Loomis's house, and spent several hours among my damaged books. Alas! alas!

Thursday, April 10th. Packed up my books, or at least part of them, to take to Ningpo. About two hundred volumes were in such a state that I must leave them here for a while, and some fifty or more are about useless. "Three removes are as bad as a fire!"

Left Chusan at half-past nine, A. M., with fair tide but light wind. Chartered a native boat, and took most of my goods and chattels, making twenty-one packages in all; paid three dollars for the boat, which is about one-third of what I should have had to pay in Macao. There were only a few passengers, as I told the owner he must not crowd the boat. Among the passengers were two inhabitants of the mainland from near Chinhai, a farmer, a Budhist priest, and a Fuhkeen merchant, decidedly the most intelligent of the whole. There were several others, but I saw none of them except one, who came to me once with his breath smelling so strong of opium, that I gave him a lecture thereupon.

Friday, April 11th. Breakfast at eight o'clock. After prayers I soon found Dr. McCartee, who is living in a monastery. Then took a walk through the city, admired the straightness and width and comparative cleanness of the streets, and afterwards went to the Pagoda, or Tower of Ningpo, an immense tall tower, a hundred feet or more in height. Vast numbers of swallows have built their nests in holes in the walls. Going up to the top, I enjoyed a magnificent view of the country around. Ningpo is in a vast plain, a perfect level; but high hills are in sight on all sides but one. The plain is so level that the hills look quite near, but they are really from fifteen to eighteen miles distant.

At six o'clock, P. M., took a walk with Way and Culbertson, and their wives. There are but few houses in this part of the suburbs, and we walked about perfectly unembarrassed with people. The vegetation is very luxuriant here. Saw several tombs erected in the time of the Ming Dynasty; there was first a pair of stone rams; then of dogs; then of horses saddled and bridled; then of monks; and then of tombs. I have seen many of them at Shanghai.

April 14th, 1845. After a visit to the city, we sailed some distance up the north branch of the river, whose course is quite crooked a short distance above the North Gate. At the distance of twelve *le*,* we passed a large distillery, known by the usual sign

* Three *le* are about one mile.

of a tall pole, with a small round bamboo sieve near the top, and a small flag above it. Passing three *le* further, we went ashore at a temple where the keeper received us full civilly, and gave us tea to drink. The temple contained nothing of interest, but we were amused in watching a boat as it passed over a sluice. As the tide rises and falls several feet in the river, the small streams and canals that empty into it would be nearly useless at low water. To prevent this, they are all dammed up at the mouth, and thus the water is made to stand always at nearly the same level, so that they are always useful for irrigation and navigation. To enable boats to enter the river, and come back into the canals, the dam is rounded off, and by means of two rude capsterns and bamboo ropes, the boats are hauled up to the top of the dam. It consists simply of mud, beaten smooth and hard, and rendered slippery by pouring a little water over it. As soon as the boats are once at the top, their own weight carries them down the other side, and they enter the river like a ship launched from the stocks. Each sluice is attended by two men and several boys, and it requires but a minute or two to pass a boat in either direction. By these economical locks there is no loss of water, and the wear of the flat-bottomed boats is small. The toll for passing these sluices varies from five to eight cents, according to the size of the boat.

18th. Took up my quarters at the Yu shing kwan monastery, belonging to the Taou sect, which is situated just within the north gate of the city. There are, in all, five monks, in the establishment. As soon as my baggage was brought in, the old abbot sent in a wooden waiter with a pile of sponge cakes, and four cups of tea, together with a red card, on the top of which was written "Congratulations," and beneath, "The resident supporter of the Yu shing kwan monastery. Hwang che hwuy bows his head and worships." A small present was sent back in return.

In the morning, had an opportunity of seeing a "small foot" uncovered. One of the female patients had some disease, which made it necessary to take the bandages off the foot, a thing they are commonly unwilling to do before strangers. The sight was by no means pleasant. All the toes except the largest were turned under the sole of the foot; the instep was greatly elevated, and the hollow between the heel and the ball of the foot much deeper than in the natural state. All the women here, excepting the nuns, have their feet thus unnaturally compressed, and in consequence, you never see a woman able to walk with even tolerable ease and grace. They all go hobbling about like cripples, and frequently have to depend upon an umbrella, or the shoulder of a female attendant whose feet are not quite so cruelly hampered as their own, to support their steps.

For several days past, green peas in abundance have been sold in the markets.

19th. Went to the Hwuy-Hwuy Tang, or Mohammedan Mosque. The keepers of the building were from Shantung; and one old woman spoke Mandarin beautifully. (The purest Mandarine dialect is poken in Shantung.) The mosque is a small building, with many Arabic incriptions, and we were informed that there are some five hundred Mohammedans in Ningpo. They have a larger mosque, and more numerous population in Hangchou, the capital of this province. There was formerly a Jewish synagogue in Ningpo, as well as one in Hangchou, but no traces of them are now discoverable, and the only Jews known to exist in China, are in Kaifung foo, the capital of Honan.

20th. Preached this morning to the largest congregation of foreigners that has yet met in Ningpo, sixteen persons in all.

21st. Dr. McCartee having occasion to go to Chusan to-day, I am left alone in the monastery; but a smattering of Mandarin, of which the people all understand a little, enables me to get along without difficulty. Dr. McCartee has three boys under his care, the two elder of whom are very interesting and affectionate; and his teacher is a kind-hearted, excellent man, "almost persuaded to be a Christian." We have prayers morning and evening in Chinese, when the teacher reads and explains a chapter in Chinese, and repeats or reads a prayer; after which we have a prayer in English. A-chang, the second boy, was greatly delighted with my barometer, and repeated several times, "Heaou teh fung! heaou teh yu!" "It understands the wind! It understands the rain!" and finally, he declared there was nothing so admirable in all Ningpo.

23d. Arranging my rooms, and putting my clock up. Got a servant to-day, who seems to be a very simple-hearted, good sort of a fellow, and who looked with unbounded admiration at the clock. Seeing one of the monks, he called out to him, "Here is a clock!" It has been a great object of admiration all day.

25th. Along with Dr. McCartee, and Messrs. Way and Culbertson, went out several miles into the country to see a patient of the Doctor's, who is confined with a broken leg. The country is intersected with innumerable canals, which supply the place of high roads in other countries. Much ground is also covered with tombs, so that the common saying, that the Chinese use no ground for tombs which can be cultivated, is incorrect. In the south, where barren hills abound, and only the valleys are fit for cultivation, the remark is true; but about Shanghai, Chusan, and Ningpo, it is not.

The canals are full of fish: to catch them, bamboo fences are staked across them in numerous places, with only an opening for boats. The opening itself is staked with flexible reed, which allow the water to pass through, and boats to pass over, but effectually prevent the fish. Commonly, the fences are formed into a kind of labyrinth, so that when the fish are driven to them, they enter a trap, from which it is difficult to escape, and they are then scooped up with a small hand-net. The appearance of the country is very beautiful; crops of wheat and barley nearly ready for the reaper, patches of clover, beds of rice for transplanting, young fields of reeds for mats, (a very important part of the trade of Ningpo,) water-wheels, worked by buffaloes or men, the latter sort somewhat on the principle of the tread-mill, a few water buffaloes and oxen, quiet farm-houses and numerous villages, with some old trees, form a picture of great beauty. Oh! that this were indeed Immanuel's land! that those whom we meet were partakers of the same faith and hope with us! "How long, O Lord! Return and visit these long desolations!"

30th. Invited to a Chinese dinner. The dishes were brought in bowls, everything being cut up, and ready for use. Each guest was provided with a small wine-cup, a spoon, and a pair of chop-sticks. The guests were Dr. McCartee and his teacher, the old abbot and one of the monks from the monastery, and myself. The dishes were:—stewed chicken, cold goose, duck and bamboo-sprouts, pork, fish, cherries, water-chestnuts, pea-nuts, soup, beche de-mer, ginger, preserved eggs, spinage, and rice and tea to close with; besides, hot spirits distilled from rice. It was my first effort with chop-sticks, which are awkward enough at first, especially when you try to take up a hard-boiled egg. Several of the dishes were very palatable, but one or two of the customs were not particularly pleasant, e. g., the old abbot, after putting his chop-sticks several times into his mouth, picked out a tempting piece of goose, and offered it to me with the same sticks. I begged to be excused, though it is a mark of polite attention to make such an offer; also a wet cloth was handed round after dinner to wipe the fingers and mouth, the same cloth for all.

May 3. In the afternoon a respectable and interesting-looking Chinese came to the Yu shing kwan temple to perform some ceremonies on the sixth birth-day of his son. The little fellow was dressed in his best clothes, and seemed to enjoy the whole affair. His father had brought gilt paper, printed prayers, and a large number of bowls full of various meats, rice, vegetables, nuts, cups of wine, and the like, which were spread out before the idols. The ceremonies were performed in the apartment of the *Tow-moo*, or Bushel Mother, who has special charge of young people, both before and after birth. The old abbot clothed himself in a scarlet robe, with a gilt image of a serpent fastened in his hair. One of the monks wore a purple, and another an ash-coloured robe. A multitude of prayers, seemingly little else than a round of repetitions, were read by the abbot. Occasionally he chanted a little, when the attendants joined in chorus, and every few minutes a deafening clamour of bells, cymbals, and hollow blocks of wood, was raised. Genuflexions and prostrations innumerable accompanied the whole ceremony. The most singular part was the passing of a live cock through a barrel which had both ends knocked out. This was done several times by two assistants, who shouted some strange words at each repetition of the ceremony. The meaning, as I was afterwards told, was something like this: Prayers had been offered to the idol that the child might escape certain dangers through which he must pass; and each passing of the cock through the barrel was intended to symbolize his passing safely through one of these perils. It was a melancholy sight. In conclusion, some of the prayers were burnt, a cup of wine poured out as a libation, and a grand chorus of bell, and gong, and drum, and blocks, closed the scene.

May 14. A wet, rainy day. In the evening Dr. McCartee was called in a great hurry to see a man who had poisoned himself by taking opium. On going to the house, found the family in much alarm. The man was in bed, looking very stupid, and his wife attending him with some appearance of anxiety and care. He had had a quarrel with his mother-in-law, and in revenge attempted to make away with himself by taking opium. There was, however, some reason to suppose that it was partly a feint to frighten the old woman, and after an emetic being given, we came away. The Chinese have but little to deter them from the commission of suicide, for they have very faint ideas of a future state, or of punishment beyond the grave.

May 17. A great Hwuy, or festival of *Too-shin*, all the gods, has been celebrated for the last day or two. Saw a part of the procession to-day, though the narrow crowded streets gave but a poor opportunity of seeing the different parts. There were innumerable lanterns, three or four gaily ornamented dragons, a boat, several chairs, idols, little boys carried on men's shoulders, and various other sights. The most interesting were several gaily dressed girls, who seemed to be standing on almost nothing at all. One girl standing on a chariot, carried a branch of a tree carelessly on her shoulder: on one of the twigs of the branch stood a little girl, on one foot, with the other in the air. Another girl held up in her hand a plate of cakes, and a smaller girl stood with one foot on the cakes, and was thus borne along. Of course all this was done by means of iron or brass supporters around their bodies. The crowd of people was immense, and numerous policemen seemed to be busy, or rather to make themselves busy, for I never saw so large a crowd, and so little disorder.

It was a curious sight to look over the crowd and see the forest of pipe-stems. Nearly everybody carries a pipe with a stem from two to four feet long, and when held up to keep them out of harm's way, they looked like a forest of small sticks, or perhaps like a cane-brake stripped of its leaves.

May 27. It is amusing to observe the commotion excited by the appearance of a foreigner in the retired parts of the city, where few have yet wandered. Every one cries out, "Hung ma nying! hung ma nying!" a red-haired man! a red-haired man! this being the name for all foreigners. The women and children scatter in all directions; the men stare and gaze, or pass their comments, as the fancy strikes them. It is melancholy to witness the fear of foreigners that still exists, especially on the part of the women and children. Some of the men look as if they would be glad to hide, and if you look at them, seem ready to sink into the ground. Commonly, however, this fear is giving way to curiosity; and nothing is more common than for those who see the stranger to beckon to the women to come and have a look also. One little boy, in his haste to do this, dropped his basket, overturned his playfellow, and running to the door, clapped his hands and called out, "Here's a red-haired man! come! quick, quick!" The titles they give, and the remarks they make, are sometimes amusing, and sometimes provoking. "Mantele!" for mandarin. "Wailo fuhke, wailo!" Be off with you! "Lailo!" Come here. "Hung ma nying!" are the common terms; and sometimes "Pah kwei," and "Kwei tsz," *white devil*, and *devil's child!* Some few, on the other hand, are polite enough to say, "Hungma seen saung," foreign teacher; and the beggars say, "Hungma laou yay," foreign esquire.

The sun is sometimes called *Kin woo*, or "golden crow," from its spots, which are thought to be crows; and the moon is called the *Yuh too*, or "jewelled hare," because they say a hare is distinctly seen in it. Hence, in poetical style, the setting of the sun and rising of the moon is expressed by "The golden crow sank in the west, and the jewelled hare arose in the east."

May 29. Went out with Dr. McCartee several miles into the country, by water of course. Stopped at a small village, and went into a temple, when a crowd soon came round us, and notice being given that Dr. McCartee would prescribe for the sick gratuitously, a number of patients applied for medicine and advice. After this Dr. McCartee and his teacher both spoke to the people on religion, and were listened to with good attention. Tracts were then given to the eager crowd, and we took our departure, much gratified with our visit and the behaviour of the people.

Returning, saw a large house in the western suburb on fire. It seemed to be the family mansion of some wealthy person; but the Chinese have little skill in putting out fires, and the owners were removing their furniture, and leaving the house to its fate. The Cheheen (mayor of the city) and several other military and civil officers, were speedily on the ground with their retainers. Being tired and hungry, we did not stop to see the end, but were informed that by breaking down parts of the adjoining houses, the flames were prevented from spreading.

May 30. Spent part of the day in visiting acquaintances among the Chinese, then went to the house of a Mr. Lin, to see his garden, which is spoken of as very fine; but were rather disappointed, as it had nothing remarkable in it. While in the garden Mr. Lin came out to see us, and politely took us over his house, which is large, airy, and well furnished. He had some six or eight large clocks of European manufacture, but all out of order, with numerous beautiful scrolls of writing and painting. His father left him a fortune of some three hundred thousand taels, (over four hundred thousand dollars,) but his extravagance has diminished it to one hundred thousand. He smokes opium freely, and looks sallow and thin. Some friends were with him at the time, and he had an opium pipe, and lamp burning in the room to which he led us. This opium is the curse of China. It is draining out their money from the land, sucking the heart's blood of their industry, and destroying the constitutions and the lives of their people.

June 3, 1845. On Saturday, May 31st, Dr. McCartee was called to see a woman in the country, who had poisoned herself by taking opium, but she was dead before he arrived. It seems she was the concubine, or second wife, and had a quarrel with the first wife, which led to her destroying herself. This evening, another case of poisoning occurred but a few doors from our residence. In this case he was in time, and some sulphate of zinc soon relieved the man's stomach. The cause was a quarrel with some of the neighbours.

Yesterday and to-day have been wet and cold. Thermometer down to 64 deg., which is eighteen degrees lower than it was the day before.

June 5. Reading in the Kea Paou, or "Family Jewels," I came across the following sentences, which are rather remarkable. "If your parents treat you with unkindness, or even do what is wrong, you must still, with the utmost quietness, submit. And if they will not hear your attempts to correct their errors, you must not become angry, and scold them; but bear it in silence. For, remember, that below the skies, there is not such a thing as a father or mother that does wrong. Your father is *heaven*, and your mother is *earth*, and where is the man that dares to contend with heaven and earth? Is it right to do so? Therefore, it was well said, by an ancient sage, 'Although a father should ill-treat his son, yet must not the son cease his filial obedience.'" The following sentence is equally remarkable: "Let not your love for your wife and children prevent your paying all due respect to your parents. Should your wife and children die, you may yet procure others; but if your father and mother depart, whence will you replace them?" Kea Paou, vol. i. p. 6. The sentiment of this last line must remind the student of history, of the saying ascribed to a Persian lady, whose whole family had been condemned to death. The monarch, permitting her to save the life of any one she chose, she selected a brother. On being asked why she had not rather chosen to save one of her children, she replied, "I may have other children, but another brother I cannot have."

To-day being the first of the Chinese month, several people have come to worship at the temple. Several travelling monks assist at the devotions. Among the worshippers were some respectably dressed females, one of whom took her little child, that knew not its right hand from its left, and making it kneel before the idol, taught it to lift its hands and worship.

June 7. Another case of opium poisoning to-day. It was a young man who could not collect money to pay his debts on the fifth of the month, when according to custom here, all debts must be settled. The application for assistance was too late, as he was dying when Dr. McCartee reached the house.

June 16. A visit from sundry official persons, and some scholars, to-day. They were civil, very inquisitive, and not at all backward in asking for anything they took a fancy to. One of them requested a few sheets of writing paper, as a curiosity, and when I took out half a quire, meaning to give him a sheet or two, he held out both hands, and took all. exclaiming, "Oh, thank you, thank you!" We gave them tracts, several of which were printed on our own press, with the Parisian type. They expressed much pleasure at the beauty and clearness of the type, as I have more than once or twice heard scholars do, when they opened one of our tracts.

June 18. An animated discussion with my teacher to-day on idolatry. He is the most zealous defender of their idolatrous rites that I have ever met among the Chinese, and does not, as most of them do, assent to everything that we say on the subject. According to what he says, idols were not formerly worshipped in China, nor are they now, by the literati, who pay their adoration only to the souls of the deified persons, and not to the images. When pressed in argument, he admitted that it was of no use, except to show reverential feeling, for the souls of the idols being in heaven, could not hear or enjoy the worship paid to them. At last he confessed that it was only "long established custom." I rejoiced to be able to tell him distinctly, that it was only by renouncing all idols, believing on Christ, and worshipping him, that any man could be saved.

It is curious to see how they use the same arguments in favour of their worship, which the Roman Catholics urge for the adoration of the saints. Among other things, he said that it was better to worship heroes, and such like, because God is too great to be troubled with our prayers, and therefore, we must approach him by means of persons greater than ourselves. When asked if there were any good and sinless men on earth, he replied with emphasis, "There are few indeed!" When asked, "Did you ever see one?" he replied, "*Never*." At this point he seemed to feel uncomfortable, and admitted that man's natural disposition is not good, though he was hardly willing to say this, without some qualification.

June 19. Another long conversation with my teacher, on religion, in which I could not but admire his independence. He freely admitted the difference between Christianity and the religion of China; but unlike most Chinese teachers, he would not compliment me, by saying that ours was the best. He listened with interest, while I spoke of the way of salvation, through the sufferings and death of Christ. Oh, that he were himself a Christian! He is acute to detect the inconsistencies of professed Christians, and asked some questions to-day, respecting some, which were hard to answer.

June 21. Went into the main building of the temple to-night, and found all the monks busy at their devotions. Some person was making an offering, and his gifts were spread out in order before the idol. Fourteen candles were burning. The old abbot was beating the drum, and twelve monks, more than half of whom were visitors, were chanting from the *Shangteking*, or Classic of the Supreme Ruler. Each wore a long yellow, or orange coloured robe, fringed with black, and read from a copy of the book beautifully written with red ink. They chanted, beat their bells and blocks of wood, knelt, and rose again, and bowed their heads Oh, how melancholy to see it! Some of the monks were old and gray-headed. One was young, with the ruddiness of boyhood still on his cheeks. I thought of the command, "Thou shalt not bow down unto them—" and my heart sank within me, as the question rose, "How long, oh Lord, how long?—" Will this kind go out except by prayer and fasting?

June 26. Several conversations with my teacher, of late, on religion, which seem to have made some impression on him. He was much struck with the idea of missionaries coming here, not to make money, but simply to teach religion, and after a pause, said seriously, "It requires great faith to do all this. I do not think our Chinese would do it." Giving him an account of my being shipwrecked some years ago, he was much interested, and remarked, "Truly you would not have escaped, if Jesus had not preserved you."

July 1. The warmest day we have yet had. Thermometer at 91° for a while, and now at nine o'clock, P. M., at 88°. Little wind, and weather very damp. It is what the Chinese call the *wang may teen*, or yellow plum season, because the plums are then ripe, when the atmosphere is so overloaded with moisture, that even when the sun is shining, the stone and wooden floors are as damp as if they had but lately been scrubbed, and had not time to dry.

July 6th, Sabbath. Greatly disturbed in our

morning worship, by a number of Chinese carrying alum, the property of a *Christian* merchant, out of a neighbouring store-room to load a ship, the property of a *Christian* owner. Verily, there is but little fear of God in the eyes of many who do business in this heathen land. Alas! for our work among this people, who know not how to distinguish among the professed and the real followers of Christ.

Very rainy, damp weather for some days, and so cold, notwithstanding the heat a week ago, as to render thick clothes and woollen stockings comfortable. But it is the last, probably, of the cold weather for a while.

July 24. Had a visit to-day from a Mr. Lefevre. a French Roman Catholic missionary, who has spent five years in Keangse, one in Nankin, and three in Macao. He seems to be about fifty-five years old, and is now on his way to Tartary, to take charge of their theological school at Siwan. He speaks Chinese, the court dialect, fluently, and tolerably well, but with rather a French accent. As he knew no English, and I but little French, we talked together in Chinese. He goes first to Shanghai, there changes his garments and puts on a queue, with Chinese spectacles, to conceal his eyes. From Shanghai he goes by the grand canal, and expresses no fear of being detected on the way. Though he speaks fluently, he knows but little of the written language, not being able to write so common a character as *Kung*, (noble,) which he has occasion to use every day.

He speaks in the highest terms of Mr. Ramaux, Roman Catholic bishop of Keangse, and says he speaks Chinese better than even his own language. (I have since heard that Mr. Ramaux was lately drowned in Macao. From some of his letters, I had formed a good opinion of him.) The Roman Catholics in China call their priests *Shin foo*, spiritual fathers, and the bishops, *Choo Keaou*, lords of the religion.

July 25. Went into the temple with a bundle of thirty or forty gospels and tracts in my arms, and found many worshippers. Presently some came and asked what books I had. On giving one away, there was instantly a crowd of eager applicants, and in a few minutes all were disposed of. A hundred more would have been taken, if I had thought fit to give them; but it seemed better to stop while they were eager for more, than to give them to satiety.

July 28. This is the birthday of the god of thunder, though, as my teacher laughing said, "No one knows how old he is." A crowd of men and women were in the temple. My teacher says, "Most of the worshippers are women, who greatly fear the thunder, though there are some men. The women like these worshipping days, because it gives them an opportunity to see, and to be seen in their fine clothes; and most of the men who come, come to amuse themselves, and look at the women." Among the crowd of the common folks, there were many men and women in silks and embroideries. Stalls were at every corner, where men were selling candles, incense sticks, and paper for offerings. The temple was full of smoke; and the crowd, together with the smoke and the burning paper, renders the place almost insupportably hot. I took some forty or fifty tracts, but the crowd was so great, and the eagerness to get them so excessive, that there was little satisfaction in distributing them.

In the *Kea Paou*, vol. i., line 562, is this sentence. "Ancient men have well said, 'A relation afar off is not so good as a neighbour that is near.'" Almost word for word with Prov. xxvii. 10. "Better is a neighbour that is near, than a brother afar off."

My teacher was greatly shocked to-day, when I said that "Abraham was the friend of God." "How can it be?" he exclaimed; "how can a man be the friend of God? for a friend implies equality. Such a thing ought not to be said." These poor heathen have little idea of the exceeding grace and condescension of God. The other day, talking with him, he advanced the sentiment that the affairs of the world to come, being beyond our personal observation, are of no importance to us; that if we attend to our own business in this life, the future may be safely left to take care of itself. In confirmation of his opinion that the future world is entirely beyond our knowledge and concern, he quoted the saying of Confucius, "Not knowing even life, how can we know death?" How truly it was said of Christ, "He hath brought life and immortality to light through the Gospel;" for they were not known before, and are not known where the Gospel is not heard.

Ningpo, April 30th, 1845.

Mrs. C. M. Hepburn—I have little sympathy for those who delight to say that our blessed Saviour never smiled, for when he "rejoiced in spirit," and when he heard the little children cry, Hosanna! it seems to me as if a smile, strangely and yet sweetly blending the divine and human, must have played upon those features. How pleasant, more than "pleasant," to see those features, once marked with the impress of pain and suffering and sorrow! They are not so marked now, for a glory covers them, such as the disciples saw when they were with him in the holy mount, and that glory I trust we shall ere long see.

My previous letter will have informed you of my arrival at Chusan, April 2. I stayed there a week, enjoying greatly the scenery and appearance of the place. It quite surpassed my expectations, and is vastly more beautiful than anything I have yet seen in China, always excepting Chang-Chow and the country around. You have nothing at Amoy or Kulangsu equal to Chusan.

There are some pious soldiers at Chusan, and, among others, I was surprised to see Corporal R——, who used to be such a constant visitor of yours at Amoy. He asked very earnestly about you all. They all seem very glad of Loomis's going there, and he now preaches in the chapel there every Sabbath. I left Chusan on the 10th of April, and go there the next day. Stayed a week with Br. Way, and then came over to the Yu-Shing-Kwan monastery, which is just within the north gate of the city. Dr. McCartee has been here for some three or four months, and I got a suite of rooms just like his, on the same terms.

This is a very quiet part of the city, as there are few houses near; the mass of the population lies off in other parts of the city. I calculate the inhabitants at two hundred and fifty thousand, including the suburbs at the east and west gates, which are very extensive and populous. . . .

We propose observing next Friday as a day of fasting and prayer, both for the mission, and as preparatory to the Lord's Supper, which I am to administer on the Sabbath following. Miss Aldersey has a fine girls' school, numbering fifteen pupils, and sustains herself well. I hope for much good from the organization of a church in these extreme ends of the earth. I trust that ere long we may admit some of the inhabitants of this place into our fellowship. . . .

May 1st. "The laughing month of May;" though we might almost apply to it the term given to the following month, "The rose encumbered June."

One of the monks brought me a bouquet of roses to-day, which I have arranged in a tumbler beneath my looking-glass. I have been busy fitting up my rooms to-day, and have everything now arranged much to my mind.

. . . . I hope we are all settled now, and will not have to move about any more, or make any other changes. I would like to see you all; but when shall it be? As my sister E. says in her last letter to me, "I am prepared to say, I hope you will not leave your field of labour, even to come and see us." I am sure I am so glad to be at my long-desired haven, that it would require no slight inducement for me to leave it. How nervous I used to feel sometimes, on my last trip, for fear I should not get up after all. By what strange ways we are led along, and sometimes hard ones to travel. "Oh there are some rough ways to heaven." "In the world ye shall have tribulation." So our blessed Lord himself said.

Friday, May 2d. We have been observing this as a day of fasting and prayer for the mission, and also as preparatory to the Lord's Supper. We met at 10 o'clock—only ourselves—six in all. Bro. Culbertson conducted the services, and made some very good remarks on the duties before us, and the disposition we should have. I read a long letter which I have just received from my father, in which he gives his views on several points in relation to the missionary work in China. I wish you were nearer, I would lend it to you. We all led in prayer. In the afternoon we had another meeting at four o'clock, which I conducted; subject of my remarks, 1 Cor. xi. 23; the administration of the Lord's Supper. What a beautiful and forcible passage it is! The Lord's Supper was instituted "the same night in which he was betrayed." Oh what a night was that! It was the crisis in the world's history. Had our Saviour then drawn back, had the cup passed by him, where had we been? Earth never saw a night like that. It was on that night that Satan's malice and man's wickedness rose to their highest point; and on that night the love of Christ was specially shown in the appointment of this solemn and tender ordinance. How the love of God in Christ stands in shining contrast with the wickedness of man and Satan! And what a beautiful sentence that is: "Ye do show the Lord's death till he come!" He will come again "in the clouds of heaven." Yea, he has told us, he will "come quickly." It will be "with power and great glory." We who are alive and remain, shall be caught up with the risen saints to meet the Lord in the air. Now we are expecting it. "We love his appearing," is the characteristic of Christians.

"Let the vain world pronounce it shame!——
With joy we tell the scoffing age,
He that was dead hath left the tomb.
He lives above their utmost rage,
And we are waiting till he come."

Herein is a beautiful feature of this ordinance. It was instituted in the time of Christ's degradation and sorrow, as a memorial of the same; but it is to be observed until the time when he comes in power and glory and joy. Every time we observe it we are carried back to the scene of his sorrow, and pointed forward to the time of his and our joy, when it shall be said to us, "Enter ye into the joy of the Lord." Oh that when the bridegroom cometh, we may be ready to enter in before the door is shut!

Our servants are greatly at a loss to find we have eaten so little to-day. We tried to explain it, but they could not comprehend why it was. I have a very simple-hearted servant, and as soon as I came back from the morning service he said, "Mr. Lowrie, don't you want something to eat?"

May 3. I have been witnessing an idolatrous ceremony in another part of the monastery where I live, which has made my heart sick. The old gray-headed Taou priest and three of the monks were reciting prayers, beating gongs, cymbals, and the like, and bowing before their idols. A man had come to offer thanks on the birth-day of his son, and the little boy, six years old, sat and watched the whole proceeding. Who made me to differ? Why have I such glorious hopes? What have I done to deserve them? What am I now doing for him who died for me, and called me into the ministry?

It is a rainy afternoon. The sky is all of one dull, sombre hue; the rain comes gently yet quickly down. A light wind blows the damp air into my apartments, and some noisy birds are chattering under the Kwai hwa trees in the court. I should like to have a social chat with you at such a time as this; but we are far away, and, moreover, the day draws to a close, and after hearing the boys say their lesson, I must finish my preparations for the services of to-morrow. Oh, how pleasant to sit at the Lord's table rather than at the table of devils; to hope for God's favour rather than that of idols which cannot save!

With my love to your husband, and to Lloyd and Brown, I remain yours, ever affectionately,

W. M. LOWRIE.

Ningpo, May 30th, 1845.

MY DEAR FATHER—The city of Ningpo lies nearly in the centre of a large plain, surrounded on all sides by mountains, and intersected by innumerable canals, which are nearly all navigable, and serve the double purpose of irrigation and travelling. A covered boat and boatmen can be had for a whole day for twenty-five cents, and whenever we want to extend our ramble any distance beyond the city, we find it most convenient to make use of them. The plain is at least twenty miles in diameter in its narrowest part, and much wider in other places. The whole of this great amphitheatre is thickly studded over with villages and farm-houses, and has two or three large cities besides Ningpo. Foreigners are not allowed to wander beyond the *heen,* or district of which Ningpo is the capital. Its exact dimensions we do not well know, but we can go at least three miles on every side, and in one direction as many as twenty or thirty. By a little prudence and care, we shall doubtless obtain a wider range for our excursions. For the present, unable as we are to speak with fluency, the field is vastly larger than we can profitably occupy; and whenever we can speak well, we doubt not that the door will be opened wider. Should it not be opened, the question will arise, whether obedience to a higher authority and covenant than any of human devising, will not justify us in exceeding the limits that have been fixed, and preaching in other cities the kingdom of God. On this point there is some diversity of opinion amongst us; but I am disposed to think that a blessing would attend our efforts, if carried on, occasionally at least, where the prince of this world now exercises supreme authority. Opposition and excitement on the part of the rulers would but rouse attention to our work. But it may be thought that this is looking too far ahead.

The foreign trade of Ningpo is not so great as it once was. It once carried on an important commerce with Manilla, when South America belonged to Spain, as well as with other parts of the Chinese Empire. But of late years Shanghai has greatly surpassed it, and the latter city is likely to possess by much the largest share of trade with western lands. When the treaty was formed in 1842, it was supposed by Sir Henry Pottinger, Mr. Morrison, and nearly every other person, that Ningpo would be the most important of the five ports; but it has been found, that the vicinity of Shanghai to the city of Loochow, and to the grand canal, give it great advantages over any of the other ports. The best days of Ningpo are probably past, and painful evidences of decay are visible on all sides. Still it has a considerable trade with Fuhkeen, and with the northern provinces; and numerous junks are constantly lying in the river. It offers more advantages to Americans than to the English, as it lies nearer to the green tea district, and offers a good market for the sale of American manufactured goods.

The people are as civil and obliging as could reasonably be expected, considering the severe and uncalled for treatment they received during the war, and the thoughtless course of some of the English officers, in destroying the public buildings for firewood. We are better treated here, by far, than a Chinaman would be in New York or London; though it does occasionally ruffle one's temper to hear himself called a pah-kwei, or *white devil*, with some other such choice epithets. So far as I have seen, there is little difference between this place and Shanghai in that respect; and the difference in favour of this place, which was observed not long ago, was probably owing to the fear of foreigners then fresh in mind, but now wearing off.

We have lately organized a church here, under the title, "Presbyterian Church of Ningpo," of which Mr. Culbertson has been elected pastor. It consists of seven members, to wit: D. B. McCartee, Hingapoo, a Chinese servant of Mr. Way's, together with Mrs. Way, Mrs. Culbertson, Miss Aldersey, Ruth Ati, and Christiana Kit. The two latter are Chinese girls whom Miss Aldersey has educated, and who were baptized by Mr. Medhurst in Java. Dr. McCartee was elected ruling elder, and Mr. Way and myself also act as ruling elders for the time being. The church was regularly organized on the 18th inst., when Mr. Culbertson preached a sermon on Acts ii. 42–47, and Dr. McCartee was ordained as ruling elder, with the laying on of hands of the bishop, and the right hand of fellowship from Mr. Way and myself, in our capacity as ruling elders. It was a good day to us all; and though the beginning is small, we trust the latter end will greatly increase. It is a day of small things, but a day not to be despised. As this is the first Presbyterian church in China, pray for us that the small one may become a thousand, and the weak one a strong nation.

May 31st. In regard to the facilities for distributing tracts a good deal might be said, but the nature of it would depend much on the disposition of the person who writes. Any number might be given away. I would undertake to give to eager applicants more than as many as our press could possibly print, but the misfortune is, that they would be just as eagerly sought after, if they were copies of Paine's Age of Reason, or any other book in the world. I think each member of our mission disapproves of indiscriminate distribution. We do not yet know the proportion of the people who can read, though it is probably small; yet we have an excellent opportunity here of circulating tracts and gospels, and there is rarely a day that Dr. McCartee and myself do not give away one or more, where we are pretty sure they will be read. We regard this, therefore, as an important means of circulating the principles of our religion, though greatly inferior to the oral preaching of the word.

I remain your affectionate son,

W. M. Lowrie.

Ningpo, July 22d, 1845.

My Dear Mother— . . . . Did you ever notice Psalm xxx. 5? "His anger endureth but a moment, in his favour is life. Weeping may endure for a night, but joy cometh in the morning." Is not that beautiful? But here is a literal translation of it, which is, if possible still more beautiful and expressive:

"A moment in his anger,
But lifetimes in his favour:
In the evening, weeping will abide;
But in the morning there is shouting."

Observe the force of the expression. "In the evening, weeping will abide." It "will abide." It threatens to remain long with us; sorrow seems as if it were about to take up its abode. Night is before us, and we see no sun, no day, no joy beyond. But the night quickly passes, "as a dream of the night," and what then? "In the morning there is shouting." And how true it is! Just compare Isaiah liv. 7, with 2 Corinthians iv. 17.

That a person can be a Christian, and yet afraid of death, I have no doubt. Indeed, I suppose most Christians are so. But why should it be so? It is hardly correct to say, "The Bible says 'Death is the king of terrors.'" Bildad the Shuhite said so, or something like it, for I am not sure that he meant death by that expression; but if he did, I would not like to take all he said for the Bible. The New Testament does not so represent it. It says that Christ "gave up the ghost," and that Stephen "fell asleep." The apostle says, even of the offending Corinthian Christians, "many sleep;" and of deceased Christians generally, that they "are asleep." Asleep! what is so peaceful! quiet repose in Christ! how long or short it matters little. Soon the Lord will come again, and them that are asleep will he bring with him. How soon? We know not; but *soon*, not a thousand years off, but so soon that we may not fall asleep, perhaps, before he comes....

As ever, affectionately yours,

W. M. LOWRIE.

Ningpo, August 2d, 1845.

MY DEAR FATHER— . . . . My health is better, so far, this year, than any year since I came to China. Still, however, the warm weather has a weakening effect, which we all feel more or less. There is too in this place a constant tendency to diarrhœa in summer, which needs a good deal of care to avoid it. In another month the cool weather will commence. If this year be a fair specimen of Ningpo summer, I think there is every prospect of good health here. It is said, however, to be cooler than usual. . . .

I am now engaged in preparing a copy of Luke for publication, with short notices, which I hope will be ready by the end of the year; and perhaps I shall prepare also Acts in the same way. I am losing faith in the doctrine, "The Bible without note or comment," at least as far as the Chinese are concerned, from the often witnessed fact, that the most intelligent of them fall into frequent and gross mistakes as to its meaning. For example, many think we worship our ancestors, because the Lord's prayer commences, "Our Father which art in heaven." If we only had enough of our small type, Luke and the comments might make a volume of seventy-five or one hundred pages. With Dyer's type, and the Paris type, it will be one hundred and fifty or more, and consequently far more expensive, and, as I think, not so good-looking. Perhaps if we print it, we may get enough of small type cut by hand to supply all we want. This will be expensive, but not much more so than to use so much more paper, &c., with larger type.

. . . . "The Lord reigneth, let the earth rejoice." His own cause is infinitely dear to him, and our follies, weaknesses, sins, mistakes, all things shall not retard it; no, not for one moment. His way may be in darkness and storms, and the clouds may be but the dust of his feet; but in due time, at the appointed season, all will be plain. Till then, "Wo unto the world because of offences. It must needs be that offences come;" but I pray God that they come not from us. Oh for that happy time when they shall not hurt nor destroy, nor cause to offend, in all God's holy mountain.

Ever affectionately your son,

W. M. Lowrie.

JOURNAL AT NINGPO.

August 8. Exhibiting a microscope to my teacher and servants, at which they were in great astonishment. The beautiful workmanship of the instrument itself, (a present from a kind friend in New York,) attracted much admiration; but its power in displaying minute objects was a thing of which they had formed no previous conception. The hairy leg of a fly was an object of especial curiosity, and they exclaimed frequently, "Why, the fly's leg has hairs! the fly's leg has hairs!"

The weather is now warm, and weakening in its effects. One's strength is easily exhausted, and two or three hours of close application, either to the pen or one's books, is fatiguing.

August 9. A feast for the dead, who have no surviving children to worship them, is just now (nine o'clock, P. M.) going on outside of my rooms. Two long ropes, with numerous strips of coloured paper suspended, are hung along the sides of the streets, and tables with various eatables, as eggs, water-lily roots, beans, fish, ginger, rice, cups of spirits, and the like, are spread over them. At one end is a hideous monster made of paper, and at the other a company of priests are performing some monotonous ceremonies. Budhist and Taou priests mingle together in the rites, and the little children look on it as a great "raree-show." The object is to feed the souls of dead men in this neighbourhood, who have no children left to provide for their wants. Contributions have been given by the neighbours to the amount of four thousand cash, and as the expenses will scarcely amount to one thousand, the remainder will of course fall into the pockets of the priests.

Saturday evening, August 23. A warm oppressive day. Feeling a slight headache in the evening, I went out and sat down on the wall by the north gate, to enjoy what little wind might be stirring. Several workmen who lodged in the guard-house over the gate, came up to me, and after a few questions and answers we were on the best possible terms. The conversation, where all were in a good-humour, and all wanted to talk, was very mixed, and sometimes diverting enough. After a few ordinary phrases, I began to find myself out of my depth, but still a word here and there, and half a sentence sometimes, kept us going. At last I asked them "what gods they worshipped;" to which some replied, "Yuh-kwang," (the Jewelled Emperor,) also "Kwan-yin," and various others. On this I remarked that these were all false gods, mere wood and clay; they were unable to speak, hear, see or walk. Of what use were they? Why should they be worshipped? These remarks excited frequent bursts of laughter, with exclamations, "True!" "Just so!" and the like. They then asked if we had no idols in our country, on which, "with stammering lips, and in another tongue," I set before them the only object of worship, the true God, the Supreme Ruler of all, the hearer of prayer, and his son Jesus Christ. They were astonished when told that he could see, hear, and speak, and asked various questions, to many of which I found it difficult to reply. On coming away several of them requested me to "come again to-morrow."

Wednesday, September 3. Dr. McCartee and myself started on a trip of relaxation and exploration, meaning to visit Teentung, a celebrated Budhist monastery, some twenty-five miles south of Ningpo. We engaged a boat large enough to accommodate ourselves, with my teacher, and a servant, besides the two boatmen. The charge for the boat and boatmen is about half a dollar a day.

The boat being somewhat slow in starting, we strolled through a large grave-yard near the landing. Numerous coffins were lying about on the top of the ground with no covering whatever, and some were almost fallen to pieces through age. There were three stone buildings about ten or twelve feet square, and as many high, intended for the reception of children's bones. One was the "Children's Pagoda," and the others the "Boys' Pagoda," and "Girls' Pagoda." Such buildings are common, for in China little attention is paid to the burial of children, unless they happen to be the first born. Instead of the massive coffins in which the remains of adults are laid, a slight box is nailed together, in which they are deposited, and laid anywhere, until, the frail structure having decayed, and the flesh disappeared, the bones are collected and put in such buildings as these.

Continuing our walk through the suburb, which is long and wide, and near the city very populous, we gave away some tracts, but refused many applicants, on the ground that they could not read. It soon began to rain, and getting into our boat, we proceeded rapidly on our way. We slept rather uncomfortably in the boat, and arrived during the night at the hills within six miles of Teentung.

The next morning on awaking we found ourselves at the foot of some hills, and as far as the boat could go. The country around had an inviting aspect, and we began to promise ourselves much pleasure in rambling about among the hills. But to our dismay, heavy showers of rain came up every few minutes, and it soon appeared that there was small prospect of getting comfortably to Teentung. We turned our faces towards *Yuh-wang*, a large Budhist monastery, with two high towers, which we had seen during the morning.

We reached the monastery a little before sunset, and found it so embowered in trees that the buildings were not visible till we were close to them. The Budhist priests have certainly, what is rather uncommon among other classes, a good deal of taste in the selection of their residences. This monastery is beautifully situated in a gorge of two hills, with another hill directly in front. This does not furnish a very wide prospect in any direction, but it makes the place quiet and retired. A brick wall inclosing several acres of ground goes round the monastery. Entering the main gate, we went down to the bottom of the valley, crossed a little bridge thrown over the valley stream, and ascending a slight elevation of some twenty feet or more, entered the buildings, and proceeding through one or two large court-yards, were politely received by the monks, and shown into the strangers' apartments, a set of three or four rooms, with some chairs, tables, and bedsteads. Monasteries and temples are the principal *inns* in China, though they seldom furnish more than four walls and a roof. The traveller is expected to furnish his own bedding and food, and to have some one to prepare it for him, though the latter service can generally be performed for him by *extempore* cooks, if he is willing to put up with the ignorance of foreign modes, and the dirty habits by which they are generally distinguished. It is, however, the safest and cheapest plan for the traveller to have his own servant along; and though some good friend of missions at home may ask what business a plain missionary has to carry a servant about with him, yet such would do well to consider, that here we have no comfortable inns, with separate rooms which we can lock when we go out, and where everything in the shape of bedding and food is prepared for us by attentive landlords. But this is digression.—Being wearied by the confinement of our boat, we were glad to get our supper; and after a hasty glance at the buildings, as it was now dark, we soon went to bed, but did not rest very well, for there was an abundance of fleas, and having neglected our own musquito curtains, we were fain to use some we found in the monastery, which did not shelter us perfectly from the attacks of the musquitoes.

The first building is a large high structure of only one story. Within it is about one hundred feet long by seventy broad, and the roof is supported by numerous wooden pillars, standing on stone bases.

The Chinese have not the art of supporting a roof without using so many pillars as to diminish materially the effect of a large room. The principal objects in this room were three immense figures, the Three Precious Buddhas. They were sitting with their feet drawn up like tailors at work, and were of immense size. Judging from the base of the seat on which they sat, and which, though twelve feet square, they quite covered, they must have been eighteen or twenty feet high, even in their sitting posture. They were richly gilt, and between them stood two attendants, gilt all over, and perhaps twelve feet high. They did not seem to have much worship paid to them, and the sparrows which had made their nests in the roof above, defiled the place with dirt. Behind these figures, and facing the other way, was the image of *Kwan Yin*, "She who regards the prayers of the world," sitting on a horse, (or ass?) and carrying a child in her arms. Several attendants stood round her shrine, which was altogether a curious specimen of working in clay. It represented the sea, with numerous rocks and islands, over which she was crossing on horseback. Along the ends and back of this building, sat thirty-four gilt images, each as large as the human figure, with every variety of countenance and dress. In front of the door stood the most curiously gnarled tree I ever saw. Its trunk was more than a foot in diameter; after rising up about six or eight feet it bent back in a sharp angle to the ground, and then stretched up again, while its branches stood out in every direction. It was inclosed by a stone railing, and evidently was esteemed a great curiosity. There was some story of miraculous appearances connected with it; but I have forgotten what it is.

Directly behind this building, and separated from it by a large square stone-paved court, was another sixty by eighty feet in dimensions, and in much better keeping. The principal objects of interest were two really magnificent shrines, of a circular pyramidal shape, one behind the other. Over the hinder one an immense silken canopy was suspended, lights were constantly burning before them, and some of the monks seemed to be always in the building. And for what, think you, was all this display? Because one of the shrines contained a veritable *Shay-le* of Buddh, taken from his sacred body before his deification! And what is a *Shay-le?* On this point I can get but little satisfaction. I am told "it is neither gold nor brass, nor stone, nor yet bone nor flesh. It is a small round thing, about as big as the half of a pea, and looks somewhat like a scab from a sore that is healing up." For a "consideration" the priests will allow you to see it, and if you are a good man, or likely to be prosperous, its color is red, but if the reverse, it will be black. As great honours are paid to this valuable relic, as to the blood of St. Januarius, and no doubt the priests make much money out of it. My teacher, who has of late some new views on some topics, laughs at it as an imposition to wheedle people out of their money. There are several idols in this hall, one of which is a jolly fat old fellow with a continual laugh on his face. The other buildings of the temple have little in them worthy of notice, and the rain was so violent that we were obliged to postpone to another time our purposed visit to the towers and grounds of the temple. This we regretted, as the two towers are each seven stories high, and the country had a very pretty appearance.

There are about thirty monks in the establishment. Those we saw were generally pale and sickly looking fellows, with countenances betokening very little mental exertion or worth. The routine of their duties is such, as must effectually quench every noble aspiration, for it consists in an unceasing round of prostrations and chants, generally in an unknown tongue, and almost always performed without the slightest appearance of devotion or zeal. It is marvellous how men can for years practise such insipid ceremonies, without becoming utterly disgusted with them. One of the monks had deprived himself of one of his fingers by a very painful process; he had wrapped oiled flax around it down to the middle of the joint next the hand, and burned it slowly, another monk reciting prayers all the time, till the finger was consumed. When we saw him the stump was not perfectly healed. He had also seared the flesh of one arm in a dozen places with a hot iron. He had a special vow of abstinence from covetousness, wine, and lewdness, and these were the marks by which he made his vow generally known. But notwithstanding such evidences, which, by the way, are not uncommon, the character of those who bear them is by no means good. The "forbidding to marry, and commanding to abstain from meats," by which the Buddhist and Taou sects are distinguished, are followed by just the consequences which all history teaches us to expect.

Having seen all we wanted, and being tired of staying, we began to think of going,—but how to accomplish it? The rain fell in torrents, and the road to our boat was flooded the greater part of the way by a stream of water nearly a foot deep. It was a regular scene in wading, and might have reminded one of trout-fishing in the streams in Pennsylvania. Getting to the boat, we changed our wet clothes for others, and going off in the rain, reached home shortly before dark, greatly amused and profited by our trip, though it had not turned out as we had expected.

Tuesday, October 14. In walking through the streets of Chusan, I was singularly affected by hearing a little girl, daughter of one of the English soldiers now stationed here, saying, "my mother wants you to come back directly." The familiar words and English accent spoken by a young person were so different from the "unknown tongue" spoken by every one around, that they easily transported my thoughts to a land where all speak my own mother tongue. How strangely it would now seem, to be where everybody spoke the same language with myself!

Tuesday, October 21. Started on a trip to *Poo-too,* one of the most celebrated establishments of the Buddhists in China.

Poo-too lies east of the north-eastern extremity of Chusan. According to a Chinese history of the island, it is about a hundred le, or a little over thirty miles, from Tinghai. A deep cleft or valley near the middle of the island reveals the yellow-tiled roof of one of the principal temples, from a great distance off, but the principal landing-place is at the south-eastern extremity.

No sooner does one step on shore than he has evidence on every side that the place is "wholly given to idolatry." A small worshipping place stood close by the landing; shrines and inscriptions were cut in the rocks by the roadside, and a large red gateway covered with tiles announced the approach to a temple. Pursuing the walk a hundred yards further over a broad stone-paved pathway overhung by trees, you enter the *Pih-hwa-yen,* or "white flowery monastery." Here I sought for lodgings, but the monks seemed not to desire company, and complained of having met such uncivil treatment from foreigners who had recently been there, that they did not wish to see any more. However, they finally showed me a suite of three or four rooms, or rather closets, up stairs, of which I took possession, and leaving my servant to keep watch and get dinner ready, I sallied out to see what might be seen.

The Pih-hwa-yen is an old building built on a foundation dug out of the hill-side, and almost concealed from sight by large overhanging trees and shrubbery. It is now in bad repair, and has an old and faded appearance. The number of monks is said to be about forty, but I saw not more than ten or twelve. The idols and ornaments of the temple are all old and shabby, and it has little to interest a visitor. In one of the main courts under the verandah were pasted up twelve or fifteen large red cards, presented by ship's companies with other offerings in gratitude to the gods who had brought them on so far. Two or three of the vessels were from *Hwuy-Chow*, in Canton, most of them from *Chang-Chow, Tseuen-chow, and Hing-hwa*, in Fuhkeen, and only one from a seaport in Cheh-keang. In the evening a religious ceremony of some kind was performed by the old abbot, assisted by six of the monks, with several of the young candidates for the Buddhist priesthood, some sailors and myself for spectators. The abbot put on a scarlet robe and a crown, and taking an incense stick in his hand, performed numerous ceremonies, accompanied with a repetition of prayers and chanting, in the chorus of which the other monks joined. But there was not the slightest appearance of devotion, except perhaps in the manner of the old abbot. The others, in the intervals of the chanting, drank tea, gazed about, and talked with one another, while the young candidates for the priesthood amused themselves with annoying one of the officiating monks, and putting balls in his chair, to trouble him when he sat down. This called forth an angry reproof from him, and produced a hearty laugh on their part. Seeing things go on thus, I gave one of the spectators a tract, whereon several others asked for some; and finally one of the monks left his devotions and came for one. I then said something on the folly of worshipping such idols, and a hearty laugh followed the exposure of the helplessness of their gods. With some further remarks on the way to worship the true God, and his Son Jesus Christ, I left them, glad to get away from the sin and folly of their unmeaning ceremonies. They kept them up with the beating of gongs and drums during the greater part of the night.

From the Pih-hwa-yen, a paved stone walk, about

five feet broad, extends over a hill and down to the central valley of the island, where the principal establishment, called the *Seen-sz'*, is built. On several of the large rocks along this road, inscriptions are cut in large letters, and shrines are built against, or carved out of the rocks. At one place is a little shrine with some characters in a language I did not know, probably the Sanscrit, and beneath *Nan woo oh me to fuh*, words that are constantly and "vainly" repeated in the religious ceremonies of the Buddhists. Several paths branched off from the main road, leading to smaller *yen*, or monasteries, in the recesses of the hills.

Arrived at the bottom of the valley, you pass through a large gateway, composed of four massive stone pillars, each a single block of granite about twenty feet high. Beyond this a few steps and you pass, at right angles, on the left another gateway leading into the main buildings. Before coming to this gateway is an inscription carved in stone to this effect: "Every officer, whether civil or military, and all the common people, on arriving at this place, must dismount from their horses." The reason of this soon appeared, for just within the second gateway, and inclosed within an octagonal tower, covered with yellow tiles, was an immense marble tablet, with a long inscription, presented by the Emperor Kanghi. It is the custom in China for all to dismount and walk when passing before anything that comes from the Emperor, though there was but little occasion for the order in this instance, seeing there is not a horse or ass upon the island.

Beyond this is a pond of water, with many of the broad-leaved lotus plants growing at each end, and a beautifully arched stone bridge across it. Beyond this again, reaching clear to the base of the hill, were several large yellow-tiled temples, with open courts in front, and two-storied dormitories at either side of the courts for the monks. In the temples were any number of huge hideous idols, all once richly gilt, but now brown with age, and black and dirty with the smoke of incense. Just within the door of the main building was a shrine for drawing lots, and telling fortunes, with the inscription above, "*Yew kew peih ying*," "He that seeketh will certainly find an answer." About two dozen monks were kneeling and chanting in the main building, among whom were several older than any I have ever seen. Outside one or two monks were superintending the winnowing of some paddy; others were watching men splitting up the roots of an old tree for fire-wood, and others were doing nothing. So lazy and good-for-nothing a set as the Buddhist and Taou priests, I have never seen; and I could not but admire the simple truth with which one of the boatmen described their occupation, when I asked him what they did, "Why, sir, they eat rice, and read prayers." In one of the side buildings, which is three stories high, there is a bell five feet in diameter, and more than seven feet in height. It is beaten with a wooden hammer, (the Chinese bells rarely have clappers,) and its sound when gently struck, amidst the chantings and chorus of the monks below, was far from being unpleasant.

Everything about these buildings showed signs of age, neglect, and decay. The yellow tiles, the gift of imperial favour, were falling from the roofs, grass was growing in the stone-paved court-yards, weeds encumbered the sacred lotus pond, windows and doors were falling to pieces, and the curtains and ornaments of the idols were even browned with smoke and dust. Here, too, there was but little evidence of devotion in their worship, and one of the monks stopped in the midst of his chanting to ask me when I arrived. I left the place with an aching heart; for the sight of these old men bending over the grave, and yet chanting the praises of these wooden gods, was a painful subject for thought.

The next morning I went around to several of the smaller monasteries, but saw little in them of interest. In one, the monks were so busy divining for some sailors, that they had not time to speak to strangers; in another, they were all gone to some other part of the island, and in a third I found no person except one old monk, suffering from disease. He was sitting in a sheltered verandah, with a little boy waiting on him, and received me quite politely, ordering tea to be brought. He said he was seventy-one years old; and was as intelligent a man as I met on the island. In answer to my inquiries, he said that the beginning of the monastic establishments on the island dated as far back as the Leang dynasty, about eight hundred years ago; but that the Seen-sz' and the How-sz' were built in the Sung dynasty. The total number of monks on the island, he affirmed, did not exceed seven or eight hundred. I had been told the evening before, at the How-sz' that there were fifteen hundred, but the old man's statement is probably correct. There are four large, and one hundred and two small establishments on the island. Allowing one hundred monks for the largest, and thirty for the other three, each, we have about two hundred. All accounts agreed that in the smaller establishments there were not over five or six in the average, being about seven or eight hundred in all. This differs widely from the accounts of former visitors, who make the number amount to "six thousand;" but I am satisfied that those accounts are much larger than is correct. There is not room in all the buildings on the island to accommodate so many.

As the monk with whom I was now talking was old and sick, and might soon die, I felt it to be a duty to point out to him, however imperfectly, the way of eternal life beyond the grave; but though he understood the most of what was said, and assented to it as very good and proper, it seemed to make little impression upon him. He said that after death he expected still to abide among the hills of this island, which had now been his home for more than fifty years. When asked how he expected to secure happiness beyond the grave, he replied, "By worshipping Buddh, and making many prayers." I set before him as well as I could the way of life through Christ,—to which he listened attentively, and remarked, "There were some foreigners here several years ago, who taught the same doctrine that you do;" referring doubtless to the visit of Messrs. Medhurst and Stevens. On coming away I gave him several tracts, which he received gratefully. Oh that the truth which he has thus heard more than once, may be blessed to him, even in this, the eleventh hour! After strolling about a little longer, I left the island at eleven o'clock, A. M., and reached Ting-hai near sunset.

Nov. 26. Saw a wedding procession, which must have been several hundred yards long, and numbered several hundreds of people. A crowd of men and boys bearing banners and inscriptions went in front, some trumpets and cymbals followed, then seven or eight men on horseback, then a couple of officers, one bearing a white, and the other a gilt button in their caps; then the bride's chair, a really beautiful article, elegantly painted, carved and gilded, borne by eight men; but the bride was quite too well inclosed to be seen; then several men bearing ornamental bedding-clothes and pillows, which form a part of the marriage presents, and are always ostentatiously displayed; while no less than twenty-one sedan chairs brought up the rear. The lady was said to be the daughter of an officer of rank.

Dec. 1. I congratulated my teacher on the birth of his daughter. "No, no, we do not congratulate here on the birth of a daughter." "No! why not?" "Oh, they are a great expense, and very little profit to us." This led to some conversation on the treatment of females, and finally to the question, whether there was such a thing as female infanticide in this part of the country, he replied quickly, "No, not here, but there is in Canton, and in some parts of

Fuhkeen." "Is there none at all here?" "No, not in Ningpo, but in the city of Funghwa, (a city about twenty miles off, and under the jurisdiction of the Che-foo of Ningpo,) there is. It is called *neih-sz'*, or death by drowning, for when the child is born, if it be a girl, the parents or assistants often heap water on it, in pretence of washing it, but in such a way that it dies!" He made this statement very unwillingly, and with many exclamations of horror, and finally added, "But of late years, since the Funghwa people have begun to understand right reason and propriety, there is none of it." Notwithstanding this assertion, there is sufficient reason to suppose that this horrid custom prevails, not only in Funghwa, but in other places in this province; but to nothing like the extent in which it is common in some parts of Fuhkeen.

TO THE SOCIETY OF INQUIRY, PRINCETON THEOLOGICAL SEMINARY.

Ningpo, November 1st, 1845.

DEAR BRETHREN—In a letter from the Corresponding Secretary of your Committee on Foreign Missions, dated October 16th, 1844, which has been lying by me since April 19, 1845, there are three definite questions and a *carte blanche*, the answers and "filling up" of all of which would occupy more time and paper than I have to spare; and, probably, more patience than you have to give. Perhaps I shall not err in answering the questions first, and then adding what may come uppermost, or find room.

In regard to Morrison's translation of the Bible into Chinese, a singular misconception has long prevailed among the supporters of missions, both in England and America. It is not three years since one of the warmest, and generally speaking, one of the best informed friends of missions in England, asserted, in opposition to the united and unanimous voice of the Protestant Missionaries in China, that "Morrison's translation of the Scriptures was nearly perfect, and another was unnecessary." This was, to say the least, rather a venturesome remark from one who did not know a word of Chinese! . . .

I can answer your question, "Is the translation useful or intelligible?" by saying it is useful, but is not adapted for general circulation. When we are explaining the Scripture history or doctrine in private conversation, it is of use, because it is sufficiently intelligible, with such cautions and explanations as we can give orally, to give those with whom we speak a fuller idea of the truth. It is of use to give to our converts, for you know the converted man finds good when the impenitent turns away in disgust; and the converts will naturally come to us for explanation. And it is also of use to those who may prepare a new translation. But it is not, as I think, adapted for general circulation, nor would I willingly give a copy to a heathen, except under favourable circumstances. These same remarks apply in great measure to Dr. Marshman's translation, which was finished about the same time with Morrison's, and has never had an extensive circulation.

You also ask, "What progress has been made towards remedying its defects?" A good deal as regards the New Testament; but as it regards the Old, almost none. We have two other translations of the New Testament; one by Gutzlaff, which is not much used; and another by Medhurst, assisted by John R. Morrison, Bridgman, and others. The latter is the one in common use; and it is in general intelligible and good, though paraphrastic sometimes, and far from being perfect. A number of the missionaries, both English and American, are now engaged in a revision of it; but it may be several years before it is completed. When the Old Testament will be revised and published, I have no idea. I hope to live to see the time, and, perhaps, to take some part in it, but it will not be soon. There is yet a great work to be done in this respect, and perhaps some of you may be called to assist in it. The translation of the Scriptures into Chinese is a great, difficult, and most important work, and the preparation of Comments and Notes upon them will require the labours of many men for many years. You can have but little idea of the strange notions they gather from expressions that are as common to us as the air we breathe. . . .

I have gone over the Gospel of Luke very carefully with my teacher, who passes for a learned man in Ningpo, and his mistakes and misconceptions have been both amusing and painful. This arises in part from the imperfection of the translation; in part from an utter and characteristic ignorance of the geography and history of every other nation but China; in part from the use of figures and comparisons unknown in China. Some people say, "The Bible is an Oriental book, and the Chinese are an Oriental people, therefore, they can easily understand it." But unfortunately the Chinese are as much beyond "the East" on one side as America is on the other; and therefore the remark is very unfounded, in part from inattention and want of interest in the subject, and in part from the "thick darkness" with which idolatry and superstition have enshrouded even the mental, and much more the moral perceptions. Oh brethren! if you were here but a few days, you would understand something of the necessity for the Spirit's influences to open the understanding, and pour light into the heart; and of the feelings of the prophet, when commanded to prophesy to the dry bones. Pray for us. So thick is the "veil of the covering cast over" the minds of the heathen, that were it not for what God can do, the Missionary enterprise would be as fantastic a scheme of folly as the brain of man ever devised. If it were not for the hope, the belief of what God will do, I would not be a missionary for another day. It requires but a few years' experience in the missionary field to learn that it is not talents nor learning, important as these are, but piety and prayer, that are chiefly requisite in a missionary. "Not by might nor by power, but by my Spirit, saith the Lord." Oh that my own heart and practice were more deeply influenced by this conviction, and that the churches at home felt it more!

You ask for my "impressions regarding the climate of China." Having not yet had a full experience of the climate so far north as my present residence, I cannot answer you so fully as may be desirable; but what I know is briefly as follows: In the Canton province, and the climate at Amoy is not materially different, warm weather prevails for nine months in the year; of which four or five are oppressive, while the months of December, January, and February, are pleasant and cool. The natives and the Portuguese at Macao do not use fires in their houses, but the English and Americans find them very agreeable. During three years, the lowest I ever saw the thermometer was 45°, while it generally in the cool weather ranged between 50° and 60° of Fahrenheit. I never used a cloak but once or twice, except in my room, where, as I sat without a fire, it was needful. In the long warm seasons my health suffered, and I became languid and thinner than usual, in August and September. Most persons suffer in the same way, but the winter, or rather the cool weather, for ice and snow are almost never seen, is invigorating, and many enjoy better health than in their own land. I consider the climate at Macao and Canton as decidedly healthy; and excepting the indisposition above referred to, which, however, never confined me a whole day to the couch, I never was better at home. The circumstances which have made Amoy and Hong Kong unhealthy, I do not think will have a permanent influence; nor should

I have the slightest hesitation or fear in going to either of these places. It would seem, however, from facts already observed, that northern men bear the climate better than southern, though reasoning *a priori* many would think differently.

In Shanghai and Ningpo, the climate is different. We have pleasant, cool, and cold weather, for nine months, and warm weather for three, July and August, and parts of June and September. Of the warm weather six weeks are uncomfortably hot, if anything, worse than at Macao. I have not yet had the pleasure of experiencing the cold weather here in its perfection, though I retain a vivid recollection of the coldness of my fingers and ears on approaching Shanghai in March, when the cold weather was nearly over, and of the strange sensations excited, by seeing my breath come out in thick steam, and sleeping under a load of bed-clothes, things to which I had been a stranger for more than three years. The thermometer falls below 25° ; ice and snow are seen every winter ; and fur clothes, which are cheap and good, are worn to an extent that would surprise you. Yet even here, the inhabitants do not use fires, but content themselves with abundance of cotton garments, (ten and fifteen jackets worn at once are not uncommon,) wadded clothes, and furs, with small foot-stoves, and finger-stoves. But I do not see how we can do without fires. The climate is subject to frequent and considerable changes. I have seen the thermometer rise from 34° to 84° in a few days in March, and fall back to 40° in forty hours; and after experiencing warm weather in June, I have put on woollen stockings in July. A fall of twenty degrees in a few hours is not uncommon, and is sensibly felt. It is now quite cool, the thermometer being below sixty, except in the middle of the day ; and the merchants' shops present a busy and rich scene, from the quantity of fine furs displayed in them. I am looking forward with some interest to the return of snow and ice, things which

I have not seen for nearly four years. My impressions of the climate of Ningpo are very favourable, though the last summer being cooler than usual, did not afford a very good opportunity of knowing precisely what it is. . . . . There are also two or three disagreeably damp seasons in the summer, of two or three weeks' continuance, when rain pours down in torrents; and if it does not rain, you feel as if the very air was damp and cloudy; and the perspiration will gather on the stones in the wall, even when the sun is shining outside. Such weather is hard on books, clothes, and animal spirits; but it is of short continuance.

We get plenty to eat here, but not a very great variety, as the inhabitants have not yet learned to provide for foreigners, as they have at Macao and Canton. Goat's flesh, pork, hams, chickens, ducks, and geese, are our principal meats; though in winter, wild-ducks, pheasants, and hares, are cheaper than anything else. Fish of several kinds we have all the year round; wheat, rice, and a little buckwheat, form the staff of life; sweet potatoes, turnips, egg-plants, bean sprouts, bamboo sprouts, taro, beans, peas, *Kaou-bah,* onions, and greens, are our chief vegetables; and for fruits we have peaches, pears, plums, lichees, persimmons, pomegranates, and oranges, with walnuts, chestnuts, and pea-nuts. You will say, "This is a goodly list." True, and we are thankful to enjoy so many of God's good gifts here; nor do we complain when we remember that few of them are so good as those you eat in the United States; whilst beef, such at least as may be called good, Irish potatoes, and apples, are seldom seen. I have tasted none of either in many months, nor apples, which are worth all the oranges of China, for years; nor do we get all these things *at once.* I find in my market-book, (for we bachelors have to attend to such things ourselves oftentimes,) that for weeks together, Dr. McCartee and I sat down together to a table, of which the chief dishes were, chickens, or fish, bamboo sprouts, turnips, and bean sprouts, with bread, rice and eggs. It is hard to say what we should do without eggs. When the egg-plants came we were delighted, and when the sweet potatoes were fit to eat, we were satisfied! The married missionaries do not fare any better than we bachelors, though they doubtless have some things nicer!

For the particularity of the above statements, I do not think it necessary to make any apology, though the pronoun "I," occurs with a frequency that is somewhat startling; perhaps it may be some excuse, that they are written in answer to the question, "What are my impressions?"

Your last question, "The magnitude of the field and the prospects of the mission?" is one on which a volume might be written, but the space already consumed warns me to be brief, the more so as I may have an occasion hereafter to refer to it. I can only say this: Few have any idea of the extent of the ground that is opened and opening to our labours, and none know where the things will end, whose beginnings we have lived to witness. The opening of China to foreign intercourse, is an event which finds few parallels in the history of the world. This country is a world in itself; and the thought has often occurred to me, while traversing its beautiful plains and crowded streets, "What a world has been revolving here of which Christendom knows nothing!" I have been led to make excursions of twenty or thirty miles into the interior, from each of the cities of Amoy, Shanghai, and Ningpo, and everywhere the country is like a vast beehive, swarming with inhabitants. It is the same about Canton, where I have also been, and doubtless the same about Foo-chow. I have not known what it is to be out of sight of a human habitation since I have been in China, and where there is one there are commonly ten. I have scarcely ever seen a little valley, or a hollow among the hills, where industry could cultivate a bed of rice, or a crop of greens, that was not occupied. It is scarcely an exaggeration to say, that temples and monasteries are as common here as farm-houses in Pennsylvania, and I have seen the streets of Ningpo crowded with many ten thousands of people, to see an idolatrous procession in honour of "all the gods." Now all this vast and teeming population of idolaters must have the gospel, or perish. Books will not do the work. It is the living teacher who must speak unto them the words of life. Such is the field we cultivate. As to our prospects, you have them in the concluding verses of Psalm cxxvi.:

They that sow in tears,
With shoutings shall gather the harvest.
Going he shall go, even with weeping, burdened with the seed to be sown:
Coming he shall come, and with shouting, burdened with his sheaves.

It is nearly midnight, and I must draw to a close without referring to other topics, which, if this letter were not already full enough, might be of interest. Full notices of the mission you will probably see in the Chronicle before long, and I have omitted them here.

Brethren, whatever your own course may be, whether to come to the missionary field, or to cultivate the vineyard of the Lord at home, there is one thing we pray you to bear in mind, "It is God who giveth the increase," and if success do not attend one's labour, the reason will probably be found in the fact that He is not inquired of by his people respecting this thing, to do it for them. Pray for us.

I am yours in the bonds of the Gospel,

W. M. Lowrie.

Ningpo, December 5th, 1845.

My Dear Father— . . . . I have my commentary on Luke, which with the text will make a handsome volume of a hundred pages, ready for the press, and trust it will be of use. The style is pure and good Chinese, for it is written by my teacher, and I know the sentiments to be correct, though sometimes not as full or clear as I could have wished. My teacher said to me, I suppose, twenty times while preparing it, "How can you expect us to understand this book? *I* do not understand it, who have been reading books all my life, and how can less learned persons comprehend it?" The doctrines, historical allusions, geography, customs, e. g., washing the feet, comparisons, everything is strange; and when joined to an imperfect translation, it is not to be thought that a careless heathen can understand such a book. At the risk of being thought a heretic, I must say I think the oft-repeated phrase, "The Bible without note or comment," is in danger of being pushed so far, as to fall over and do harm. However true it is and correct under limitations, it is not correct in itself. It is not true in fact, that our people at home read it "without note or comment;" for there is no one who does not hear many a note and comment from parent, teacher, friend or minister, and there are few who do not form their opinions of most of it from such "notes and comments." If these and innumerable commentaries besides, are needed in a land of so much light as America, what must be the case in China? "Without note and comment" is true, so far as authoritative and infallible exposition is intended; and also, if it be meant that the simple text, when understood, is to be carefully studied and pondered in the Christian hours of devotion; but I humbly conceive there is danger if it be extended much beyond these limits. However, I ought to reflect that you have thought on the subject long enough not to need such a "lesson" from me. . . . . I was deeply grieved to hear of the accident you met with but thankful it was no worse. How many strange accidents we miss, within a hair's-breadth of them, though unawares. We shall doubtless often wonder when we get to heaven, and look back on our past life, that amidst so many dangers it was prolonged so long.

. . . . After a good deal of thought, I am about settling down to the opinion, that I ought to aim at a pretty full knowledge of books and writing in Chinese. In a mission so large as ours, and where we have a press, there must be some one tolerably at home on some points. Now, I have been so circumstanced, as to be obliged to turn my thoughts much that way, somewhat to the disadvantage of my speaking fluently, and I am so still. I have laid such a foundation of acquaintance with the written language, as enables me to go on with some ease, and such as the other brethren can scarcely be expected to do in some time. They are accordingly outstripping me in the colloquial, though I have the advantage in the books, and can easily keep it up. My education and previous habits are also such as fit me more for this than for mingling among men, unless actually obliged to do so. I propose, therefore, not to neglect the colloquial, but to lay out a good portion of my strength on reading and writing Chinese; keeping in view, chiefly, the translation of the Scriptures, and works explanatory of them, and perhaps the preparation of elementary books, and it may be a dictionary, a thing we are greatly in want of. What do you think of this plan? You will not think I mean to neglect the *great work* of preaching, for I trust to be able in the course of next year to undertake regular services. I might do it now, if I had no accounts to keep, letters to write, and advice and assistance to give to others, especially in the matter of the printing office. That you may see how much I have been hindered one way and another since coming to China, I may say that though it is nearly four years since I left you, yet I have had a teacher, and by consequence have been studying the language effectively, only twenty-three months, and of those, three are hardly worth counting from the interruptions I met. I sometimes felt quite discouraged, and now feel ashamed to think I have been here so long, and done so *little*. . . .

With many affectionate remembrances and prayers,

I am, as ever, your affectionate son,

W. M. Lowrie.

CHAPTER VII.

1846.

Missionary Labours at Ningpo—Heathen Customs—Superstitious Fears—Preaching in Chinese.

During this year the missions in China were further strengthened by the arrival at Canton of the Rev. John B. French, and the Rev. William Spear and his wife, and at Ningpo, of the Rev. J. W. Quarterman. The British troops were this year withdrawn from Chusan, and as the Chinese authorities would not permit foreigners to reside there, Mr. Loomis and his wife removed to Ningpo.

Mr. Lowrie's study of the Chinese language, while in Macao, as already stated, was much interrupted by the business matters of the different missions. The Mandarin dialect, which he studied at Macao, is not spoken in the south of China, and hence he could converse in it with his teacher only. This he found to be a serious disadvantage. The Ningpo and Mandarin dialects are as different from each other as the French is from the Spanish. In learning to speak the former, he had therefore to begin anew, with the advantage however of hearing it daily spoken by the inhabitants. But here also his time was a good deal taken up with the business of the Ningpo Mission, and correcting the proof-sheets of works issued from the press. So many, and such long-continued adverse circumstances, at times almost produced discouragement in his own mind, as it regarded the spoken language. But even in it his progress was not slow; in less than eighteen months he commenced preaching in Chinese. His knowledge of the written language was more satisfactory to himself. In August he wrote several essays, which were published in the Chinese Repository, on the proper Chinese words to be used in translating the name of God into Chinese. These were among the first pieces that were published on the side of the question so ably sustained since by Doctors Boone and Bridgman.

In September he commenced the preparation of a dictionary of the "Four Books," and afterwards he decided to include also the "Five Classics." These books contain the body of the Chinese language, and if his life had been spared, he would, no doubt, have made it a dictionary of the whole language. He became much interested in this work, and had even to guard himself against being drawn aside from his appropriate work of preaching the gospel.

The letters and journals of this period throw much light on the interior working of the mission at Ningpo, and still further tend to elucidate the state and condition of the native population. Other subjects are occasionally adverted to. One of much importance, in relation to the return of missionaries, is noticed in a letter to one of the members of the Executive Committee. It would be out of place here to examine the views there presented; but the whole subject is worthy of far more consideration than it has yet received from the Church at home.

About this time his views on the Millennium underwent a change. After examining the subject, he was led to embrace the opinion that our blessed Lord would personally appear on the earth, before the blessings promised concerning the Church would be fulfilled. His views on the subject, however, conflicted in no degree with the present duty of the Church to preach the gospel to all the world; and that as the Millennium would not come till the gospel was so preached, it was an additional inducement to Christian effort, in tending to hasten the glories of the latter days. He held these views calmly to the last; and when he spoke or wrote on the subject, it was without bitterness, and more with a view to present the spiritual than the controversial aspect of the questions involved.

Ningpo, January 1st, 1846.

A happy New Year to you, my dear mother, and very many of them! is a wish that, if I had the power, would certainly be accomplished; and yet, though I might have the power, I might not have the wisdom necessary to make it a blessing. So I will change it to the prayer, that He who knows what is best for us, and loves us far better than any earthly friend can love another, would give you such length of days, and such enjoyment therein as will make you most useful here, and most blessed hereafter. New Year's morning! Although it be only an arbitrary distinction that makes this day more important than any other of the year, for *each* day is the point of "confluence of two eternities," yet consent has erected it into a sort of elevation to look back over the past, so rapidly fading from view, and to strain our weak eyes into the unknown future. How little we can know of the one, and how feebly we estimate the importance of the other!

Although I always look forward to the New

Year with some such feelings as these, yet it always takes me by surprise, and I find it difficult in looking back to the last one to realize the events that have occurred and passed away. How many events must have occurred in your larger circle of friends! Here, few as are those I know, yet I find strange alterations in the last year. A fellow-passenger in the Huntress (Mr. King) died, and was buried in the Red Sea. One of my warmest friends, Mrs. Sword, has been called home. She was always exceedingly afraid to die, and yet when called away, though fully sensible of it, fear had entirely departed, and peace reigned. It makes me feel desolate sometimes to think of such friends departing, and she is not the only one whom the last year has removed me from, though the others are not dead, but only farther off, and to remember again that I am a stranger in the earth; but then it is pleasant, too, for the separation is but temporary. I have no patience with those stoics who maintain that we shall not know our friends in heaven. Certainly the Spirit of Christ alone would fill our cup of joy even to overflowing, but why should not those who in tears and temptations and prayers served him here, and encouraged each other in the upward course, rejoice with joy unspeakable together there? We shall remember the way by which we were led through this "great and terrible wilderness," and shall we forget the kind words spoken, the cup of water, the look of affection and encouragement more eloquent than words, and more soothing than the sweetest harmony? I do not believe it. Christ said to his disciples that those who had "continued with him in his temptations," should sit with him in his glory, and if we hold communion with Him in this respect, why not with one another? We shall have bodies as well as souls in heaven, "spiritual" it is true, but "bodies" still; we shall have human affections, too, freed from all sin; and if such affections form our sweetest and most satisfying solace here, what will they be there? But I did not mean to write all this, for I was thinking of other things when I commenced.

Here I am, after voyaging and tossing about again on the rough sea. I am now settled down in the field I have long been looking to. I have made some little progress in the language, and begin to feel at home among the people; but shall I remain here? I do not know why it is, but I seem constantly to have a voice saying, "Arise, this is not your rest!" Nor should I be surprised at any time to receive an order to depart. Yet as such feelings are not the rule by which we are to be guided, I endeavour to work on as if this were to be my earthly home; and be my abode long or short, to be in readiness when He comes, whose coming will not tarry.

My teacher has just come in, and knowing that this is our new year, he has been cogitating a salutation for me, which was as follows, *Seen sang, shangte pongdzooe ne taou teendong chèaw*, "Sir, may God assist you and enable you to arrive at heaven!" I was not a little surprised and gratified too, for I never heard him utter such a sentiment before. Oh that the wish, which in politeness he made for me, were fulfilled in reality to him! If he were but a Christian, or if I might but see him one, it seems to me I should almost be ready to depart in peace; for his talents and acquirements are such, that if they were sanctified they would be invaluable. But alas, he is proud of his learning, temporizing in his policy, and averse to know the plague of his own heart. The doctrine of human depravity, he cannot away with; it is a very abomination to him, and after all the instructions he has received, if he repents not, how much greater will be his condemnation! I fear we shall prove a "savour of death unto death," to more than we shall be the means of saving, in this land. . . .

Believe me, as ever, yours in kind remembrances,
And sincere affection, W. M. Lowrie.

Ningpo, April 21st, 1846.

REV. JOHN LLOYD—MY DEAR BROTHER:—It is now near four months since I wrote to you, but you will believe me when I say, that if I have not written I have at least not forgotten you, and often try to remember you, where I trust you remember me, at a throne of grace. I could give you the usual string of apologies; Chinese, reading proofs, keeping accounts, answering letters; but I fear if I did so, it would make you think I was doing a great deal, when in fact weeks pass away and I seem to have done nothing, to have really made no progress, and have to cry out for mercy to the unprofitable servant. How would Calvin, or men of half his mind, smile at the idea of all I do being called work! I fancy that hundreds of men do as much before breakfast as I do in a whole day. I find it a very serious drawback in my study and acquirement of the language, that so much of the best part of my missionary life was spent where the dialect I was studying was not spoken. Although I know more of books than any other here, yet McCartee speaks incomparably better than I do, and both Culbertson and Loomis will probably be preaching before me. What in the world should I do among the "tones" of your delightful dialect? I fancy I should be among them like a certain Presbyterian clergyman, who attempted to conduct the Episcopal service once, and had it reported of him afterwards that "he wandered up and down among the prayers, like a blind man among the tombs."

This reminds me that in your last you speak of our having no tones in this dialect. This is to a great extent, but not entirely, the case. The tones are necessary in some words; but generally speaking, if you get the idiomatic expression, you need not bother your head about the tones; and none of us pay any theoretical attention whatever to their acquisition. It is a pretty good proof of their not being necessary, that the Fuhkeen men, of whom there are many here, cannot learn to speak this dialect well. The remark is often made that "you foreigners speak Ningpo dialect better than the Fuhkeen people;" and imperfect as my acquirements are in speaking, I have been told a dozen times that I pronounce better than the Fuhkeen men. If I could only get among the people, and not see a book or a foreigner for six months or a year, I think there would be some hopes; and I often half wish some person would run away with me, and keep me captive for a while, for otherwise I do not see how I am to get away. Well, all this is egotism, and much of it is nonsense; but I beg you to receive it as a proof how much I care for you, that I let you see such effusions, and how much I do not care for you, or I would not let you see them.

I have just been interrupted by a long talk from a couple of Chinese, who talked so fast that the words came out like a mill-stream, and all I could do was to gather the drift of their discourse and let the particular words vanish into thin air. I wish I could talk as much as I can understand! But patience, perseverance, and prayer! Oh to be kept from growing weary or careless in God's work! I did not feel afraid of this in the first year or two; but now it requires much watchfulness and prayer, lest I become weary or discouraged. You have much reason for thankfulness that you got to your field so soon, and have not quite so many letters to write, as I had during my first two years; but I ought not to complain of them, for it was my appointed work, since the providence of God repeatedly prevented me from taking any other course, and perhaps it was the best on the whole. But as I look over my past life, and especially that part spent in the missionary ground, I have to pray, "pardon the unprofitable, erring, sinful servant!"

It is so late, having been so interrupted by the

conversation above referred to, that I must close my sheet for the night, hoping to be able to finish to-morrow, though I know not when a letter can be sent from here. If the overland route answers, we will try and send in that way.

I think Mr. Smith has led you into a mistake, on the point of the "two dialects." As far as I know, in all parts of China, the written and the colloquial dialects differ so widely as to be really two languages. This is the case here, for Ningpo colloquial cannot be written with Chinese characters. True, many words, perhaps one-half, are the same in the two; but you never can tell from seeing a character in a book whether it can be used in speaking, unless your teacher tells you. *Jin* is spoken *nying; urh tz* is spoken *'ny tz; chay-ko* is spoken *kihko,* while *Jootsze* which is book Mandarin, and *chay-yang* which is colloquial Mandarin, meaning, "so fashion," or "in this way," in one dialect is *sz'-ka-go,* which cannot be written at all, i. e., has no characters to express it; though characters might be arbitrarily employed, which would give the sound. This is the case with hundreds of words in common use.

I was both pleased and surprised to hear how much missionary work is done in Amoy. Would that we could report the half of it here! But except tract distributing, at which we all do a little, there is no preaching excepting by Dr. McCartee, who has a service every Sabbath, and talks to the people frequently during the week. I have tried once or twice, but, like the man who tried to swim before he had been in the water, succeeded so poorly, that I feel afraid to try again. I conduct service with my servants morning and evening, and hope I shall soon be able to set up a meeting which might be called "a parish meeting," i. e., not a regular preaching service, but a preparatory one, which will prepare me for preaching. I have been much thrown back by not having been able to get a teacher on whom I could depend for giving me the colloquial expressions. The one I had for nine months after coming was a capital scholar, but proud, disobliging, or rather unobliging, and took no interest in anything of the kind. After bearing with him till I could bear no longer, I turned him off and got another, who was so stupid that I kept him only a month. Yesterday I got a new one, and he has taken such "strong hold" as quite astonishes me. "A new broom sweeps clean;" but this man is a scholar, appears to be a gentleman, is quite obliging, lively, patient, apt to teach, and on two days' acquaintance I am greatly pleased. I hope he will hold out, but I greatly fear. If he does well, and if he becomes a Christian, Oh, how I should rejoice! With a good teacher, who was a real Christian, I think I might be of very much more use than I am now.

You speak of "feeling as safe as if in New York or Philadelphia." I feel the same here. I live a mile from any foreigner, and have frequently walked two miles through the city after eight or nine o'clock, P. M., without a lantern or any company, with less apprehension than I would go through many parts of New York city. The people here are generally very well behaved, and very civil.

As to mandarins, we see none of them; we do not visit them, and are not visited by them. The English consul has discouraged visiting, and foreigners, except officers, seldom go near them. There is a white-buttoned one whom Dr. McCartee and I have called on, and been called on by; and last year we had frequent calls from travelling mandarins with gilt and white buttons, who came to see the strangers; but of late I have seen none, and do not feel any anxiety to meet them. You get in with them at Amoy, because of the important fact that Abeel and Boone and Cummings have had to act as interpreters, when there were none but missionaries to interpret, and as the mandarins of course know of no difference between you and others, they keep up the acquaintance.

We are all moving on very quietly and pleasantly. The weather is getting pleasantly warm, but even yet I like to sit with my fur coat on in the mornings and evenings, and have as yet laid aside neither flannels nor woollen stockings. It has rained almost every day this month, and in consequence of so much rain now, and the probability of very little next month, when it will be much wanted, fears of a scarcity of rice prevail, and it is already rising in price. As to ships, there has not been one here, except men of war, since last August. I do not know how we are to get our funds after Chusan is given up. Our letters we shall manage to get overland from Shanghai.

We have bought a *burying-ground* here, about one hundred feet by fifty, for fifty dollars. Abraham's first possession in the land where he was a stranger, was a burying-ground.

Your brother in Christ.

W. M. Lowrie.

Ningpo, July 9th, 1846.

My Dear Father—Your two most acceptable letters of November, 1845, and February, 1846, came, one in the end of May, and the other to-day. I cannot tell you how much I am obliged for your good long letters: the journals of your trips to Washington and to Albany, were deeply interesting. I wish I could give you an account of half as much done by myself, but all my performances seem to me of small account. Here is a specimen of to-day's employment. Rose before six. Our nights are warm, and following on warmer days, I do not derive the refreshment from them that I could wish. After breakfast and prayers, went over the river to see after the printing office, got a proof to correct, and came back; it was ten o'clock when I got home, and thermometer then at 90°; sat down with my teacher and went over Acts xvii., on which he wrote comments by my explanations. Then read some in Mencius, and looked over some points in Chinese history, and some notices of two or three of their sages. By this time it was one o'clock, and the thermometer had risen to 98° in my coolest room. I was pretty well tired, and told my teacher that was enough for to-day; came up stairs, corrected the proof for the press, and finished the first draught of a letter, one of a series which I am preparing for the Foreign Missionary. This and dinner kept me till three o'clock; all this time the thermometer at blood heat; and though a pleasant breeze blowing, yet coming in at times as if out of a furnace. I have never known such warm weather since I have been in China, and it so relaxes the whole system, that a very little labour is quite sufficient to lay a man by. At three I felt so tired that I lay down, and between reading a little and dozing, whiled away the time till five; then got up, found it a little cooler, sat in the breeze and read an account of the synod of Dort till six. Went out then for a walk; went through a number of streets, and found everybody out of doors, men all half naked, and many of the children entirely so, and the heat given out from the stones and houses so great as to be very oppressive. This, and the foul odours arising from the filth common to every Chinese city, were such that I was glad to get on the city wall, and turn my steps homeward. Somewhat of a breeze on the wall, and getting to my own house about sunset, I sat down to enjoy it. Presently a man came along and seemed anxious to say something; so he asked if I would take a smoke. I told him, no, I did not smoke, and asked him to sit down. Then he asked how old I was. Where I came from. Where I lived, &c. &c. By this time others came, one, two, five, ten, and soon there were about fifty persons collected to see and hear the Hungnan-nying, (Red-haired man, as they call all Englishmen.) Asked a good many questions, and in the course of the talk, gave me an opportunity of saying several things very pointedly about the folly of idolatry, the importance of attending to one's soul, and the way of salvation through Christ. Speaking of Jesus, one of the men remarked that he supposed Jesus was much such a person as Confucius. "No, Confucius was only a man, but Christ was far superior to men." Was listened to with as much attention and interest as I have been at any time, and found it gave me some access to them, when they found that I had read and could give the sense of their own books. There was one man there from Shangtung, but I could understand very little of what he said. He seemed, however, to have no difficulty in understanding all I said, and seemed much interested. Gave away some tracts; gave a copy of "The Two Friends" to one whose appearance had pleased me. He looked at it and asked if all I had were alike, and begged for a copy of another kind. Came away, all of them giving me a hearty *good-bye*, and one or two joining their hands and thanking me for the books and doctrine. Came back home, got my tea, and sat down to this letter, which I suppose will take all the rest of the evening. The thermometer is now down to 91°. I am sitting in a thin grass-cloth suit, and feeling comparatively comfortable after the hot day.

In some of my previous letters, I have probably given you to understand that I was much discouraged about learning to speak this language. This arose in a measure from the unfaithfulness of a teacher whom I employed after coming here. For a while I learned a good deal, and as he was a capital scholar, I wanted to keep him. But after being with me a few months he found out what words I knew, and would use no others, so that during the last four months I had him, I scarcely learned a new phrase. I disliked to turn him off, because in some things he suited me admirably, being good at explaining the classics, and besides he was poor: but at last I could endure it no longer. It was then nearly two months before I could get a good teacher. If I could go about as some others can, I should be less dependent on a teacher, but my disposition does not lead me to delight in promiscuous company; and somehow I have the knack of getting a large share of the writing, book-keeping, proof-correcting, &c., of the mission into my hands, which gives me less time than I could wish for visiting and going about. However, I have been favoured in getting a first-rate teacher, and have gained so much in the last two months as quite encourages me; and it is my present expectation (Deo volente) to commence a regular religious service in Chinese when the warm weather is over. I might do it now, but prefer not undertaking what would necessarily require a good deal of labour in preparation, until the present oppressive season is past; and in the mean time, go about a little and talk as I did to-night, which is a help in perfecting my pronunciation, and enabling me to speak without embarrassment. In the course of the present year, I hope we shall have several of our number actively employed in preaching.

. . . I quite agree with you in the general principle, that a wife should not always take her husband home. Still in many cases, a wife *cannot* go alone. Dr. and Mrs. H—— (of the London Missionary Society) went home last year on account of her health, and she died before she got to England. Mrs. J. S—— went *without* her husband, and took her children; (five or six, one very young;) she died on the voyage. I have not heard how the children got home. It is this that makes it so difficult for a woman to go alone. Few missionaries have left China of late for their health, till they were well nigh broken down, and it requires no small resolution to send off a sick wife on a long voyage, especially if she have children to take care of. What is to be done? For a while I was tempted to wish that missionaries could live without wives; but after more experience and reflection, I am satisfied that all men cannot receive this saying. Even if unmarried men could be contented and happy, yet there are other, and serious objections. I have seen more than one or two cases in which I thought the bachelor missionary, merry and cheerful as he professed to be, would have been not simply a happier man, but a more humane, thoughtful, sober, useful missionary, and a far better example to the heathen, if he had been married; and where example is of such vital importance as it is here, whatever conduces to render it better, is not to be overlooked. . . . .

Your affectionate and obedient son,

W. M. Lowrie.

Ningpo, August 10th, 1846.

Rev. John C. Lowrie—My Dear Brother:—. . . I heard of Mr. Dod's death, but had not heard of Mrs. P.'s. How many gaps there are already in the circle of my acquaintances at home! You will not perceive it so much as you are constantly making new ones, but mine are only decreasing: so be it. "I am a stranger in the earth," and never so happy as when I feel it most.

This has been an oppressingly hot summer. I will send you a notice of it soon. I doubt whether you saw the equal of it in India. For days together we have had the thermometer up to 100°, but most providentially, it always fell 12° or 14° at night. June, July, and the first week of this month were *roasters;* but the worst is over now, and it felt quite delicious to-day when the thermometer got up only to 88½°. Then we have had a drought all summer; rumours of poisoning; alarms of evil spirits, and an earthquake, a veritable earthquake, which shook the houses right merrily, and wakened every man, woman and child in Ningpo. Such screaming! and beating of gongs! and firing of crackers! I will send you accounts of all these presently. I have them all in my journal. The earthquake was on the 4th instant, about three o'clock, A. M. It did no harm, but it frightened the people terribly, especially as they were then under extreme alarm, from a panic occasioned by the belief that there are thousands of evil spirits bent on mischief in the city. With all the melancholy arising from seeing them so wholly given up to such superstition, it is yet most ludicrous to see what tales they can invent. The panic is dying away now, but when we found the people giving credence to such tales, we began to fear that evil might come out of it. There is no joke in it, however, for Mr. and Mrs. Loomis have just come over from Chusan, not being allowed to remain there, and can get no house here, on account of the panic and fear of evil spirits, which are supposed to have some connection with foreigners. . . .

Pray for me, and believe me ever,

Your affectionate brother,

W. M. LOWRIE.

Ningpo, August 26th, 1846.

MY DEAR FATHER—. . . . Our excessive hot weather is now over, and though the days are sometimes warm, the nights are delightful, and we are all in the enjoyment of excellent health. My appetite and strength are returning rapidly, and the summer, notwithstanding my fears in June, has been the most comfortable I have spent in China. I have not done much for two months past, however, for it is really too much labour to study or work with the thermometer at blood-heat.

Of late, I have been busily engaged in collating notes and quotations, on the proper word for expressing the name of the Supreme Being, in Chinese. The weight of authority, i. e., most of the most learned missionaries, have given their influence in favour of using *Shang-te*, but many others dislike the term exceedingly, as being the proper name of the chief Chinese god; and when we use it, the people at once say, "oh yes, that's our Shang-te." I have satisfied myself pretty well that *Shin* is the proper word to use. . . . If this word is adopted, it will then become almost necessary to use the word *Poo sa* in colloquial, though many have taken up a strange prejudice against the word, as if it meant an idol, and was a contemptuous or dishonourable term. Nothing can be more contrary to the fact, and I have found myself in my efforts to talk to the people, almost compelled to use it, there being no other term in the language which expresses so well and so intelligibly, what we mean by God. It is a little troublesome in preparing articles of this kind, not to have the proper books at hand for reference. My library is, I believe, the best in Ningpo, (unless Mr. T—— has a better, which I doubt,) but I found it quite insufficient for my wants, as I know of several books which would have materially helped me, but had them not.

Everything goes on very pleasantly and harmoniously in the mission; but the great things, life, and vigour, and zeal, are lamentably wanting. How easy it is, even for the missionary, to seek for pleasure in everything but in God. I am often cast down, and sometimes deeply discouraged, to find in me so little love for my Saviour, and so little disposition to active exertion. Instead of coming nearer and nearer, and being more conformed to God, I seem to be going farther and farther away. I trust that no one else here is so low or so useless as I often feel myself to be. The sense of my own worthlessness often makes me unwilling to send for such things in the way of books as I need, (and there is very little else that I feel any want of,) and even unwilling to receive all the kind presents and letters that are sent to me. Oh, for more purity, and zeal, and love—to be like Christ! Do not cease to pray for my spiritual well-being.

Believe me as ever, your affectionate son,

W. M. LOWRIE.

Ningpo, September 3d, 1846.

MY DEAR MOTHER—The clock has struck eleven, and I ought to be in bed, but I feel as if I wanted to write to you, though I do not know that I have much to say. I was writing a sermon this evening to preach on the next Sabbath, for I still write sermons occasionally, and getting it finished before eight o'clock, I was a little at a loss to know what to do, for I did not feel like reading or studying after that. So I took out a package containing the letters received from father and you, during the first two years of my life in China. Getting interested, I kept at them till nearly eleven o'clock, and then felt as if I wanted to thank you more heartily than I had ever done for all your affection, and sympathy, and kindness to me. Of course I could not read them all over, but I glanced over each, and read parts of them, and many a tear fell as I recalled the scenes through which I had passed, and your deep sympathies with me. It is good to weep sometimes, and I often wish I could weep more over my own sinfulness and uselessness. It is nearly five years since I have seen you; sometimes I catch myself asking, "Shall I see you again?" and then again, "But how is it possible?" I was discouraged a few months ago, for fear I never would learn this language, but for the last seven months I have made such progress that I should be loath on any account to leave this field of labour. I think now my prospects of acquiring a pretty thorough and extensive knowledge of it are quite fair; and if so, then here is my field, and here would I gladly labour, and die.

Yet if I may be of a little use here, it will abundantly repay me; and at present I can conceive of scarcely anything that would be so painful as to go back to the United States without an unmistakable call to do so. It does seem to me as if I could not do it. How much of this may be from a desire to preserve my reputation, I will not pretend to say, but among other motives, I trust that of preaching Christ to these poor idolaters is not the least. How wretched is their condition! I stood at my window the other day, and saw an idolatrous procession go by, till my heart asked, "Oh, Lord, how long?"

But I am wandering from my purpose, which was more immediately to tell you how I felt in recalling the trials and events of the first few months of my life out in China. Somehow, they seem to have happened much longer ago than is really the case. Most of them seem to have occurred ten years ago; and I sometimes think of them as if they had happened to another person. How much goodness and mercy were mingled with them all! I was much struck, too, in reading your letters, to notice how many that I knew when with you are already dead. Some that were careless then, are pious now. Changes, breaking up, and settling down:—I am more at home here than I should be in the United States.

I am commonly very happy, all but in one thing; I have so little grace. Pray for me. It is a hard thing to keep the flame of piety burning bright when the sickening blasts of idolatry blow on the soul, and there are few to speak of Christ. He came once, and though he came to suffer and to die, yet even then the "groaning creation" was on tip-toe to receive him. The winds heard his voice, the waves became solid beneath his feet, the fish came at his command, the tree shook down its leaves when he spoke. Good angels hovered near, and devils fled at his word. If all this happened when he came to be "a servant," what will it be when he comes "to reign?" and we shall reign with him.

Yes, for ever and ever. "So shall we be ever with the Lord." It makes me wonder, how can he condescend so low? how is it possible we can be lifted up so high? But "fear not, little flock, it is your Father's good pleasure to give you the kingdom." It is his "good pleasure," and so we shall have it. If it were our "good deeds," we might despair. Thanks be unto God for his unspeakable gift.

I do not write so much and so freely as I used to; and I sometimes fear you may think I am forgetting, or losing my affection for you; but it is not so. I have more to do than I used to have, though I do not seem to accomplish much, and it is often of such a kind as indisposes me for the free and easy letters I would like to write. But nothing brings tears more easily to my eyes than to recall past hours with you, and I sometimes seem to live them over again. Well! here is the last corner of the sheet, and though I have not said much, yet it seems like a relief to say even this, disjointed as it is. It is nearly midnight,—high noon with you. How often is it so in life! Bright noon and joy with one, and perhaps his dearest friend at the same moment in midnight gloom, but the Sun is still in his place, as bright and cheering as ever; and "when I awake, I am still with thee." I presume you know my meaning. I have not space to enlarge it, and so write here

Ever affectionately yours,

W. M. Lowrie.

Ningpo, September 15th, 1846.

My Dear Father— . . . . You will unite with us in thanksgiving, that we have been permitted to receive a Chinese, a native of this place, into the church. He was for a long time, eight or ten months, under pretty constant instruction and examination, and gave us every satisfaction before being admitted to the church. He is employed by Miss Aldersey, who has been very faithful to him in teaching him.

. . . . I got my head full of a notion of preparing a Dictionary of the Four Books the other day, and may perhaps try to make something out of it. There is no existing dictionary by which a Chinese student can read even the Four Books with satisfaction. Morrison's is the best. My plan would be to make a Dictionary, 1st. Of all the words in the Four Books, about 2500: this would be the great body of characters used in the language—Dyer's list having only 3500. 2d. To give all the meanings of each word that occurs in the Four Books, which, as they are the foundation of the literature of China, would be by much the greater part of the important definitions needed. 3d. To give pretty full biographical notices of all the persons, and notices also of the places mentioned in the Four Books: this would give nearly everything that is important in ancient Chinese history. The above is the better half of what I have cut out. To do it, without interfering with my more direct and more important missionary labours, would require between two and three years. Should this plan succeed, I might afterwards try my hand at a more important and ambitious effort, i. e., a Dictionary of the language; but this is so vast an undertaking, that at present I have little idea of trying it. The Dictionary of the Four Books I think I can manage, and it would be an important contribution towards a general dictionary. I have not spoken of it to any one, and do not wish to do so, as so many things may interfere, but I should be very glad to get all the assistance possible in it, even if only for my own advancement. I should like to get the translations published at Paris and Berlin. I do not know where the money is to come from for all these, but if you can manage to get them for me, or for the mission, all the same; I should be very glad. I hope you will not say I am engaged in any such work, for I am not yet so committed to it that I feel myself bound to continue it, even to myself; and if I did commence it, I would not want it known, till I was in a situation not to fear the reproach of beginning without counting the cost.

I have been a good deal encouraged of late in my hopes of learning the language, and if God spares my life, and gives me health, I think there is a reasonable prospect of my becoming a tolerably thorough scholar. My early education, for which, under God, I am most indebted to you, gives me some qualifications for it, which, I trust it is not vanity alone tells me, are not possessed by all those who have gone before me to this field. . . . .

Ever your affectionate son, W. M. LOWRIE.

Ningpo, December 9th, 1846.

JAMES LENOX, ESQ.—MY DEAR SIR:—Your letter of April 20th has been lying by me for some three months, a longer period than usually elapses before I answer letters; but my time has been much occupied with writing appointed me by the mission, and with the preparation of my weekly Chinese discourses, which take much of the time that I once gave to correspondents.

I am exceedingly obliged for your kindness in regard to the books. On several occasions we have been very glad to have some at hand; and I have no doubt they have been a means of doing good, by being put in the hands of persons who would otherwise have had few or no religious books near them.

I do not think the books for the blind would be of service here. They are, of course, in the English language, and it could hardly be considered a profitable employment for us to turn from the multitudes around us, and spend time in teaching a few blind persons to read a strange language. One or two at each station, as a curiosity, and to show the Chinese the comprehensive benevolence of Christian society, which regards even the dumb and the blind, would doubtless be interesting. My teacher was exceedingly astonished the other day, when I showed him a hymn for the blind, which I happened to have, in raised letters. The idea had never occurred to him before. I fear it would be impossible to adapt it to the Chinese language. Even with "the skin burnt off," the fingers could not appreciate the fine lines of our many thousands of characters. They are trying enough even to the eyes.

I have been trying to teach my teacher lessons in music, partly with a view of finding thereby what are their ideas of music; but the experiment has not been very successful, partly, no doubt, because I know so little of music myself. I wish (when will wishes end?) that we had some missionaries here, who were adepts in musical composition, to study the nature of Chinese music, improve it, and compose tunes suited to Chinese poetry. It seems to me rather incongruous to tack Ortonville, Old Hundred, &c., tunes composed for English words, to Chinese poetry. In Luther's judgment, music composed for Latin poems was unsuited to German verse; and if so, foreign music must be still more unfit for Chinese verse. But I feel at present comparatively little interest in singing Chinese poetry, from the fact that it is so utterly unintelligible to the mass of the people. This language, I mean as written, is one of the greatest possible barriers to the spread of the gospel here. I may be mistaken, but to me the conclusion seems irresistible, that till a change as great as that which came over the languages of Europe at the Reformation, comes over this language, it will be unfit for the extensive dissemination of truth among the mass of the people;—I mean, of course, the written language. We can now preach the gospel in the spoken language; but the spoken language is not a written language; and thus, as far as the mass of the people are concerned, we have no means of reaching them, except by the living preacher, or such of their own educated people as may feel interest enough in our books to explain them to the people. Why not write the spoken language? It may be done, but not in a day, nor in a year. I hope to see a beginning made in my day, but it must come gradually, and against strong opposition and contempt from the literati of the country. We think of preparing some books, or rather sheet tracts, in the colloquial language of this province; and, as a means of making them attractive, in spite of the contempt of the people for what seems to them so low, we want to have them illustrated with pictures. Pictures are like the corks which hold a man up in the water oftentimes; at least, many a book is read at home for the sake of the pictures, and there is no reason why it should not be so here; and we shall soon make an application to the Committee to send us out a good supply of the pictures of birds, beasts, utensils, and various figures, prepared by type-founders, which are precisely what we want; and I feel disposed to speak for your vote in the Committee beforehand. Some might laugh at the idea of sending such things to a mission-station; but really, a picture of a steamboat, or rail-road car, with a suitable description, or pictures of the costumes and customs of different countries, with short accounts of them, would do more to arouse a spirit of inquiry, and awaken the dormant mind of this people, than a person at home, accustomed from infancy to such things, could well imagine. Such a book as the New England Primer, well translated into the colloquial dialects of this country, and with good pictures, would be a national blessing. The book would be eagerly taken and read for the sake of the pictures. It may be said, this is treating the Chinese like children; but the fact is, the wisest of them are ignorant of things which every child knows at home; and amidst all the diversity of talents which we require, and can employ here, scarcely any is better than aptness to be an "instructor of babes."

....Much as the return of missionaries is deplored by our friends at home, it can hardly be felt by you so much as it is by us; its effects here are almost always more sensibly felt than at home. Our little number diminished, men of experience taken away, the remaining parties discouraged; the heathen, judging from one, that all are equally uncertain to remain, and hence feeling less interest in us; are only a part of the difficulties. But has the question ever been fairly studied and looked at, at home? It is felt that something is wrong, but who knows where to lay the blame? or where to apply the remedy? A thought has often occurred to me, which yet I feel some delicacy in expressing. The difficulty, or one difficulty is, that the Church expects of the missionary what the mass of church-members would not do themselves. Now it is hard for the stream to rise higher than the fountain; and missionaries generally possess very little, if any more piety than Christians at home. It does seem unreasonable for those who stay at home, and know comparatively little of the pains of separation from friends, of loneliness and isolation among the heathen, to say to their missionaries, "Good brethren, go; and the blessing of God go with you. We will support you, and pray for you, (?) and think of you, and read your letters;—*but do not come back here.* If you do, it must be at the risk of losing much of your influence, and being thought to be tired of your work, and you had better not come." Doubtless, many of the best friends of missions would be far from using such language, and yet if I am not mistaken, it is the feeling of the mass. It is a serious question whether those who use such language, or feel such sentiments, are entitled to use it; or whether they should not, first, pluck out the beam before they spy the mote. Now it strikes me that it would be better to say, "Go brethren, and labour faithfully, and as long as you can. We will do our part. We do not expect, and we do not wish, you to forget your father land. You have the feelings of men and women, of sons and daughters, and it is natural and right, that you should at times long for Christian intercourse with the great congregation, and the family fireside. Should these feelings become strong in you, we shall not interfere with your once more visiting your aged parents; but shall welcome you among your friends, and endeavour to fit you to go forth again with renewed vigour to your work. Only remember you are the Lord's, and may not needlessly or extravagantly use his time, even for objects so sacred, as cultivating the kindlier feelings of your hearts." Some such language as this, expresses the feeling I would like to see among the churches. My meaning is, that it ought to be understood and allowed, and in many cases approved, that a missionary, after a certain time, should have the right to return home on a visit. The Church ought not to require *exile*, as many seem disposed to do. I am satisfied that to have it understood on all hands, that a man had a right to see once more, those whom he cannot but long to see, would have no tendency to increase the number of returns home. It would make most men and women better contented to stay and labour ten years, if they felt that at the end of that time there would be no obstacle to a visit home if desired. And a person who had spent ten years in heathen land, would not, after that, want to leave it finally, if he had the smallest portion of true missionary spirit. If he did, it would probably be better that he should. It seems to me, that the prospect of a cheerful visit home would encourage many a man to labour on, and to form his plans for life here, who might be appalled by the idea of a lifetime, unrelieved by any such prospect; nor do I see how the mass of Christians can object to this, without either condemning themselves for their own want of self-denial, or else requiring of their missionaries to renounce many of the finest feelings of their nature.

In the English army in India, the officers are allowed after ten years' service, three years' furlough; and after twenty years, to retire finally. I should be sorry to see the latter regulation applied to our warfare; but at present it strikes me, that the privilege of a visit home, after every ten years of service, for a much less period than three years, would be a saving both of men and money in the missionary cause. There are some who would not embrace it; most persons probably would. It would make their first ten years pass more pleasantly away, and it would revive them bodily, and mentally, and *spiritually*, for the next ten years; and at the end of twenty years, if they wanted to leave the missionary field it would probably be for sufficient reasons.

Believe me, my dear sir, very truly yours, in Christian bonds, W. M LOWRIE.

Ningpo, September 13th, 1846.

TO THE REV. JOHN LLOYD—DEAR BROTHER JOHN:—You will judge from the date of this letter (Sabbath evening), that it is not to be about everything under the sun. I do not know how it strikes every person, but occasionally I like to spend a part of the Sabbath evening in Christian conversation with an absent friend, and I do not know that it is more improper to converse with pen and ink, than by word of mouth. . . . Your note of July 1st, inclosing a letter from J. M. L., came two days ago, and your note of Aug. 27th, reached me this morning. . . . In several notes you have spoken of a wish to be near me. I heartily wish it could be so, but I fear you would find only a very weak and bruised reed to lean on, if you expected any good from me. You would not expect much if you knew me better. God is showing me of late in a very painful way that in myself I am nothing,—can do nothing, and am utterly sinful and vile; and the way he shows it is by leaving me to myself, to walk on in my Christian course, and to do my duties without any sensible support of his grace; and the consequence is, that I am very low. Oh, how many bitter things I write against myself! but the worst is, my utter deadness—no life or delight in prayer, the Scriptures, or meditation. What dreadful things these hearts of ours are! It amazes me to think that God can be gracious to people naturally so vile, and who sin so grievously after conversion. I preached a week ago on the prodigal son's departing from his father's house. I felt the subject a good deal myself, and several of the little audience were in tears; but alas, I do not seem to have "come back" yet. To-day was our communion, but I found little or no benefit. There has been much strangeness between God and my soul for many months past, and often a great reluctance to close and faithful dealing with myself. So dead that I have lost the savour of spiritual things, and the perception of the beauties of the Bible, and seldom draw nigh unto God. I seem to satisfy myself with very faint services. Oh to be revived! and yet this lazy heart would be revived without effort on my own part. Awake, thou that sleepest! Alas! I am so soon wearied in my efforts. Like the little flying-fish, but a moment up, and then back in the troubled waters of this heaving, restless world. Oh Lord God, give me wings, and enable me to breathe the pure and spiritual atmosphere of heaven. I find myself by nature diseased by sin, which, like the leprosy, affects my whole frame. Yea, "the plague is in his head." Yea, the "whole head is sick, and the whole heart faint;" and thus I neither properly appreciate, nor comprehend spiritual things, nor feel them aright; therefore I am unclean, separated from the society of the holy, dwelling without the precincts where the people of God's love are. How deep should be my sorrow, and self-loathing, and abasement! and how should I come to him whose word can cleanse.—Lev. xiii. 44–46.

But I trust I am one of God's people, and yet even this is but renewed reason for humiliation. "My people have committed two evils." "Forsaken God, the fountain of living waters;" what greater despite, contempt, unbelief, and sin, than this? And "hewn out broken cisterns which can hold no water." How true is this! It is so with me. Made for God; heart disquieted till it rests in him; and yet unwilling to come to him; and on the contrary, seeking rest in creatures! Well may heaven and earth be astonished at this!—Jer. ii. 12, 13.

I trust I have not wholly forsaken God's service, but there is small comfort in this. It has been with but half a heart that I have served him. I have sought happiness in my study, books, correspondence, business, friends; and with a half heart to them and a half heart to God, how miserably have I gone on! Oh Lord, unite my heart to fear thy name! Psalm lxxxvi. 11. It is impossible to serve God if the whole heart be not his. If with a half heart, then as good none at all. Thus with my half heart I have fallen asleep, and am become dead. Oh let me now awake, and arise from the dead, and may he who is the light of the world give me light! Eph. v. 14. None but he can do it. Blessed Jesus, raise me to thyself and shine into my heart with the light of the knowledge of the glory of God, of which I now know so little. 2 Cor. iv. 6. Let me rise with thee, and being risen, let me seek those things which are above where thou sittest, Col. iii. 1. I have too often forgotten that he who is risen with Christ, must still seek and labour. Oh let me forget it no more, and thus labouring and believing, praying and trusting, I beseech thee show me thy glory. Ex. xxxiii. 18; xxxiv. 6, 7.

You will ask, why do I live thus? Because, I am "sold under sin," and "the good I would I do not." I know I ought to do it, and am guilty for not doing it. "Oh, wretched man that I am, who shall deliver me from this body of death?" Jesus Christ our head? Yes, but there is the worst of it. Like the prodigal departing from his father, I have gone away from Christ, and therefore have no life. Pray for me. I will continue this strain no longer.

We have much reason for gratitude in not being left entirely destitute of a blessing here. As many as three persons have hopefully experienced a change of heart here during the past year. One of these is Azin, Miss Aldersey's Chinese servant, a native of this place, who was baptized to-day. He has been inquiring for nearly a year, and after a very satisfactory examination, was received by the Session into the Church. God be praised for this! Oh for more! There are others who sometimes give us hopes, but we are often grievously disappointed. My servant seems to be somewhat serious, but I dare not hope that any real impression has been made on his mind. I think my teacher thinks more than he is willing to admit, but I have as yet no hopes of him. What a dreadful thing a backwardness to speak on religious topics is! There is no one thing that has troubled me in all my intercourse so much as this. No duty I find so hard to perform, or which I oftener fail in attending to. Nothing has caused me to doubt my piety so much as this one thing, and now I almost despair of ever overcoming it. "Out of the abundance of the heart the mouth speaketh," but if I am judged by this rule, I shall stand very low. I am glad others are not so deficient in it as I am.

Monday, 14th. Your summer has been very cool, and ours excessively hot. Such hot weather, *and so long*, I have never known. After having the thermometer up to 98° and 100° every day for six weeks, it was quite a luxury to find it rising no higher than 88° and 90.° It is now, however, and has been for three weeks, very pleasant, and has been down as low as 74° at night, now generally below 80° at night, and even at the warmest there was always a fall of 10° to 15° at night. I do not think we could have lived through it if it had not been for this.

Walsh, at Mynpurie, speaks of 122° *in the sun*, as very hot. We have had it much higher than that in the sun here; but in India the hot weather lasts much longer than it does here.

Why do we never see your *lucubrations* in the Chronicle, or Foreign Missionary? A man who holds as ready a pen as you do, is bound to let it speak *pro bono publico*. Tell Brother Brown I am very glad he has commenced at the right end, and I hope he will keep on.

I am engaged of late in preparing a report on the word to be used in speaking the name of God. We are pretty unanimous here in disapproving of the word Shang-te, as it is perpetually confounded with the Chinese idol of the same name. I believe we are all in favour of Shin, and I have been quite surprised at the amount of authority, I mean from the Chinese classics, in favour of its use. What words do you use? and how do they take with the people? I would like much to hear what your custom is.

Believe me, ever yours, in the gospel and ministry of Christ, W. M. LOWRIE.

Ningpo, December 31st, 1846.

REV. JOHN C. LOWRIE—MY DEAR BROTHER:—Your truly welcome letter of June 22d, came to hand to-day. I know not why it was so long on the road. A letter from another person in New

York, written on the same day, reached me six weeks ago. But we have to submit to some inconvenience up here about our correspondence.

By God's grace I am preaching, though it be with stammering lips, and my prospects of mastering the language are now so fair that I would be very unwilling to leave this mission. I am, therefore, satisfied and anxious to remain; and my present feeling, which indeed has almost always been my feeling, is not to leave unless the Committee, who took the responsibility of sending me to China, will take the responsibility of sending me away. I am glad and happy to be here. It is true I am lonely, sometimes very lonely, but this loneliness is appointed to me by Him who knows better than I do what is best for me. I have not sought it, nor run into it rashly, and in due season it will be diminished; or if not, then it is best that it be so, and I will, if not gladly, at least resignedly, or if not resignedly, at least praying to be resigned, confess myself a stranger and a pilgrim on the earth.

The clock strikes twelve, P. M., and 1847 has begun. I have disobeyed your injunction; but, in the first place, it is very seldom that this happens. I am almost always in bed before eleven. Second, I was anxious to write as much of this letter as possible, for it must be closed to-morrow or next day. I must confess I did not mean to spin it out so long. Third, I do not disapprove of seeing the New Year in, and commencing it with prayer. I wish you, and yours, a happy New Year.

I am always interested in the accounts of your church, and pray for a blessing on it. If you are ever "disheartened" with any among the people you have to deal with, just fancy what kind of congregations *I* have. I will try and give you a peep at one, some of these days, and you will not dare to say a word after that. That leads me to ask, how much *egotism* is allowable occasionally in articles for the Chronicle? I could write an article now, on preaching to a heathen audience, which might surprise and edify some of your readers, and give them juster views of the real nature of missionary work, than fifty Tabernacle speeches. I am not boasting, for I grieve over a vast many speeches about missions that are published; they are well meant, but all wrong. But to give such an article, I must enter into my own feelings pretty deeply, and write just as I would talk to you, or any other dear friend, and the little pronoun "I" must come forward pretty often. This is rather hazardous; some really humble men, like Brother Sawyer, could do it very well; but there are very few who can do it. Yet really, as far as I can see, such relations of one's own experience are among the most interesting and profitable articles; for many a man, if he has only the right spirit, may write an article of that kind well, who, if he attempted to write an edifying article on general principles, would soon become very dull. . . .

Your affectionate brother,

W. M. Lowrie.

JOURNAL AT NINGPO.

June 11th. There has been some talk of poisoning of late in a district about a hundred miles from Ningpo, and some placards have been sent here and pasted up in conspicuous places, warning the people not to take up articles of food that may be found in the streets, lest they should contain poison. To-day my servant came in great trepidation, and said he had heard people say that a man in the city, having eaten a cake, became suddenly ill, and his body becoming black all over, he soon died. This has aroused suspicion that the poisoners are abroad here. In consequence of this, some persons have had a large number of the above mentioned placards printed off here and distributed about. This is considered a very meritorious act, though almost the only effect it can have, will be to create a panic terror among the people.

June 12th. The talk of poisoning is more general than ever; and a man having been taken sick after eating a cake bought in a shop, the shopkeeper was taken before the mayor of the city, and sentenced to be beaten with forty strokes of the bamboo. This was chiefly to pacify the people, for many say that even if the cake was the cause of the sickness, there is no proof that it was not left in the shop by some evil-minded person without the knowledge of the shopman. Among a multitude of reports that are flying about, for the people are fairly panic-stricken, is one which says that about one hundred persons have lost their lives in Seaou-shan, and another, that a Buddhist priest there being detected, or at least suspected of being concerned in the nefarious business, was seized by the people and on examination was found to have cakes and rolls, and drugs of various kinds concealed about his person. In all probability the whole affair is a panic.

The summer of 1846 is likely to be long memorable in Ningpo, on account of the many calamities, some real and some imaginary, with which it was accompanied. The year has been fruitful in terrors, and some were so wide-spread that it was impossible to collect all the facts, or a tenth part of the reports concerning them. Some of us heard one set of stories, and some another, and even contradictory statements, which must account for some of the discrepancies between the following sketch and some others that you may have seen.

The month of April was distinguished by a season of unusually rainy weather. There were but one or two fair days in the whole month, and most of the time the rain fell in torrents. It is in the month of April that the rice is transplanted, and though some rain is required for this purpose, a superabundance is a great evil, which was the case this year. In consequence of the rain, the officers of the city, about the middle of the month, appointed sacrifices, and, by way of further propitiation, ordered that for the space of seven days no swine should be slaughtered for food. This is called the *Kin-too*, or prohibition of slaughtering, and is frequently resorted to in times of distress. But their miserable idols did not hear their prayers, and, as a last resort, about the end of the month, some of them were put out in the rain! The rain ceased soon after this, and the people continued mad on their idols.

During the month of May but little rain fell, and the weather became rather warm, though not oppressively so. The summer of 1845 had been so mild and pleasant that we did not think of the weather becoming unusually hot this year. But the months of June, July, and August, were dreadfully hot. None of us had before experienced such long-continued hot weather. During the three years that I was in Macao, although that place is eight degrees farther south than this, and in the torrid zone, the thermometer never rose so high as it did here day after day.

From the experience of the past summer, we have been completely convinced that good houses are indispensable to health in this climate. We are at present all living in Chinese houses, which are not made for constitutions like ours. The low rooms and thin roofs and walls, are miserable defences against the heat of such burning suns. It is true we are not likely to have many summers so hot as the past, for even the natives spoke of it as "extraordinarily hot;" but we shall have them occasionally, and houses built under our own inspection, might be so arranged as to diminish much of their oppressiveness.

Next added to the oppressiveness of the heat, was the fearful drought. I have spoken of the abundant rains of April. They were followed by a four months' drought, which, like Pharaoh's lean kine, devoured up every remembrance of the preceding rains. During the months of May, June, July, and August, but one copious shower fell; and most of the time the heavens over us were as brass, and the earth as powder and dust beneath our feet. Clouds sometimes sailed over our heads, or gathered on the hills around the city, and sometimes the thunder and a few drops of rain excited our hopes, but they passed away again, and more than once I have heard natives of the place say, as they saw them disappear: *Teen puh kung lo yu*,—"Heaven is unwilling to drop rain." Vegetation suffered exceedingly. The deepest canals were drained dry in the vain attempt to supply the wants of the growing rice-crops. The canals being dry, the internal navigation of the country was in great measure stopped. Deep anxiety sat on many faces. Public processions were appointed in honour of the gods, and the officers of the city, on two or three separate occasions issued the *Kin-too*, which was at last observed so rigidly, that for nearly a month a pound of pork could be obtained only by stealth and previous arrangement.

"When shall we have rain?" It assumes a very serious aspect, now that for so long a time we have had none.

As if the real evils of the heat and drought were not enough, the people added others from their own folly and superstitions. I have already spoken of the alarm caused by the report of poisoners. This foolish story gradually died away during the month of July, but was succeeded by another equally appalling, of which the following extracts, entered in my journal at the time, will give some account:

August 1, 1846. There has been no little excitement here for a few days past, on account of a supposed visitation of evil spirits. It seems that some persons living in the main street were awakened a few nights ago by a great noise, as though a large body of disorderly men were marching and carousing through the streets. On looking out, however, nobody was seen, and the conclusion drawn was that the noise had been caused by *che jin*, paper men.* The story spread, and it was speedily reported that there were three thousand evil spirits, that they had been to Yuyaou and Funghwa, and have now come here, and will soon visit Chinhai and Chusan. Of course they can have come for no good purpose, and to drive them away, gongs and drums have been beaten and crackers fired for several nights, filling the air with a deafening noise for hours together. This has caused a great demand for gongs, and it is said that the gong shops in the city have disposed of nearly all they had on hand. In default of gongs, brass kettles are supposed to be nearly as efficacious. Strips of yellow paper with four mystical characters, whose sound and signification no one pretends to know, have been sold by myriads, and pasted up over every door and window, hoping to prevent the entrance of the evil spirits.

The reason for beating the gongs is thus explained: There are two great principles called the Yang and the Yin, under which all substances material or im-

* These paper men seem to hold the same position in the superstitions of China that the "familiar spirits," held in the times of the Old Testament, or the "evil spirits," under the control of conjurers and witches of our own and other Christian lands. In the History of the Three States, which is probably the most popular book of light reading in the Chinese language, is the following notice of them: "When the battle began, Chang-paou commenced his magical arts, whereupon arose a great tempest of wind and thunder; the dust flew about; the stones rolled over; a black cloud overspread the heavens; and, as it revolved, men and horses came down from above. Thereupon, at a convenient place, Heuenteh gave the signal, and his men poured out the mixture of the blood of swine, sheep and dogs, previously prepared. By doing this the power of the magic spell was broken, and nothing was seen in the heavens except paper men and straw horses rapidly falling. The wind and thunder ceased to sound, the sand and stones became quiet again, and Chang-paou seeing his schemes confounded, turned his head to flee, and his followers were defeated with prodigious slaughter." In the colloquial dialect of Ningpo, *che jin* is changed into TSZ' ANE, and may be expressed in English either by witches or evil spirits.

material are supposed to be arranged. These two are in perpetual opposition, and if either one of them attains too much ascendency, great confusion is the inevitable result. It so happens that the evil spirits which cause all the present disturbance belong to the Yin principle, while the sound of brass vessels belongs to the Yang. By beating the brass vessels the Yang principle will be enabled to resist the too great ascendency of the Yin, which is shown in the present incursion of evil spirits, and thus it is hoped order will be again restored. Great excitement prevails in the city, and all the higher officers are going in state to the temples, to pray that the evil spirits may be driven away.

August 3d. We were aroused shortly after three o'clock, A. M., by an earthquake. Having been sound asleep, it was some moments before I became aware of the real cause of the disturbance. There was a dull heavy roaring in the air, coming from the north gate of the city, and the roof of the house moved as if being gradually lifted off by a strong wind. Thinking it was a strong wind, I was about to get up and close the windows, when I perceived that the bed and the whole house were moving from end to end. Jumping up, and going to the window, I observed that the motion still continued, and being now sensible of what it was, and fearing lest the house should fall, I ran down stairs and out of the doors, and called to my people, who were all awake, to come out. The motion, however, had ceased before I got out. All this took up probably less than a minute, though how long the shock might have lasted before I was awaked, I do not know. The consternation that prevailed in the city was indescribable. Owing to the rumours and panic caused by the fear of the evil spirits, many people have been sitting up for several nights past, and when the shock came it was so violent that even the sleepers were awakened, and the universal idea was that the evil spirits were coming to take the city by storm. The inmates of the house next door to mine set up a terrific shriek, and in an instant the whole city with its quarter of a million of inhabitants, rang with the beating of gongs, the firing of rockets and crackers, and the shouts and crying of men in terror. To increase the alarm a bright falling star shot from the zenith to the north, leaving a long train of light behind it, and to many terrified imaginations it doubtless seemed as if the Yin and Yang principles were wrapped in endless confusion, and heaven and earth about to end. The noise and beating of gongs continued so long and loud that it was impossible to distinguish any other sounds. I regretted this, for once or twice I fancied there was the same dull, heavy roar that struck me on first awaking, and the Chinese, thinking it was the shouting of the evil spirits, cried out, "There they are! They are coming!" It may have been, however, only the blended sounds of rockets and gongs, and the cries of men in terror, as they rose over the night air. It was with difficulty I could prevent even my own servants from joining in the uproar, and one of them asked me, with a trembling voice, "Teacher, *is* this the evil spirit's coming?" Many cried like children when in fits of the extremest terror. It was a solemn thought to think, if such the terror occasioned by a single shock of an earthquake, what will it be when the heavens and the earth shall pass away with a great noise?

August 9th. In consequence of the earthquake, and especially the strange sounds accompanying it, the belief in the presence of evil spirits has taken a still firmer hold on the minds of the people. Multitudes of them have prepared green branches of trees, supposing they would be of use in warding off the invisible foes, and the most absurd rumours are abroad as to the cause of this visitation. Many attribute their coming to the Roman Catholics, who are about rebuilding the chapel which they possessed here in the reign of Kanghe, while others attribute them to the Protestant missionaries.

One of our missionaries lives in the western part of the city, and the people around him look with much suspicion on him, and on his wife. Among other things, they have it reported that when he and his wife walk on the wall of the city near his house, in the evening, they carry a bottle containing a number of these invisible people with them; it is further reported, that when they take out the cork a number of evil spirits, of different sizes, come out and kneel down to receive his commands, and then, on a signal, disperse themselves over the city. Another of our missionaries is reported to have forty-nine of the evil spirits under his control, and some of the worthy citizens who have seen me walking on the wall about sunset, have reported that they saw a long white devil walking there. All this is very unpleasant; the people are becoming excited and alarmed, and if they were at all of the disposition of the mobs in Canton, it would not be difficult to arouse them to wreak vengeance on the few defenceless foreigners here, whom they suppose to be the occasion of their calamities. One immediate effect has been, quite to break up my soirees on the wall. I had been in the habit, for some weeks, of sitting down to enjoy the cool breeze at twilight, on the wall near my house, and very frequently had quite a little congregation of the people to talk to, and converse with on religion and general topics, but now, when I sit down there, not one comes near me.

The sound of a shaken leaf terrifies them. My next door neighbours heard their paper windows rattling last night, and supposing the evil spirits were coming, they commenced the usual shrieking, shouting and beating of gongs, much to my discomfort; and there is scarcely a night in which I am not waked several times by the noises around. Last night and to-night are perhaps the crisis of the affair, for there is a report abroad, that six persons of particular classes, will die to-night, if they happen to fall asleep. In consequence of this, all belonging to those classes (such as were born under the influence of certain constellations) sat up all last night, and will sit up this night, fearing that if they sleep, they will be of the number of the six that must die.

Verily, "gross darkness covers the people."

August 21. The rumours about the evil spirits have taken a firmer hold than ever of the people's minds, and the most ridiculous stories are in circulation. Some men have had their queues cut off at night—of course by the witches, and the people are becoming excited. The drought still continues; we have been tantalized by clouds, and a drizzling mist, yesterday and to-day, but they are clouds without rain. The delusion about the witches has spread all over the province, and it is everywhere attributed to foreigners. Placards have even been posted up at Ningpo, saying that there will be no peace here till the foreigners are extirpated. My teacher went home a few days ago, and found his family in the greatest distress. He had not gone home for nearly a month, and they thought I had either locked him up, or bewitched him that he could not go. When he laughed at his neighbours for their folly in believing in the spirits, they said, "Oh yes! you are eating the bread of the foreigners, and it is very well for you to say so." One of Miss Aldersey's adopted orphan children died a few days ago, and the common report is that she murdered it. It is common here to keep the dates of people's births in the temples for astrological purposes. It has been reported that some foreigners have been copying these registers, and that all whose names are copied will surely die. In consequence great numbers of the people have gone to blot their names out, lest the foreigners should lay schemes against their lives.

August 22. A little rain last night and to-day supplies us with water to drink, and is very reviving to the crops and to the hopes of the people.

But still there is not enough to fill the canals even partially.

August 25. As a last resort to drive away the evil spirits, a procession has been got up in honour of Kwan-te, the god of war. Two companies of it went past my house *on the wall* to-day, in one of which the god was carried along in great state, in a chair upborne by eight bearers. There were dragons, lanterns, gongs, &c., &c., as in other processions; firing of crackers, and guns, and noises of all kinds. Two or three companies of soldiers formed part of the procession, marching in beautiful disregard of time and order. The neighbouring foo city of Shaou-hing having been cleared of evil spirits by a procession in honour of Kwan-te, the people of this city are induced to seek deliverance in the same manner. How dreadful to see them so given up to idolatry! I was deeply pained as they passed my house, bearing their earthen gods, and performing their silly rites. Oh Lord, how long?

August 26. The procession is still kept up, going through nearly every street in the city. As the neighbourhood around my house seems to have been particularly infested with the evil spirits, probably on account of my being here, a second detachment came past my house after eleven o'clock at night. The effect of the numerous lanterns was very pretty, but it is sad to see such worship paid to men. This Kwan-te flourished about sixteen hundred years ago. He is one of the three great heroes in the San kwo che, or History of the Three States, and was a native of the department of Shaou-hing, which borders on Ningpo.

Nothing was heard of the evil spirits after the procession. The people having full confidence in the power of Kwan-te, their imaginations were at rest, and the evil spirits departed!

September 4. Rain at last! More rain has fallen to-day than all that has fallen since the first of May. It is a great blessing. "He sendeth rain on the just and on the unjust."

September 5. In consequence of the rain the *Kin-too*, or prohibition of slaughtering animals for food, after being in force for several weeks, has been withdrawn. Images of the gods from all the different temples had been collected at one place, for the convenience of the chief officers of the city, who went there daily to pray to them altogether to send rain. In consequence of the rains, they have now been all taken back to their respective temples.

October 3. The long drought of the summer has been followed by a month of rains, nearly as fatal to the hopes of the husbandman. The canals are full and overflowing, and the fields are flooded. Withal it is cool, and it is now doubtful whether the crops will ripen. The first crop was short, and the second crop, after being withered by the drought, and nearly drowned by the rain, is not in a condition to come to maturity in the moderate and cool weather now coming on. A plain-looking man, in the ferry-boat, as I crossed over to-day, was expressing his belief that the gods pay no attention to what is done on the earth. "In the spring they heard not the prayers for dry weather. In the summer they heard not the prayers for rain. Now it is raining too much. I believe that heaven rains just to please itself."

In consequence of the cool weather, but a very small portion of the second crop of rice was worth anything. In many fields the farmers did not attempt to gather it.

October 4th, 1846. To-day commenced a Chinese service in my house. Put up a notice at the door, inviting *choo pang yew*, "all the friends," to come and hear; prepared seats for about forty; and about the hour my servant went to the door and invited the passers-by to come in. Except that the words were spoken with a totally opposite intention, they were remarkably apropos. See Prov. ix. 15, 16, to call passengers who go right on their ways. "Whoso is simple let him turn in hither, and as for him that wanteth understanding," &c. Some came in with their burdens; some looking half afraid; some ran right out again; some stood up; some sat down; some smoked their pipes; some said, "what is the use of staying, he is a foreigner, and we do not understand foreign talk?" the attention was none of the best, for it required all my courage and presence of mind to keep going, and the people feeling quite free to talk and make remarks, I got along no better than I anticipated. I am not discouraged, though by no means flattered by the result of this day's experiment. There were about forty persons present.

October 16th. A revolting instance of cruelty occurred opposite my window. A poor beggar who had only a coarse thin pair of trowsers, and a straw mat for his shoulders, in weather when I find woollen clothes comfortable, had by some means obtained eighty cash, equal to five cents, from a Chinese of this place. This morning the creditor came upon him for the money, and as he had not wherewith to pay him, began to beat him unmercifully. First, he struck him on the head and face with his fist; then he caught him by the hair, and beat him on the arms; then he took his queue or tail in one hand, and putting his foot on the poor man's back, pulled till I thought the man's hair would have come all out; then he struck him again fiercely in the face; and finally taking off his shoe, he began beating him on the bare back. The beggar all this time made no resistance, but uttered piteous cries, and falling down beat his head on the pavement, asking mercy! Several Chinese passed, and some looked on, but none made any attempt to interfere. Finding the brute continued his beating, I could stand it no longer, and going down, I laid my stick on his back not very gently. He looked up in some surprise, and seemed half enraged and half frightened, to find a foreigner interfering. I asked him what he meant, and why he beat the beggar so? He sputtered out some words, but began to edge off, as if he would like to be away; so I told him to clear out, and gave him another blow with my stick. I had half a notion to break it over his back. He seemed glad to get off so well, and went away in a hurry. The poor beggar's gratitude was inexpressible. He lay down, beat his head on the ground, and between his sobs and tears and bleeding face, let me know how much he was obliged to me. I gave him a few cash, and one of my servants, who seemed much interested, gave him an old garment. Quite a crowd had come around us, who seemed quite pleased at the turn affairs had taken.

October 18th. A larger and better audience than I have yet had, and very attentive. Oh, for a blessing! Otherwise it is only speaking to dry bones. One young man among others who stayed after the service, was anxious to defend himself from the charge of the folly of idolatry, and declared the monks and the nuns were a great nuisance; that he thought the monks had better marry the nuns, let their hair grow, destroy the temples, and follow the advice of Confucius, to "honour the gods and keep them at a distance."

October 25th. Service not so well attended today; more disorder, fewer persons, and less attention; must expect difficulty in keeping up the services. If it is hard to command full and attentive audiences at home, how much more so here, where the preacher is at best but imperfectly understood, speaks of strange subjects, sanctified in the mind of his hearers by no familiar or early associations, and of which they see no possible use? Surely were it not for the word of God, the missionary enterprise were the most foolish experiment of the age. Oh, for God's Spirit! What can man do?

November 1st. A rainy day, but a good many people in the street, going past my house: though the most of them carried burdens or bundles.

There are many weddings about this time, and I expected a small audience; made all my preparations, however, and went to my chapel; sat awhile, and one man came in and sat down; determined to keep him if I could; I commenced a conversation, but he seemed frightened at finding himself alone, and remarked, "nobody has come yet, and I'll not stop now, I'll come back soon!" So off he went, and came no more. Many passed the door, a few looked at the notice, but all went their ways, one to his farm, another to his merchandise. After waiting till I was satisfied that nobody would come, (my servant had already invited a number of the passers-by to come in,) I shut the door, and went and prayed. Then prepared a somewhat attractive card, both to paste up on the door, and to distribute about, stating that there is preaching here, &c. If this does not succeed, then I see no way but to get a better location, or to go out into the streets and by-ways, the highways and hedges, and speak unto them. Probably a chapel in any place, after the novelty wore off, would be deserted; certainly, I suppose, unless the Spirit be poured out from on high. Oh Lord, visit this people!

Quite cold to-day; thermometer down to 51°, and a foot stove quite comfortable.

November 2d. Quite a wintry morning; thermometer down to 43°, which is much lower than we saw it during this whole month last year; not prepared for it, not having my stove up, nor cracks stopped; but it has moderated somewhat towards evening.

Went to call on the Sz' family, the head of which has recently died. He was, take him all in all, the most respectable man I have known in Ningpo. He died of apoplexy; might probably have been spared, had the family been willing to have him bled; but as the Chinese have a great horror of blood-letting, they would not consent, and the poor old man died by inches. Poor, verily! for he knew enough of the truth and rejected it. Oh how dreadful is the reflection, that in the vast majority of cases, our labours only seal this people in deeper destruction! They would have perished if we had not come. We come and speak to them; they refuse to receive our words, and sink into deeper misery. But are we free from all blame in this? Do they see us so in earnest as to be convinced that we really mean what we say? I fear, often not.

November 15th. In the afternoon I preached on the miracles of Christ, to a small, fluctuating, and disorderly congregation. I was greatly interrupted by their talking, and especially by a crowd of boys, who came in, and behaved without manners. Spoke with more fluency and satisfaction to myself than I have yet done; but it seems like speaking to the wind and waves, or writing one's name on the sand. Spirit of God, breathe on these dry bones!

November 22d. Preached in the afternoon twice, on the death of Christ. Commenced with three or four persons, but more dropped in till there were twenty or thirty, by the middle of the discourse. Some were very attentive. So many kept coming in, that after the first company were gone, I preached the same discourse over a second time, and had some forty or fifty at the close. Generally pretty good attention, but I was excessively fatigued. An hour's almost constant talking in a strange language, and to an audience where there are always some unruly ones, is no easy work. Some come in and go out; some make remarks; one or two smoked pipes; and one or two were rude enough to make remarks in a very loud voice as they went out, apparently for the purpose of showing how little they cared for what was going on. I have not yet learned to talk at ease amidst all the interruptions which I foresee I must expect in this work; but give me such a day as this—I mean in regard to numbers and attention—and for a while at least I shall rejoice. Yet to many of the hearers, all they hear must be the merest scraps; something, to allude to Amos, like the "two legs, or a piece of an ear," which others, more eager for something, have sometimes got. Well, "faith cometh by hearing;" and I do rejoice, that, however imperfectly, I can yet give some of this people the opportunity of hearing. Oh for the living Spirit to breathe on the dry bones, and bless the word!

November 29th. Weather quite cold of late at night, and thermometer twice down to 34° before sunrise, but a clear day to-day, and it got up to 66°; very pleasant.

Preached in the afternoon twice, on the resurrection and ascension of Christ, with pretty good attention both times. One man, who came too late for the first service, said, "I don't care about books, but I want to hear you talk." Yet there was more eagerness for the books than I have often seen. How delightful to be able to speak with any fluency! There were some old men there, tottering on the brink of the grave; will the seed thus sown ever spring up?

When I was in Macao, my great anxiety was to get here; arrived here, and was satisfied for a short time; but then became anxious to be able to talk, and thought I would be satisfied if I could only talk; can talk a little, and for a while was almost satisfied; but now I want to see fruit. Perhaps if permitted to see it, I may be anxious to see it ripen; if it ripens, to see it safely stored away. When shall I be freed from anxiety? When but in heaven? Come, Lord Jesus, come quickly. I shall be satisfied when I see thee, or awake in thy likeness.

December 6th. Preached on the Divinity of Christ, with a good deal of satisfaction to two different audiences; the second very full and generally very attentive, and very eager for tracts.

December 13th. Had the emptyings of a theatre to fill my house, which it did to overflowing. It gave me a larger audience than usual; but those in the back seats were so incommoded by the crowd, that they could have heard but little. Preached on the Creation. One man seemed greatly struck by the account of the institution of the Sabbath.

CHAPTER VIII.

1847.

Missionary Labours at Ningpo—Voyage to Shanghai—Manchu Language—Chinese Translation of the Bible—Importance of selecting proper terms—Death and Character.

UNTIL the latter end of May, Mr. Lowrie continued his regular Chinese services on the Sabbath; and during the week he found many opportunities of making known the truths of the Christian system. A portion of each day was given, with increased interest, to the preparation of his Chinese dictionary, his plan enlarging as he advanced with the work.

Having been appointed one of the delegates for the revision of the translation of the Bible, he reached Shanghai early in June; and when his colleagues assembled, he took part with them in this important work. Much time was taken up in deciding on the proper Chinese word to be used for the Elohim of the Old Testament, and the Theos of the New. This question he had carefully examined before the meeting of the delegates, and his further researches led him very clearly to prefer the Chinese word *Shin*. It was his firm conviction, that to use the Chinese *Shang-te*, or the word *Te*, for the true God, was only to confirm the Chinese in their idolatry.

Among his last letters is one to his father, expressing his intention of studying the language of the Manchu Tartars, and requesting that the necessary books might be procured and forwarded. He did not overrate the advantages which a knowledge of this language would afford to the missionary cause; and it will be for those still labouring for the evangelization of this great people, to carry out this and other important measures of usefulness which he left unfinished.

The essay on the trials and discouragements of the foreign missionary, preceded by a note from his friend Mr. Culbertson, closes the present selection from his writings. Although some of the sentiments are expressed in his previous letters and journals, it was deemed best to publish this paper entire. His trials and sorrows were soon to cease. The work assigned to him by the Head of the Church was all finished. On the 19th of August, he was called, as we trust, to exchange this scene of conflict and of trial for the joy of his Lord. The particulars of this mysterious and distressing dispensation of Divine Providence,—the estimate of his character by those who knew him well,—and the expression of deep affliction caused by his death, are given by other pens. Whilst his relatives and friends bow in humble submission to the will of God, and whilst they know most assuredly that nothing happens by chance in the government of Him who has all power in heaven and in earth, the stroke is so severe, the wound so deep, and so many endeared ties have been broken asunder, that they cannot but mourn and weep over the early grave of this beloved missionary. He who wept at the grave of Lazarus, does not forbid the hallowed tears of his bereaved and afflicted servants.

Ningpo, January 18th, 1847.

REV. JOHN C. LOWRIE—MY DEAR BROTHERR:—I do not know that I have anything of consequence to write at present. Everything moves on quietly.

. . . . I find myself now making perceptible progress in reading and speaking, and begin at last to feel as if I had mastered the chief difficulties in the outset of this hard language. You will, I trust, join with me in gratitude for this. Mind, I do not consider myself a scholar, or anticipate no further difficulties, for I can see enough to know that it is a rough and stony path yet, and up hill too. I do not despair, however, if life, and health, and grace be given, to make at least very respectable acquisitions in the language. One of the greatest difficulties I meet now, is a temptation to devote myself too much to the merely literary part of the work. For I find I have made such progress as, notwithstanding all the difficulties, to find real pleasure in the study; and withal, there is a field of investigation and thought, of philosophy and of poetry in the language, which is well worthy of cultivation. Do not smile at this. Nothwithstanding the witty articles of the Repertory, the Chinese are no fools, and they have said and done things worthy of great renown. I begin to have a real veneration for Confucius, and to doubt whether any heathen philosopher ever saw so much truth as he did; while my tastes are becoming so Chinese, that I find eloquence and poetry, and what not, in multitudes of forms. You may laugh as much as you please at my tastes, but let those laugh that win. However, seriously, I do feel that there is danger of attending to merely literary pursuits, to the neglect of the far more important duties of one whose chief business it should be to know nothing but Christ, and him crucified. *Pray for me.*

Your affectionate brother,

W. M. Lowrie.

Ningpo, February 19th, 1847.

My Dear Mother—. . . . The weeks slip by with a rapidity that would be frightful, were it not for the calm and pleasing hope that they are wafting me to a home where in all labour there is no sorrow. I can hardly realize that six weeks of the present year are gone already, but so it is. Yesterday too was my birthday; finished twenty-eight years, and commenced my twenty-ninth; and it is more than five years since I saw you last. You will ask, what am I doing that makes me so busy? Why, I write a sermon in English about once a month; a sermon in Chinese each week; an average of two or three letters each week, (full letters, notes not counted;) correct two or three proofs in Chinese every week, each proof a good hour's work; and then to fill up and overflow every hour besides, I have this copious unfathomable language, which I find I must study in winter, and take easily in summer. I am, however, now so far advanced, as to find a great deal of real satisfaction in the study; and being thus encouraged by success, do not again apprehend the tedium of labour which I found in it for so long a time. I can now read an ordinary book without assistance from a teacher, though of course I can read much faster and easier with him by my side, and hope ere long to be able in a great measure to dispense with a teacher in translating from Chinese into English. I have not yet begun to ask, when I can do without one in translating from English into Chinese; that point is as yet many years off. I do not know how much you practise Chinese now, but a pretty little thought came into my head a few days ago; it may be in some book I have read, but I have no recollection of having met it anywhere. You perhaps know that the word *neen* means *to think*. Now just divide that character in two, and you have *kin sin*, "*now heart*," i. e., what is now in the heart, which is not a bad definition of thoughts. But perhaps this smells too much of the lamp for you. So, for more domestic concerns, I have lost my beautiful dog Fanny. She followed me out into the street one day, and got to frisking about, and got lost in the crowd. I should have felt quite melancholy had it happened a few months sooner; but the fact is, though very beautiful, she was so utterly useless that I did not regret her going. Instead of barking, she fawned on every stranger that came in, and followed everybody that called her in the street. So it seems a fair exterior is no better proof of good qualities in dogs than in men. I've got a little pup now, who yelped incessantly when I got him, until at last the cat took pity on him, and took him under her care. This comforted his heart very much, and he is now famous for eating rice and milk, and worrying the cat, and gives promise of being worth something more before long. I call him *Jim*.

Our winter has been mild, and is now pretty much over. We have had both ice and snow, but no weather so cold as a good deal that we had last year; and as we all know better how to prepare for it, we have got along very comfortably. I think too we shall not have so severe a summer. . . .

With much love and many warm thoughts,
Ever affectionately yours,
W. M. Lowrie.

ON THE MINUTES OF THE GENERAL ASSEMBLY OF 1846.

Ningpo, March 20th, 1847.

The Minutes of our venerable General Assembly, after being long delayed on the way, have at last reached this place, and are now lying before me. The General Assembly! How many precious and endearing associations are connected with that name! From this heathen land it recalls my thoughts back to the land of my birth and early youth; to the land of my first Christian hopes and preparation for the ministry. It is the land of my parents of my brothers and my sisters. It is the land where many warm friends dwell. It is the land where the departed sleep; a land of privileges and light! Its external and physical advantages are great; for it might be said as was said of Canaan in old times, "it is a land flowing with honey and milk," and "the eye of God is upon it from the beginning of the year to the end of the year." It is a land of freedom, and of peace. But its Christian privileges are greater still. It is a land of Bibles, and Sabbaths, and preaching and revivals. It has its Sabbath-schools and religious institutions. It has its missionary and its Bible societies, to extend to other lands the blessings enjoyed in its own borders. The influences of the Spirit, like currents of vital air, pervade the land. From its hills and its vales go up the voices of prayer and praise, and the saints of the Lord are resting in its graves. A land highly favoured—its God is Jehovah! Compare that land with this, and how painful is the contrast!

It is pleasant to think that the Church, the minutes of whose highest judicatory are now before me, *my own loved Church*, holds no mean place among those which, under God, have made that once wilderness land, to bud and blossom as the rose. "The *General Assembly* of the Church!" I love that name. How general and extensive, stretching far and wide, throughout the land, yet comprehending and *assembling* all together in one brotherhood. How goodly is the fellowship of the saints! The representatives of the Church throughout the length and breadth of a vast land are assembled here, and that not for any selfish purposes, but for the highest and the noblest known on earth; they are met to consult for the glory of Christ and his cause. When shall we have such a general assembly in this heathen land? When shall all the earth see eye to eye, and have one General Assembly? When shall we all go up to the General Assembly, and Church of the first-born on high?

It has been a deeply interesting employment to look over the list of ministers in connection with the General Assembly. I have gone over the whole list, pencil in hand, and placed a mark against each name of those I knew. I have looked to see how many of God's people are under the care of each; how many additions to the communion of their churches; how many baptisms. I have looked farther, to see how active, how liberal, how benevolent, the flock of each has been, and how much they have contributed to spread the cause of Christ, at home and abroad. But let me recall that word "benevolence." With most persons it signifies a free gift, or a disposition to give, where there is no claim on the giver. But surely it is no benevolence to give aught to Him of whom we receive our all, and to whom, if we give aught, we but give him "of his own." "All things come of thee, and of thine own have we given thee." To speak more properly, I have looked to see how much each church of those I knew, has realized of its responsibilities and its stewardship, and what answer it has given to the question, "How much owest thou unto my lord?" In some cases I have almost feared that an unfaithful steward has been there, and in place of requiring the full amount, has said, "Take thy bill, and sit down quickly, and write fifty, or fourscore." But charity requires me to suppose that the minutes of the General Assembly give only an imperfect account of what each church has done. The thought, however, occurs to me, man may see and record what we do, or he may not, but there is One above who sees and records it all, and he has said, "It is required in stewards that a man be found faithful." See the whole context, 1 Cor. iv. 1–5.

I love to look over the roll of the General Assembly. There are many well-known names there. The venerable father in Christ, the strong man, the gentle, loving teacher, friends of my boyhood were there: classmates and friends of my College days were there: beloved associates in the Theological Seminary were there. If I have numbered aright, there are ten with whom I met week after week and month after month, to hear the instructions of our venerated professors. With you I have sat in the same class-room, gone to the house of God in company, bowed together in the same prayer-meeting, and sat down side by side at the same table of the Lord. Tears fill my eyes, as with an overflowing heart, the memory of those favoured hours comes back; and if it might be so, I could wish for their return. Ye are dwelling in the house of God, whilst I sojourn in Mesech! Ye are going up with the great congregation, whilst I sit in the tents of Kedar! Yet will I remember thee, oh God, from the land of Jordan, and the Hermonites, and from the hill Mizar.

Years have passed away since then. Many billows roll between us now, and many billows have rolled over us since then, yet many recollections of those days come up before me in long array. What constant friendship did some of us vow, when our hearts were warmed as we communed together by the way! And there was our resolve to remember each other in our prayers on Saturday evening. Do ye remember it yet? God's blessing rest on you all, friends of my heart, associates of my earlier days, fellow-labourers in the same church, and expectants of the same crown! And ye too, venerated elders of the churches! Some of you I have known in your own homes. Some of my earliest and warmest friends were among you. Nor can I ever forget the deep feeling with which one of your number, now gone to his rest, once said to me, "Ever since I knew aught of Christ, it has been my daily prayer that I might know more of him;" or how another of your number said on his death-bed, with an emphasis which only the powers of the world to come could give, "Oh what a Saviour is Christ! He is a rock!" May the spirit of those devoted men rest on you all!

I have read with much interest the proceedings of an Assembly, to which I am bound by so many ties. How great a privilege it would have been to be even a doorkeeper there! It would be tedious, and unreasonable, to tell you half my thoughts, on reading over the proceedings. May I be pardoned for recording some of my thoughts, on reading a part of them?

It is natural for each one to feel most interest in what most nearly concerns himself and his own immediate pursuits. The foreign missionary looks with peculiar interest to the proceedings of the Assembly in relation to Foreign Missions. Shall I, or may I, say what I thought? Perhaps it may be wrong, or presumptuous, or censorious; if so, forgive me; but there was an emotion not unmixed with disappointment, on the perusal of the resolutions about foreign missions. You know best whether so many as nine resolutions were necessary, but it did strike me that they were dull,—too many words, and the sentences too long. A person almost loses his breath before he reads through some of them. Would it not have been better, if, with less of the character of a grave homily, there had been a more pointed application? If, instead of merely "grieving" and "inviting" and "recommending," they had embodied in few words a glowing resolution *to do*, and *to act?* But I will not criticise. Rather let me carefully read them over again, and may God's blessing rest on their authors, and on him who reads.

It is well. The work of missions is important; the Church should unite under their own Board: missionary intelligence should be diffused; earnest prayer should be offered; and the Jews should have an able and efficient mission. It is well that the Church, through her highest judicatory, should give utterance to these truths. I suppose they were adopted unanimously, as no notice is given of any disapprobation or dissent.

But what shall be, or rather what has been, the result of these resolutions? They are your public testimony, and not merely recorded in your official records, but recorded by one who says, "When thou vowest a vow unto God, defer not to pay it;" and who will look to see how official resolutions, which bear the nature of a vow, are performed. You have gone down from that high position in the General Assembly, to your separate flocks. If you carry not out your own resolutions, surely no others will. Have you then in your separate fields carried out the principles, and performed the duties you have publicly professed? Is interest in the missionary cause deepening among your own people? Is missionary intelligence more widely diffused? Do your flock take more copies of the Chronicle and Foreign Missionary? Is more prayer offered? Are more efforts made? Or if not, are we to understand that you have already attained to the measure of the standard fixed in your resolutions, and need not to go beyond it?

And how do your resolutions compare with those of the past or previous years? What advance has been made beyond the stand taken ten, or five years ago? The resolutions of the General Assembly of 1841 were very good. The Assembly of 1842 recommended that one hundred thousand dollars should be raised in that year; but that sum has never been raised in any year yet. The resolutions of 1844 I have not yet seen, but a kind and cordial notice of missionary operations, found a place in the narrative of religion of that year.

I fear it must be said, that the resolutions of the General Assembly mark no perceptible advance in the state of missionary feeling in the Church. There has been a slight increase of pecuniary contributions, but the Church has not yet come up to the standard fixed by the Assembly of 1842, as then practicable. Brethren, where is the fault? Your resolutions, to be of any worth, must be acted out; or in the end the people will become hardened by them, and instead of good, they will do harm, and "the rust of them" will be a witness against yourselves. Might I, with all humility, suggest that instead of a long series of resolutions, a few sentences, brief and pointed, would be much better, if each one who voted for them were to resolve that, let others do as they may, he at least would carry them out in his own church. Were this course adopted, in five successive General Assemblies, nay, in only two, what prodigious results would be secured!

But there is one sentence in the last resolution, which calls forth my warmest gratitude. The General Assembly of our Church solemnly assures us that your "daily prayer is that the Saviour may be present with us, and that the blessing of the Holy Spirit may rest on our labours." Oh ye fathers and brethren! this one sentence is to us worth more than thousands of silver and gold. Let others do as they may, we are here assured that in the daily prayers of one hundred and thirteen ministers, and seventy-six elders, we are remembered. Who would not rejoice to be held in "daily" remembrance by so many ministers and elders? Who would not feel strengthened in his work, by the assurance from the highest judicatory in the Church, that at least all those who composed that body, every day invoke "the presence of the Saviour, and the blessing of the Spirit" on his labours? In the name of every missionary of our Church, I thank you for that assurance; for surely God will hear such prayers. May they be graciously answered by Him, in blessings on our heads, and may they return with tenfold blessings on your own! You are daily praying, and doubtless daily looking for an answer to those prayers. God is the hearer and the answerer of prayer, and our hearts are revived by the thought. How glorious, how blessed to be a member of a Church, so large as ours, where such a bond of union exists, and where those who occupy the most conspicuous stations, assure those farthest off, and least known, of an interest in their daily prayers. I cannot allow myself to harbour for one moment the thought, that this assurance is a mere unmeaning form of words, passed in the routine of business, and forgotten amidst succeeding occupations or more interesting pursuits. It cannot so be.

W. M. Lowrie.

Ningpo, April 10th, 1847.

My Dear Father—Your letter of July 17–20, did not come till about ten days or more after the things it mentioned had been received. I believe everything has come safe. Some of the other brethren were not so much favoured, as some three or four boxes fell into the hands of pirates between Canton and Macao. The pirates are getting exceedingly bold all along the coast. I was told to-day that ten out of the eighteen timber firms in Ningpo had shut up their shops this year, as the pirates on the coast stopped their ships when coming from Fuhkeen province, and required such heavy ransom, that it became a losing business. I hardly know how I shall get to Shanghai this summer, as it is hardly safe to venture out to sea, in our small passage boats, when such customers are abroad. At present I propose applying for leave to go by way of Hangchou, a place I want to see on many accounts.

The convention for the revision of the Translation of the New Testament, is to meet on the 1st of June. I presume you will see the accounts of it as soon as any other person. The most interesting question likely to be discussed, is the one in reference to a proper term for "God." Increasing dissatisfaction is felt by many with the term Shang-te, which Mr. Medhurst patronizes, and the discussion of that subject is likely to be an earnest one. I should like much if you could find time to make yourself familiar with it. You will find in the Chinese Repository of 1846 and 1847, several articles on both sides. The one in November and December, 1846, and January, 1847, shows my views. I think, if the principles laid down in the article in the November number are granted, that the question is settled in favour of "Shin," and I should be glad to get the opinion of some Biblical scholars on the subject. You will see Mr. Medhurst's views in the January number of this year. I think every one of his positions is capable of a clear and distinct answer. I hope some one will reply to it. I shall probably write an answer myself, but do not expect to publish it, having already said as much as becomes so young a student of the language. As an evidence of the evil done by using the term Shang-te for the name of God, is the following:—Not long ago a very respectable man came to my house one Sabbath. I got into conversation with him, and asked him if he knew anything of Jesus? He replied, he had heard he was the son of "Yuh hwang ta te," the "Jewelled Great Emperor." This is the chief god in the Chinese mythology. His birth-day is on the first month, third day; his image is in one of our largest temples; and he is known indifferently by the name above given, or by that of *Shang-te*. I never use the term now, having uniformly found that the people supposed I meant their own Shang-te.

Sabbath evening, April 11. This has been a very pleasant day: clear warm, and comfortable. Sermon at our church by Mr. Culbertson, on "Joy in heaven over one sinner that repenteth." After sermon, the eldest boy in the school, of whom you have heard several times, and whose full name is

Yuen Ko Keun, made profession of his faith, and was received into the church, in presence of all his school-mates, and several other Chinese, by baptism. After a short interval, the Lord's Supper was administered. All the services of Baptism and the Lord's Supper were in the Chinese language, and were conducted by the pastor, Mr. Culbertson. This is, I believe, the first case in which any one whose first impressions are due, under God, to members of our Mission, has been admitted to the church. Others have, it is true, received great benefit from our mission; but, humanly speaking, they would have been savingly converted if we had not been in the field. I suppose in this case, as in the case of Apoo, baptized two years ago, that the principal influence has been exerted by Mrs. Way, and it is worthy of notice how God has been pleased to use the youngest, feeblest, (as far as bodily health is concerned,) and the most unassuming member of our mission, to effect the purposes of his mercy. To his name be the glory. As an offset to the above pleasing account, take the following:—All the time we were engaged in our services, we were disturbed by some Chinese carpenters close by, building a pleasure-boat for a European resident. I went out and requested them to cease, which they promised to do, but for some reason did not. Coming home from church, I found in one place a number of Buddhist priests reading and chanting prayers over a person lately deceased; and a few steps further on, a table full of victuals spread before a new tomb, and a widow woman wailing bitterly. They formed sad contrasts to the exercises in which we had been engaged.

After a light dinner, I preached on the Eighth Commandment, but the audience was neither large nor attentive. One man, however, evidently heard everything, and indeed so did another, who was sitting by the door outside when I began, but became so much interested, that he came close up, and sat down as near me as he could. But most paid little attention, and went away as they came. . . . .

Monday. Quite warm to-day. I hope this week to get through my collection of significations of the words used in the Four Books. There are about twenty-three hundred different characters. Most of them occur in only one or two senses; but several of them occur in such a variety of meanings, that it will take no little skill to get them properly exhibited. After getting through the Four Books, I think of laying the subject by for three or four months, as I am pretty tired of it. In the fall, if life and health be spared, I wish to resume it, and treat the Five Classics in the same manner, which will be a large job, and I suppose will occupy two years at least. . . . .

As ever, your affectionate son,

W. M. Lowrie.

JOURNAL AT NINGPO.

January 3d, 1847. Preached on the faith of Abraham, to a strange kind of an audience; most of them very respectable, but disposed to talk and make remarks; some were very attentive; but to some the story seemed amusing and almost ridiculous, and the idea of so old a man having a son only afforded matter for a laugh. How hard it is to preach to such a people—so indifferent, so insensible! I came from my address to my knees; for I am made to feel that the treasure is committed to earthen vessels.

Have some encouragement with my servants, particularly Azhih, whom I am training carefully in religious instruction. They take a good deal of interest in it, and I cannot but hope are beginning to feel a little. Oh, for God's Spirit to be given to them!

January 10th. Preached on the character of God; audience much as usual. It is no small trial of the spirit to one accustomed to address attentive audiences, to have such as I commonly find; people coming in and going out, some making remarks, some laughing, some ruder, and only few attending, and yet some of even these few taking up the strangest notions from the plainest truth. To human eyes all such preaching must seem very foolishness. Well, be it so. "The foolishness of God is wiser than men," and by "the foolishness of preaching he will save them that believe."

The external evidences of Christianity are of little use here. The people have as many and as famous miracles as we to boast of; and their minds are not so trained as to perceive and appreciate the evidence, which proves the truth of ours and the falsity of theirs. Hence they make no scruple of believing whatever we tell of deeds of wonder by Christ and his apostles. They can produce parallels in their own history. I spoke of the miraculous conception of Christ. "Oh, yes," said one, "that is true, it is just like a similar event in our history; let me see, where was it?" And after some thought, and assisted by one or two others present, he produced the circumstance. How should he believe my story, or feel more interest in it than I in his? Oh, Spirit of Life, come down!

Jan. 24th. A wet, rainy day, and apprehended having no congregation again; however, on going down, found a very respectably dressed middle-aged man named *Chuh*, who lives somewhere in the city; he was very polite and respectful, told me he had long "desired to see me, looked up to me for instruction," &c., according to the usual routine of Chinese ceremonial speech.

We had some talk, and as there were three or four persons present, I delivered my discourse to a very attentive, though small audience. The man took a copy of Luke with comments, and promising to come again departed. I was very glad of the opportunity of talking which was afforded, for I sometimes feel greatly cast down, especially when I find little opportunity of speaking for Christ.

Knowledge that there is such a thing as Christianity is increasing and spreading in this part of the country, as I frequently meet persons who have heard at least the name of Jesus.

Feb. 21st. For the last three or four Sabbaths, nothing special has occurred; audiences varying from ten to fifty; commonly sit and talk more after giving my sermon than I used to do, which gives an opportunity of more pointed and personal application, but also opens the door for any and every kind of question, and is very sure, in half an hour, to get off to questions about food and clothing, &c. The natural man "understandeth not the things of the Spirit." One man to-day seemed a very merry sort of a fellow, but withal, as respectful as a man could be whose only object was to make sport; asked a number of questions, and started a hearty laugh after each of them, in which he was joined by several others, who seemed to urge him on. At last, I asked him why he asked such questions; and whether his only object was not, to make sport of what I considered a very serious matter. He was quite abashed: several persons around him told him to be quiet, and he got up and went out. Had quite a full house as I talked the second time; but, alas! it is preaching to dry bones. O, Spirit! Breath of the Almighty! breathe on these dry bones!

Feb. 26th. Took a long walk into the country, to some places where I have not before been; was exceedingly stared at in one place, where the whole village turned out to see me, and the women were the most forward and curious of all. Quite abashed a little girl by asking her what her name was, as it seems she had none. It is not common to give names to girls. But it is melancholy to see the dissipation of morals here. . . . . Oh when shall purity prevail, where there is so much vice?

Went afterwards and had a pleasant little talk with some men in a little resting-house, and then came home, well-tired. Some little yellow flowers are in blossom now. I saw dandelions in full bloom a month or more ago, though there had been a hard frost before, and plenty of it since then; but the cold weather must be nearly over now.

March 14th. Preached in the morning in English, on Gal. iv. 7; in the afternoon in Chinese, to some thirty or forty persons, on the Fourth Commandment; was favoured with as much fluency as I have ever had, and fully as good if not better attention. Indeed, the congregation to-day would not have done discredit to any similar congregation in a Christian land. One man came in talking, and I supposed meant to keep on talking, but he behaved very quietly, only putting in a word now and then. After I had said that no work was to be done on the Sabbath, he asked, "Then what shall we do—go to sleep?" This brought on the next part of my subject—Duties to be done on the Sabbath. He stayed after service. I talked some; but there were many who wanted to talk about the news and trifling matters, and I found so little opportunity of saying anything profitable, that I soon left them. The man above referred to, seemed a man of some learning. He insisted on it, that since I was so generous, as to come out here, and preach to the people, and advise them to do good, I would surely become a god at last! But how hard it is to get a Christian idea into their heads, to say nothing of impressing it on their hearts. After repeating over and over again, the statements about God as eternal, true, and holy, they are sure to confound all you say with their own gods. This is not because they do not understand what I say, for I find that I am pretty well understood; but because, first, they cannot conceive how it is that their own gods are false gods; and, second, they have no idea of the importance of the subject, to induce them to give a serious thought to what they hear, and hence, when they hear of the "true God," they take it as a matter of course that their own gods are intended.

March 21st. Opened my doors at three, P. M., and went down as usual, but there were few passers-by. I sat alone for nearly half an hour, having only one little boy carrying a baby in his arms, to come near me. After a while, two or three well-dressed men came in and one sat down, but the other two went away. I asked him his name and residence, but he did not seem disposed for a conversation. I then opened a copy of Luke and began to read it. He asked what it was, and we had something to talk about it. Others came in; he praised my fluency of utterance and correctness of speech: and in answer to some questions, I had a good opportunity of giving some outlines of creation and redemption. But the subject had no charms for the natural heart; and as soon as I was done, one of the men asked, "Is your sovereign a man or a woman?" Quite a crowd had now collected, and I gave them my sermon as well as I could, which was not very well. Some heard it all; some got enough before it was half done. One quite respectable looking lady came in and sat down, and she at least heard everything that was said. Oh for a blessing on her!

It is hard preaching, for the audience changes so much, that I must go over the same simple truths every day, treating all the time of first principles; and this displeases the few who come more than once, for having already heard all this, they want something else.

I am teaching the Shorter Catechism to my servants, but find it hard work; first, the Chinese language has no suitable terms for many things, and second, my command of the language is not yet sufficient for the circumlocution in such a case. There are more terms in the written language than in the spoken, but they are of no more use to the common people than the Latin and Greek terms in theological and philosophical books are to the unlearned at home. I know of no term in the language to express precisely "chief end." For "decree," there is a good word, *ming*, in the written language, but not in the spoken. For "covenant," *yo* is a good word, but it is understood only by scholars, nor is there any good word for it in the colloquial. "Providence," "fall," "redemption," "original sin," "effectual calling," "justification," "adoption," "sanctification," "privilege," "holy," are all very hard words to be put into intelligible Chinese. Most of them may be expressed after a sort, in the written language, which is very copious, but when it comes to the spoken language one is at a loss, and a great deal of circumlocution is unavoidable. One of the great difficulties in our work lies in this very want of proper terms, and I see not how it is to be remedied excepting in long and patient use of the most suitable terms we can find; thus, at length, "converting" them from their heathenish uses and associations to Christian purposes.

How true are those words, "Sin has reigned unto death!" Its power is shown even in forms of speech. The application of terms to evil, is an evidence of sin reigning. This language is an instrument in Satan's hand to blind men to their ruin. But as sin hath reigned, so shall grace reign, even in the terms of this language, unto everlasting life. Wherever sin hath set up its throne and swayed its sceptre, there shall grace come in and set up a higher throne, and sway a mightier sceptre. Would that I might do something for the conversion of this language, and through it of this people unto God!

Monday, 29th. Busy in the fore part of the day with my teacher, and at the Four Books. At three, visited Mr. Culbertson. Coming back, was barked at unmercifully by several dogs. As soon as I am three steps beyond them, they follow for a square or two, barking and yelping without ceasing. It does make one feel as a stranger to be barked at in this way, for they do not move their tongue to a Chinaman.

March 31st. All day at my Chinese studies, and at the Four Books. At five, P. M., took a walk for relaxation. Gathered some spring flowers, for my flower-pot; a few wild lemon flowers, some clover, some yellow primroses, some parsley, and one or two others. In one place came across a dead dog, and two other dogs lying by him. In a few steps beyond, saw a flowering almond in full and luxurious bloom. So it is in this strange, melancholy world of ours. When most pleasantly engaged, you are wounded and grieved by some revolting spectacle, and again in a moment delighted with some scene almost too fair and beautiful for aught but heaven.

April 1st. In the evening looked over my Chinese sermon. At first it took me three evenings to prepare a discourse, but now I commonly get through very easily in one evening. I find I am generally understood, but mistakes are often made by beginners. I often wonder how the Chinese can keep such grave faces, when they hear such queer combinations as we foreigners sometimes make out of their language. The only time they ever laughed at a mistake I made, was when I spoke of "Peter's mother's wife," instead of "Peter's wife's mother." Even then some of the elder hearers seemed scandalized, that the young ones were amused at a mistake of "the guest."

April 3d. Looked a little into a work in Chinese, on astronomy, geography and watch-making, by some of the Roman Catholic missionaries of former days. It gives the Ptolemaic system of astronomy, that the sun and stars move round the earth. In the numerous books they published in China, they always explained astronomy in the old style, and published books and plates, representing the sun and stars revolving round the earth. I have seen some of these books.

April 25th. Preached to some twenty or thirty persons on the Tenth Commandment, and was favoured with a good deal of fluency in speech. Several were very attentive; and after sitting down, I got into a conversation which lasted more than an hour, in reference to idolatry, creation, redemption, the creed, &c. On the whole, it was a very satisfactory meeting, yet alas! without the Spirit of God, of what avail is it all? The people laugh at their idols, but go and worship them still.

After dismissing the audience, I found a couple of natives of the place, a Mr. Tai, and a Mr. Leu, waiting to speak with me. I had seen them both before, and the first of them several times. He was first led to think about Christianity, by a Chinese who came up here with Dr. Macgowan, and who first brought him to my notice. Last week he sent me a letter requesting baptism, and came to-day to speak about it. He said that himself and his friend, Mr. Leu, and another, Mr. Chow, whom I have also seen, are all pretty much decided for Christianity; and though, as he says, he is much laughed at and reviled by his friends, yet he professes a determination to persevere even until death. I had a tolerably satisfactory conversation with them, and we prayed together.

Worship of ancestors is one of the great features of the Chinese religion; every family has a picture of the father and mother, to which incense is offered, and religious worship performed. Mr. Tai asked what he should do. He said he had taken down the pictures and laid them away, and has fully determined not to worship them any more; "and if I should deceive you by saying I do not worship them, when I do worship them, yet I could not deceive God." He has, however, been told he should burn the pictures. Now this seems hard, for being portraits of his parents, he wishes to keep them just as we would. Does this case fall under the rule of destroying every vestige of idolatry, no matter what it be?

April 18th. Finished the first draught of the Shorter Catechism in Chinese, and May 11th, finished revision of it with teacher.

May 16th. Preached to-day on heaven; but it was talking of things in which the people seemed to feel that they had little concern. Had more satisfaction in a short extempore address I made afterwards, on the main object of Christianity. Two or three inquirers were present, who have been attending at Dr. Macgowan's, but of late have shown a disposition, entirely of their own, to come to me. I asked two of them to make some remarks, as I knew they had been in the habit of talking on the subject of Christianity. They both did so; what they said was good enough, but it did not seem very direct or impressive.

I find the Commentary on Luke takes very well; one of them inquired with much interest, if any more or other books would be published, remarking that it was very hard to understand our Scriptures without them, which is true. The drought still continues.

Shanghai, June 3d, 1847.

My Dear Father—In some of my previous letters, I mentioned to you my expectation of visiting this place. The object is to be present at the Convention for the revision of the translation of the New Testament, to which I have been appointed one of the delegates. The other delegates are Drs. Medhurst, Boone, Bridgman, and Mr. J. Stronach. I do not yet know of any others, and presume there are no others. Bridgman and Stronach are not yet here, but are expected daily. I supposed the Convention would not sit more than six or seven weeks, but every one here seems to think that six months is the shortest possible time, and a year is spoken of as more probable. The work is important enough, no doubt, to deserve so much time, though I have some doubts as to the expediency of it just now. However, as I am the youngest and least skilled in Chinese of all the members, I do not expect to do very much except to look on and see what is done. In the mean time, I expect to pursue my Chinese studies, much as at Ningpo, except that I fear I shall lose in the practice of the colloquial of that place. The dialect here is a good deal like that of Ningpo, and yet so much unlike, that while I can make myself tolerably well understood, I find a good deal of difficulty in understanding others; but a little practice will assist me.

I left Ningpo, May 24th, but owing to adverse winds, had to lie at the mouth of the river till the 29th. I then came by way of Chapoo to this place in three days, one of which, being the Sabbath, was spent at anchor in the canal. I did not apply for a permit to come by the way of Chapoo, and met no molestation or hinderance in passing through that place. The route from Ningpo to Shanghai, via Chapoo, may now be considered an open route, as several foreigners have passed both ways, and no notice has been taken of it by the Chinese authorities. It is a great convenience to us, and is one among the many evidences how the country is opening. Chang-Chow, where the visit of Mr. Abeel and myself made so much noise, some years ago, has been visited several times of late, and I have no doubt that the country will be as wide open in a few years as we can desire it.

Your letter of December 17th reached me last week, also two mission letters of November and December. . . . .

I have referred so often to my Dictionary, that I am afraid you will be tired of the very mention of it, but I will trouble you once more. I have collected all the significations of all the words in the Four Books, and have concluded to go on with the work so as to include the Five Classics, though perhaps I may not include the *Le Ke*, a large and for the most part very trifling and useless work. In the Four Books there are in all two thousand three hundred and forty-five different characters, and in the Four Books and Five Classics, the *Le Ke* excepted, there are rather more than four thousand and two hundred. I may perhaps send a list of them some day, from which you will see that the great body of the language is contained in them, i. e., the great body of the really useful characters. Now, my plan is to give each of these characters with its pronunciation in Mandarin, and in the dialect of each of the five ports now open to foreigners. Then to give the etymology of the word from native dictionaries, where I think such etymology worth notice. Then to give the different significations, whether as verbs, nouns, adjectives, &c., and at least one quotation to illustrate each signification, with reference to the page and line where found. This will be the body of the work: but my plan includes a good deal more, for as the whole of the ancient history, geography, &c. of China, is contained in these Four Books and Five Classics, I want my work to be a sort of "Classical Dictionary" on these points. Hence I propose short biographical, historical, geographical sketches under the appropriate characters, with references to such native and foreign authors as may give the student fuller details. You see this is a pretty extensive plan. As to time, I have no idea that I can do it in less than five years, without neglecting other works, which I think are entitled to the first place.

But here I am met by a great difficulty. We have few books in Ningpo. My library is by far the best there, and yet it is a poor thing compared with some that are in China, and it is miserably deficient in works relating to China, many of which are quite essential to me in carrying on my undertaking. Is there any way of supplying this want? The books I refer to would cost I suppose some five hundred dollars, and would be of great service, not merely to myself, but to all our mission, and I think ought to be possessed in a mission like ours. I will make out a list of them in a few days, and send to you by next mail. I mentioned several of them in some former letters, which I hope you will be able to procure. They are all to be had in Paris or Berlin. . . . .

My health is very good, and I remain as ever,

Your affectionate son,

W. M. LOWRIE.

Shanghai, July 23d, 1847.

REV. JOHN C. LOWRIE—MY DEAR BROTHER:—I am in your debt for several letters, which I must now endeavour to repay. I have been here nearly two months, and as yet I am quite unable to give any definite idea when we shall get through. Owing to the uncertainty of travelling up and down this coast, some members of the Convention did not get here till the 28th ult.; while I, who was punctual to the day, had to wait on my oars from the 1st ult. After we got together, all went on well for a week, when we were stopped by a question which has excited no little talk and writing for some time, "What is the proper word for God in Chinese?" Morrison and Milne have adopted the word *Shin*, which, according to the best judgment I can form, means *God*, or *Divinity* in general. Mr. Medhurst for many years used the same term, and even so late as this present year, 1847, has published a dictionary in which he says, "The Chinese themselves, for God, and invisible beings in general, use *shin*." But some twelve years ago or more, he began to use Shang Te, *Supreme ruler*, for the true God, and *shin* for false god. Mr.

Gutzlaff also did the same; and these two being the best and most experienced Chinese scholars, had of course great weight. And most of the missionaries were carried away by their example. For some years past, however, there has been a good deal said on the subject, and a strong disposition manifested to return to the old way. *Shang Te* is objected to, first, as being the distinctive title of the national deity of China, and hence something like the Jupiter of Rome; and second, it is not a generic term, and cannot be used in such passages as "Chemosh thy god, and Jehovah our God," "If Jehovah be God," &c. "The unknown God, him declare I unto you," &c. In fact there are many verses where the point and emphasis rests on the use of the same *generic* word all through, as in John x. 35, 36, 1 Cor. viii. 6, &c. Hence of late many of the missionaries wish to return to the old word, and a good deal has been written in the Chinese Repository, and a great deal said on the subject. Dr. Medhurst, however, has taken up the cudgels in earnest, and printed a book of nearly three hundred pages, in which he maintains that *shin* never means god, much less the supreme God. This, by the way, is in opposition to three dictionaries of his own, published in the last ten years. And he further maintains that *te*, which properly means *ruler*, is the *generic* term for God in Chinese; and that *Shang Te*, "High or Supreme Ruler," is the proper word to translate *Elohim* and *Theos*, when they refer to the true God. So the case stood when the Convention met. We went on with the revision very well, till we came to Matt. i. 23, where the word *Theos* occurs. Dr. Bridgman then proposed that we use the word *Shin*. Bishop Boone seconded this; and it was well known that my views coincided with theirs. Dr. Medhurst and Mr. Stronach took decided ground for *Shang Te:* and so we have now been discussing this question for three weeks, Medhurst and Boone being chief speakers. The latter is a superior debater, and having a very quick and logical mind, pressed Dr. Medhurst so closely, that he declared he must have all down in black and white. We agreed to this, and Bishop Boone and myself worked hard for a week, and wrote out an argument for *Shin*, covering twenty-six folio pages. Dr. Medhurst, who had spent five months in writing his book, and scarcely allowed us ten days to answer it, took our answer so seriously, that he said he must have some weeks to prepare a reply. So he and Mr. Stronach are now engaged on this. I greatly fear that the result of all will be, that each side will hold their own views, and Dr. Medhurst and Mr. Stronach will secede. In that case there will be two versions or none. A large majority of the missionaries in China, I believe, are for *Shin;* most of our missionaries are strongly for it, though one or two hesitate a little; all the Baptists; all the Episcopalians, both English and Americans; most of the American Board missionaries, and several even of the London Missionary Society. This of itself is a strong proof for *Shin*, for it shows that even the acknowledged Chinese scholarship of Medhurst and Gutzlaff is not able to command assent for *Shang Te*. But I did not mean to write so much on this.

. . . This summer, so far, has been very pleasant; nothing like so hot as last year. I am staying at Bishop Boone's, where they make me feel very comfortable. Hitherto our agreement of views on the question we have been discussing, has made us the best of friends. He is of course a strong Episcopalian, but withal very catholic, and speaks very cordially of "other churches" and their ministers as "ministers of Christ." He has shown an excellent spirit, thus far, in the convention.

Mr. Milne often speaks of you with much kindness. He and Medhurst and Stronach, are all well. Believe me ever,

Your affectionate brother,

W. M. Lowrie.

Shanghai, 29th July, 1847.

My Dear Father— .... I think it probable that we shall have the remainder of the discussions respecting the term for God next week. It is my daily prayer that we may be directed to a right conclusion. The importance of the subject seems to grow the more it is examined, though this is often the case, even in unimportant matters, when the mind is intently fixed on them; and the more examination I give it, the more I feel satisfied that without the *generic* term for God, it will be extremely difficult to give the Chinese correct ideas of our theology. If that word be not *Shin*, I am utterly unable to see what it is. Dr. Medhurst now says it is Te, but this is an idea taken up within the last five months, and is in opposition to all his own dictionaries, and translations, and to all the experience of all who have ever written in or on the language. I make my remarks in this sweeping style, because convinced of their truth. Even the Chinese say, "We don't use the word Te in that sense." Oh for the Spirit of wisdom and grace to direct us! It is a matter of much thankfulness that Dr. Boone's health permits him to take an active part in the discussion; as the character of his mind and acquirements, and his readiness as a debater, are of the utmost importance in discussing with Dr. Medhurst. Having no fondness for such contests, I say but little; but spend a good deal of time with Dr. B. in examining the subject in the native Chinese authors.

I hope in the next overland to be able to give an account of the close of the discussion. In the meantime, I suppose it will be better not to publish anything about it, beyond the general fact of the Convention being in session.

I am anxious to study the *Manchu Tartar*, a language not studied as yet by any one of the missionaries, but of great importance in explaining Chinese, as the French scholars have shown in their books published in France; and which, as this country becomes open to us, and allows us to go further north, will be found to be of great utility. See an article on this subject in the Chinese Repository of 1844, by Mr. Cushing. For this, I would like the following books:—Gerbillon, Elementa Linguæ Tartaricæ; Amyot, Grammaire Tartare Mantchou; Langles, Dictionnaire Tartare Mantchou Français, 3 vols. 4to; Klaproth, Chrestomathie Mandchou: Paris, 1828.

So far the summer is very pleasant, and my health better than in any previous summer....

Your very affectionate son,

W. M. Lowrie.

Shanghai, August 8th, 1847.

Rev. Joseph Owen—Dear Brother:—I wrote to you some time ago a letter which I hope you have received. I now write on a special occasion, and shall be very glad if you can give me a pretty full answer by return mail. I am here attending a Convention for revising the Translation of the New Testament into Chinese. We are divided on one point of great importance. Some of us in translating אלוהים and Θεος, wish to use the word *Shin*, which is the Chinese term for God, or Divinity in general. It is applied to all their gods, from the highest to the lowest, and to the spirits of ancestors, which are always deified and worshipped by their descendants; and the being who is supposed to be in all their idols is also called *Shin*. Hence it is the *generic* term for God, just as Θεος, ("Gods many and Lords many, but to us one God," &c.) Others of us prefer the term *Shang-te*, which means *Supreme Ruler*, and is the name or title of the chief divinity worshipped by the Chinese. This is not a generic term, nor capable of being applied alike to true and false gods, nor of being used in the plural. Such is the state of the case.

What I want to ask is, what is the custom in India? Do you find any term applied by the natives to all their gods? And do you use this term, and say, "You worship many *gods*, but they are false, and we preach to you the *true God?*" Or do you use a distinct term, in speaking of the true God, from that used to designate false gods?

Some say that in Arabic there is one term for the true God, which is used for him alone, and others for false gods; and that in such sentences as "Chemosh thy god, and Jehovah our God," (Judges xi. 24,) different words are used to express the word אלהים. Is this so? Any light you can give us will be very valuable. Please direct to me at this place, care of Rt. Rev. W. J. Boone, D. D., Shanghai, as I shall probably be here when your answer comes.

The question is a very important one here, and has been a good deal discussed. Medhurst, and Gutzlaff, and John Stronach are the chief advocates of *Shang-te;* Legge, Bridgman, Boone, and myself, are among the supporters of *Shin,* as were Morrison and Milne before, and a majority of the present missionaries in China.

My health is very good, as is that of most of the members of our mission, saving the languor produced by the heat of summer. Poor Brother Speer has lost both his wife and daughter. Dr. Medhurst preaches three times every Sabbath, and twice during the week, to audiences varying from one hundred to four hundred persons. Two or three persons have been baptized here, and as many in Ningpo, and on the whole, we are encouraged.

With kind regards to Mrs. Owen, and a kiss to your son, believe me, in haste, ever

Affectionately yours, W. M. LOWRIE.

From the Rev. A. W. Loomis, of the Ningpo Mission.

Ningpo, August 25th, 1847.

WALTER LOWRIE, ESQ.—HONOURED AND VERY DEAR SIR:—It has become my painful duty to act on this occasion as the bearer of mournful tidings, and may you, my dear sir, and your family be enabled to say, "It is the Lord, let him do as seemeth him good." I need not attempt to hide anything from you: for your God, who has enabled you cheerfully to consecrate one after another of your dear children to his service here below, will enable you submissively to resign them when they are called to his service above. I trust you will be able to say, "The Lord gave, and the Lord hath taken away: blessed be the name of the Lord."

Our brother, Walter M. Lowrie, whom we loved, is no more, for God has taken him. We have confidence that our loss is his unspeakable gain. The stroke has fallen heavily upon us, yet He who loved him infinitely more than we could, saw fit to take him to himself.

The news of this melancholy event reached here yesterday, brought by Mr. Lowrie's long tried and faithful servant, and by another Chinaman in the employment of the mission. [Mr. Loomis then mentions that this man had been sent from Ningpo to Shanghai, where Mr. Lowrie was attending the Convention for the revised translation of the New Testament, requesting him to return to the station at Ningpo, with reference to certain occurrences at that station.] Mr. Lowrie, with these two attendants, set out from Shanghai on Monday, August 16th, by the canal to Chapoo. They arrived, all well, at Chapoo, on the morning of the 18th. A boat was engaged, one of the regular passenger boats, and on the evening of the 18th all went on board with their baggage, to be in readiness for an early departure next morning. During the day of the 18th inst., he had been about through the city without anything unpleasant having occurred in his treatment by the Chinese. On the morning of the 19th, the boat in which they had taken passage set sail very early. The wind was unfavourable, being strong from the South. Accordingly it was necessary to beat, and the boat sailed, as is supposed, about twelve miles in a south-easterly direction; when suddenly a vessel was seen bearing down upon them very rapidly. It was a craft like those which belong to Chapoo, with three masts and eight oars. At the sight of this vessel the boatmen and other Chinamen (passengers) in the boat, were greatly terrified, and were for turning back, but Mr. Lowrie endeavoured to allay their fears. As they drew nearer, he showed a small American flag which he had with him, but still they came on, and soon discharged their fire-arms. Upon this, he went to the inner part of the boat, having been previously standing in the open part of the boat in the bow. When the pirates came, they boarded the boat with swords and spears, and began to thrust and beat all who stood in their way; especially they seemed to seek out and maim the sailors, or the strong and able-bodied, to put an end to their interference. All agree in stating that they did not see a *single* blow inflicted on Mr. Lowrie. He is said to have seated himself on a chair or box, and remained quietly; and when they were breaking open a trunk with their heavy spears, he took out the key and gave it to them, saying, "There is no need to break it open, here is the key." The pirates continued their work of plunder, breaking open everything and taking out such things as they wished, and stripping even the clothes from the Chinamen. Yet they did not touch anything that was on him; even his watch, and perhaps seven or eight dollars that were in his pocket, they did not take. They stripped and beat his servant, which he requested them to stop, as the poor man was sick. Being probably unable to stay and witness such cruelty, he then went out and sat on the bow of the boat.

Before they had finished plundering, something seemed to have awakened a fear in the minds of the pirates, lest when he reached Shanghai they would be reported to the authorities, whereupon they debated for a moment whether they would kill him or throw him alive into the sea. They hastily determined upon the latter, and two men seized him; and they being unable to effect their purpose, another came up, and he was thrown overboard. One of the boatmen, who was near him during his last moments, states that while the pirates were ransacking the boat, he was engaged in reading his pocket Bible, and when they seized him on deck, he had it still in his hand. As they were in the act of casting him into the sea, he turned himself partially around, and threw his Bible upon the deck.* He had also the presence of mind, as he was going overboard, to throw off his shoes, and he swam about for some time in the water. He was seen to turn several times, as if he would struggle towards the boat; but as one of the pirates stood with a long pole, having an iron hook at the end, in his hands, ready to strike him when he approached, he desisted, and soon sank. Such has been the sad end of our dear brother. . . .

I will not add to your distress by alluding to the deep gloom caused by this most melancholy news. May our Lord remember us in this bereavement. May his parents and relatives be able to say, "Though he slay me yet will I trust in him."

With much respect,

I am yours in the Lord,

A. W. Loomis.

* This Bible was afterwards found and taken to Ningpo. It is a copy of Bagster's 12mo. edition in Hebrew, Greek, and English. It is the same copy he preserved with so much difficulty and care in his shipwreck in the Harmony.

From the Right Rev. W. J. Boone, D. D., of the Protestant Episcopal Mission at Shanghai.

Shanghai, August 31st, 1847.

WALTER LOWRIE, ESQ:—MY DEAR SIR:—I cannot resist the strong impulse of my heart to commune with you, and to mingle my sorrows and tears with yours at this time. Our merciful and loving heavenly Father has seen good, in his infinite wisdom, to afflict us all in a very tender point. To you especially, my dear sir, he has sent a very heavy trial. May his grace be abundantly bestowed to enable you to bear it with entire submission to his will. Indeed, my dear sir, he is too wise to err: too good to do what is unkind.

In his infinite wisdom it has seemed good to him to take to himself your beloved Walter; and that, too, under circumstances which have wrung our hearts with anguish. My heart's prayer for you is, that when you hear the sad story, you may be enabled to say with the aged Eli, "It is the Lord; let him do whatsoever seemeth to him good."

He has done so, and, in this case, not in wrath, but in mercy and in loving kindness. He has removed your dear son from his vineyard on earth to a nobler service in his sanctuary above.

His work was done. The time of his removal arrived, and the circumstances thereof I am persuaded were ordered for the benefit of us who survive, rather than for anything to be effected thereby on our dear brother himself.

You will no doubt receive full particulars from your brethren at Ningpo, but lest their letters may not reach you by this overland mail, I will mention them. You are aware that he was at Shanghai as a member of the translating committee. On Saturday, the 14th day of August, he received a letter from his brethren at Ningpo, requesting him to join them immediately. [Dr. Boone here relates the particulars of this melancholy event, as given in the letter of Mr. Loomis.] . . . His servant escaped to Ningpo, and communicated these particulars, which we devoutly thank God he has permitted to reach us, so that we hear of him to the last moment, and that these violent men did not mangle his body.

Oh, my dear brother, I feel that these are sad tidings to write to an affectionate father of a son, and of such a son; but for our consolation we can surely say that the finger of God was never more manifest in the removal of any of his servants than in this case. To my mind, the very *slightness* of the *secondary causes* upon which his life and death seemed to turn, manifests the *clearness* of the *Divine Decree* to take him to his Heavenly Home.

This event has thrown my family, who had the privilege to enjoy his company for the last two months and a half of his earthly existence, into the deepest affliction. Dearly as I know he was beloved by the mission with which he was connected, yet I believe no one in China mourns his loss as I do. We were together daily for two months and a half, labouring together in what we both believed to be the most important matter connected with our Master's cause in China, with which we had ever been connected.

Circumstances occurred when he was under my roof which drew our hearts very closely together, and which now, as I look back upon them after what has just transpired, I cannot but regard as a merciful preparation to him for his sudden death. Whilst he was with me I was twice threatened with attacks of the brain, which I thought would prove fatal in a few days. On these occasions we had much conversation on the subject of a sudden summons, and how a Christian should live and feel in view of such an event. The person whose call was supposed to be near at hand was myself. We never dreamt that he was so near the confines of eternity; but he entered into the subject with me with all his heart. Never have I heard any one converse, who had a more delightful state of child-like simplicity of heart in relying upon the Saviour. I remember particularly our conversation, when we were sitting alone one moonlight night, upon my terrace. We were speaking of the case of a man removed from his field of labour in the prime of early manhood, when he gave promise of daily increasing usefulness. His train of thought was striking, and much impressed my mind; it was intended for consolation to me. God grant it may prove so to you, my dear sir, when you read it. He said he could not view this matter as most Christians seemed to do. He could not call it mysterious, *peculiarly* distressing, as was commonly done. On the contrary, to his mind, there was something peculiarly cheering to survivors in such a death. In the case of an old man, he was removed in the common course of events. Even to our eyes his work was done. But not so with the case of which he was speaking. The peculiarity of it was, that there was promise of much more to be done here for the glory of Christ. This world, however, we may be well assured, is but the first stage of our existence: God's children are employed in services infinitely more glorious, and that conduce much more to the glory of his holy name, in the sanctuary above, than any employments entrusted to them on earth. Should we not then, said he, use their early manhood, their manifest capacity, for usefulness in the vineyard here below,—indeed, every argument which can be pleaded, derived from their prospective usefulness to the Church on earth, to assure ourselves that God has called them to a more than common post of usefulness in the Church triumphant? His modesty and deep humility would have prevented his applying this to his own death, but from my heart I adopt it as the *true interpretation* of our Heavenly Father's dealing with him and with his cause in China in this instance.

If this be the true view of the case, most cheering indeed is the assurance it affords us of his present happy state and glorious position.

No one in China promised to do more for the cause of our Divine master than he. Just brought out by his brethren's choice to a participation in the work of revising the translation of the Scriptures, this call upon him was having the happiest effect in overcoming his disposition to modest retirement, and making him feel the necessity that was laid upon him, to take a more prominent stand among those whose attainments in the language qualified them to participate in all of a general character that was doing to advance the Saviour's cause. In the unhappy division of opinion which exists with respect to the proper word by which to render *Theos* (God) he took a prominent part in the discussion, and wrote on this subject one of the ablest articles that appeared in the Chinese Repository.

He was daily growing in power, and the field of usefulness was continually opening wider and wider before him; but God had work for him above this vale of tears, and now leaves us mourning and sorrowing, to do the great work without his aid. O, that by the Spirit's gracious influences he may more than supply this loss to us, and that the work, for which our beloved brother was labouring with all his powers when he was taken away, may be so accomplished that his own most holy name may be glorified thereby.

We had promised each other, that if *my life* was spared, we would labour much together to set the plain doctrines of the cross, by means of tracts, before this people; but, alas! he is not, for God has taken him.

May we not suppose that the object of our gracious Saviour, in giving us, in addition to the general promise of the resurrection of all at the last day, the special assurance that "the sea shall give up its dead," is to assuage the grief of those who have been bereaved as you are, and whose precious ones lie buried in the deep.

Believe me, my dear sir, very sincerely yours, in the hope of a common resurrection with our beloved brother. WM. J. BOONE.

---

*From the Rev. John Lloyd, of the Amoy Mission.**

Amoy, September 17th, 1847.

WALTER LOWRIE, ESQ.—MY DEAR MR. LOWRIE:—Yesterday, I received the sad, the very sad intelligence of Walter's death. I need not tell you how much I was affected by this afflictive event. Walter was very dear to me. I loved him with a brother's love. He was my dearest earthly friend. We were born into God's glorious family about the same time. We entered the church on the same day. We formed the resolution of devoting ourselves to the work of foreign missions about the same time. We often took sweet counsel together, and walked to the house of God. We often talked together of God's kind dealings with us. We often spoke of our hopes. I recollect one instance of this kind which occurred at Jefferson College. We went out into the groves to commune with each other, and as we talked by the way, our hearts did burn within us. Walter often alluded to this walk and talk in the groves of Canonsburgh in his letters, and spoke of it as an antepast of the joys of heaven. All this intimacy with him while we were in college, gave me opportunities of learning his worth. I knew his inward mind on those subjects which were nearest and dearest to his heart, and I can most freely say that the more I knew him the more I loved him.

* This able and beloved Missionary has also finished the work which his Master had for him to do in China. He died at Amoy, of typhus fever, on the 6th day of December, 1848. Thus after a short interval, these two friends met, as we trust, in the presence of the Saviour, to be separated no more for ever.

After Walter left college, I saw no more of him till I met him in Macao, in October, 1844. In the providence of God our meeting was of short duration. I soon left that place for Amoy. What I saw of him there gave me higher notions of his piety, of his sound judgment, and of his intellectual character, than ever I entertained before. My love and admiration could not but be increased. I heard him preach and address religious meetings only two or three times. He was very solemn, and his solemnity was contagious, if I may use the expression. It possessed the rare quality of radiating from its centre, and entering the hearts of all around. Hence his discourses, which were plain and practical, always took hold of the feelings as well as the intellect. One never wearied listening to them, and one always left the meeting feeling that he had received both instruction and spiritual benefit from what he had heard.

My dear Mr. Lowrie, it is not my intention to write an eulogy upon Walter; but I cannot but feel that you, and I, and the Church of God have sustained a very great loss. This loss more nearly concerns you, and though I cannot fully appreciate a parent's tender feelings and yearnings in behalf of his beloved offspring, yet I can realize in some degree the depth of that grief which the news of this severe affliction will produce in your mind. I most deeply sympathize with you. My heart bleeds for you. I feel totally unfitted to administer consolation. The blow is too heavy to admit of alleviation by anything that I can say. I can but weep with you over the loss sustained. But, though I cannot afford relief to your mind in this season of sorrowful bereavement, yet there is one who sympathizes with you, and who is fully able to console you in this hour of heavy affliction. That Jesus, whom Walter loved, knows the depth of your grief. He knew it before the sad event occurred. He has consolation for all the sons and daughters of affliction. He is a tender comforter. The bruised reed will he not break, the smoking flax will he not quench. To him you can go with all confidence. He is waiting to hear your cries. What a privilege God's dear children possess!

When God afflicts them, he does it as a tender, loving parent—he does it for their good. This affliction is for our good. I feel it to be intended for my good. I had wrong views in relation to God's work in China; I almost felt that it could not go forward without Walter. I felt that we must have him to control and counsel us, to manage our operations, to rebuke us when wrong, to encourage us when right. I felt that we needed him to oversee the press, to prepare tracts, to assist in revising the Scriptures. I knew that God had endowed him with a noble intellect, had given him a sound judgment, had bestowed upon him much grace, and had eminently fitted him for a high station in this great harvest-field. I knew all this, and felt that we could not spare him. But God's thoughts and ways are not as ours. He has taught me that he can do without us, even the best of us. He has no need of our poor assistance. When he sees fit, he calls us to himself. He has called Walter thus. We idolized him. God has rebuked us. But he has taken Walter to himself. This is my consolation. I have no doubts on this point. I feel as sure as I can on any subject based on moral evidence, of the safety of Walter. He is happy beyond conception. We mourn his loss and feel our spirits depressed, but he is beyond the influence of sorrow's pains. Walter wrote me not long ago a letter, in which he spoke freely of his feelings. He was mourning over inbred corruption, and found all his hope in Christ. I thought for a moment of sending this letter to you, but what need is there for this? You have many letters from him, the spirit and sentiment of which leave your own mind free from all doubt as to Walter's personal interest in the blood of the precious Saviour.

I love to think of Walter. Many of the sweetest spots of my existence teem with delightful recollections of him. It may seem strange, but it is true, that the thought of being saved with Walter and dwelling with him for ever in heaven, has often filled my soul with peculiar emotions of joyful satisfaction, and has aroused into life a sweeter affection for the blessed Saviour, who was pleased to give me a title to the same inheritance which he has conferred on him. Walter has already entered upon the enjoyment of that inheritance, and is now employed with the patriarchs and prophets, with the apostles and martyrs, and with the general assembly of the first born in heaven, sounding the high praises of him who loved him and washed him in his own blood, and made him a king and a priest unto God and his Father. He was ripe for the kingdom and his work was done, and so God took him to himself, and now employs him in the upper sanctuary in a higher and holier service.

Would that I could fill up the void which this sad bereavement will make in your parental heart! But I have hopes that God will sustain you. He enabled you to give up Walter with cheerfulness to the work of Missions. He enabled you to bear up under the distress of a long separation. Surely he will not now forsake you in this the extremity of your grief! I trust you will feel that the cause of missions still needs your aid; that the Church has work for you still to do; and especially that God, by this dark and mysterious dispensation of his providence, is preparing you for more self-denying labours in the station which he has called you to occupy. God may intend by this event to accomplish more for that cause which Walter so dearly loved, than (speaking humanly,) could have been accomplished by him if he had been spared many years. Of one thing we are sure, God does nothing wrong. He brings good out of evil; all his ways and all his dealings with the children of men are right and holy.

May we therefore be submissive; may we bow and kiss the rod and him that hath appointed it; may the blessed Spirit save us from all murmuring on account of his dispensations; may he give us meek and lowly minds; may he sanctify to us all his heavy afflictions, and may he make them work out for us a far more exceeding and eternal weight of glory! May the God of grace sustain you.

Yours with all sympathy,

JOHN LLOYD.

From the Rev. Joseph Owen, of the Allahabad Mission.

Allahabad, November 19th, 1847.

MY DEAR MR. LOWRIE—We have just received from China the distressing news of your beloved son's death, and there is in the Mission a deep and universal feeling of sorrow and sympathy, which I have been requested on their behalf, to express to you. Some of us knew your dear son personally, and are thus in some measure prepared to appreciate the loss to you and all your family and friends, caused by his death. We all knew him, through the Missionary Chronicle, as a faithful ambassador for Christ, in perils often, perils of water, perils of robbers, suffering shipwreck, and spending nights and days on the deep. I had the privilege of knowing him as a beloved fellow-student, and, since we have been in the eastern world, as a dear friend and correspondent. Four days ago, on the 15th inst., I received from him a letter, dated Shanghai, Aug. 8th, where he was attending a Convention for the revision of the New Testament in Chinese. He wished an answer by return mail, to some inquiries respecting the terms we use in the India dialects to represent the Supreme Being, and wrote in good health, and encouraged with his prospects of usefulness. On the envelope I found with sad surprise, the following lines from Brother Harper, dated Canton, Sept. 21st. "You will excuse my opening this envelope to inform you of the lamented death of the beloved writer of this note. He was murdered by pirates, when returning from Shanghai to Ningpo, Aug. 19th, near Chapoo. They threw him into the sea, and he was drowned. All our Missions are in deep grief. Our ablest and best man has fallen." These sad tidings were confirmed the next day by the Friend of India, in which we found an extract from the China Mail of September, which I have had copied, and will send to you with this. You will no doubt have heard directly from China before this reaches you, yet every scrap of intelligence on the subject will be valued by you, and therefore I send you all that we have.

This is indeed a mysterious dispensation of Divine Providence. Truly God's ways are not as our ways, nor his thoughts as our thoughts. Dear Walter was qualified in no ordinary degree for the great work in which he was engaged. His excellent scholarship, ripe judgment, extensive and matured knowledge of China, the deep foundation which he had laid in its difficult language, and above all his unwavering and ardent love to the Redeemer and his Church, prepared him to be very extensively useful in that immense field. But God has again shown us, that the excellency of the power in the great work of the world's conversion, is to be, not of us, but of Him, and given another illustration of that great truth, "Not by might, nor by power, but by my Spirit." I feel that another tie to earth is broken. I loved Walter most sincerely, and have known and loved him ever since he was nineteen years old. Many of our pleasant interviews I shall never forget, and I trust we shall with delight converse about them hereafter. In particular, I remember the kind visit he paid me, at my father's, a short time before I left America. We took a long ramble together in the fields, enjoying the sweet fresh air of spring, part of the time on the winding, beautiful banks of the Croton, and conversing of our future prospects. His heart was then towards Africa, but subsequently God directed him to that glorious field in which he has now fallen. His usefulness, however, has not terminated with his sojourn on earth. His name is precious, not only to those who intimately knew him, but it must be to thousands. His career was short, but very eventful. He was called not only to do, but to suffer much for the Lord Jesus, and he did it as a good soldier, falling eventually as a leader in one of the foremost ranks. A breach has been made by his fall, not easily filled. God grant that his example of labour and patience, of zeal and wisdom, of faith and love, may call forth many dear youth from our American Zion, to count not their lives dear to themselves in publishing the glorious gospel to the land of Sinim. He has been removed from a lower to a higher sphere of service. Though he rests from his labours, yet he is not inactive. But we see through a glass darkly. We know little, and in our present state are capable of knowing but little, of the glorious service in which he has joined the redeemed around the throne. The dark, fearful billows that closed above him as he sank into the sea could not contain his spirit. In a few minutes his ransomed soul was with the blessed Redeemer, for ever beyond the violence of earth and of hell. And if the kind, considerate authorities at Ningpo should not succeed in recovering his remains, it will matter little after a while; the day will soon come when the sea shall give up its dead, when the members of Christ's body scattered throughout its immense, dismal caverns, shall all be recovered, brought and joined to their Head, and for ever made like to his glorious body. We may be sure that the Omniscient and Omnipotent Saviour will not allow one particle of his purchased possession to be lost. We hope soon to be with him in the midst of the glorified throng. We are repeatedly and emphatically reminded that the fashion of this world passeth away.

The tidings that you conveyed to me a little more than two months ago, were some of the most painful that I ever received. I was looking forward with very great happiness to having my own dear brother with me here. But the disappointment, with the almost certain prospect of his speedy death, is a deep affliction. I bless God who has not allowed a murmuring thought to arise in my heart. He knows what is best for his Church, infinitely better than we do, and the multitude of his ransomed ones in India and China, shall surely be brought home, though we and all others now on the field should fall. God is trying his Church by terrible things in righteousness. He has taken to himself some of our most useful fellow-missionaries of late. On the 19th of Aug. your son; on the 1st of Sept. the Rev. J. Macdonald of the Free Church Mission, Calcutta, a very holy, useful man; on the 7th of Sept. Mrs. Hill, who had been for twenty years a faithful missionary at Berhampore; and not long ago Mr. Whittlesey, a very useful missionary of the American Board, died in Ceylon. Other useful labourers are obliged to leave the field, as dear Brother Rankin, and Mrs. Scott. And others God is keeping from coming. Ought not the Church to think of these things? These are loud calls to us here, to the Committee at home, to the ministers and elders, to the sons of the prophets, to every individual in the Church, to humble ourselves under the mighty hand of God, that in due time he may lift us up.

Yours affectionately,

JOSEPH OWEN.

From the Rev. John M. Lowrie.

Wellsville, Ohio, January 26th, 1849.

DEAR UNCLE—I enclose several letters to me from cousin Walter. As we were so much together while he was in the College and in the Seminary, our communications were chiefly personal and not written. I will therefore give you some of his religious experience and views during these periods.

If I were drawing off a sketch of his character as a student at College and in the Theological Seminary, I would notice some such points as these.

His first care was attention to his own spiritual wants. I never knew a man more scrupulously careful to maintain punctual and deliberate habits of private devotion. We were for a short time occupants of the same room; and it was arranged that our hours of exercise should leave the room private to each of us in turn. Many times when this arrangement was interrupted, I have known him enter a little closet in one corner of the room, that no eye might see him while he sought his Father's face.

It was chiefly his desire to secure uninterrupted hours and seasons unknown to any, for devotional duties, which led him to secure a room by himself during the greater part of his course, after his profession of piety. His seasons of fasting I sometimes knew, because we ate at the same table; but at other times, I think, he so arranged them in connection with visits to friends in the country, that we supposed him not yet returned from a visit, when, in truth, he had exchanged his social intercourse for a season of solitary communion with his God. And I have often knocked at his door for admittance, when I knew he was within, but he would not reply, for he wished uninterrupted his seasons of devotion and of study. It seemed also remarkable to me that he so well maintained his devotional habits when absent from home. I have no knowledge of any friend whose habit of meditation upon the Bible after reading it was so fixed. At the foundation of his Christian character, was an ardent love for his closet.

Next to his attention to private duties, I would rank his affectionate concern for the piety of his fellow-professors of religion. There was at Jefferson College a small religious society, still in existence, bearing the name of the missionary Brainerd. Of this he was an active member, and he ever regarded it as a means both of profit and influence. But outside of this little band, he exerted no ordinary influence upon Christian students. He was especially beloved by those who were associated with him in the support of Sabbath Schools and prayer-meetings, for he was naturally more with them. And as from the very first his was a missionary spirit, so those brethren both at Canonsburg and Princeton, whose minds turned towards the great field whitening to the harvest, were his peculiar companions. There was one room at Canonsburg that was the place of many a conference for the land of Sinim, and many a prayer that it might be opened to the heralds of salvation. And there are brethren in China and India, and I believe in heaven too, who will long remember room No. 29, in Princeton Seminary, hallowed as it has been by conference, by tears and prayers. I scarcely know one whose influence upon the piety of the institutions, both at the College and the Seminary, was more consistent and healthful than his was.

His influence was also exerted over those who made no profession of religion. He was deeply impressed with the truth, that to every young man the period of College life was the golden opportunity to secure salvation, or to strengthen pious habits and a pious character. He was well aware, also, of the many insidious and dangerous snares which beset those who are so early in life set free from the restraints and the wholesome discipline of a parent's control. Many a time has he expressed deep anxiety on learning that some interesting and inexperienced youth had taken his boarding in dangerous company.....

Worthy of notice, also, are his zeal and devotion to improve opportunities for usefulness. The Sabbath School at Miller's Run, where he attended church, and of which he was superintendent, was about six miles from Canonsburg. Under his control it was a thriving and most interesting school. Accompanied by a band of affectionate teachers, his fellow-students, he went to the school, sustained meetings for exhortation and prayer, visited the sick, and was ever welcome to the firesides and the tables of an attached people. Beyond doubt, there are precious souls in that congregation, who retain the sweet savour of his memory. They will remember the crowded prayer-meeting, the solemn Bible-class, the simple address, and the fact that many young persons, almost all from the Sabbath School, united with the Church during his sojourn with them, as evidence of his influence and usefulness among that people. These labours were a delight to him, though they were toilsome. Often he would walk as many as eight miles on Saturday evening to hold a prayer-meeting, and return to the church on Sabbath morning to the school.

There remains one other matter which I have in lively, and I may add, grateful remembrance,—this is his faithfulness in discharging the important but unpleasant duty of admonition. I have lying before me a letter, which cannot be made public, but which is an excellent instance and evidence of his watchfulness over his brethren, and of his kindness and prudence to warn and correct. Nor was he less ready to receive than to administer reproof.....

Yours affectionately,

J. M. Lowrie.

REMARKS ON THE DEATH OF THE REV. WALTER M. LOWRIE,

By the Rev. A. Alexander, D. D.

The mournful tidings of this disastrous event has sent a pang of grief to the hearts of thousands in our Church and in our country. The loss of such a man, and in such a way, is, indeed, a deplorable thing. Christianity was never intended to destroy the natural feelings of humanity, but to regulate and refine them. In Holy Scripture we find that the pious gave free indulgence to their feelings of sorrow, on account of the death of good and great men. When Abner was treacherously murdered by Joab, king David "lifted up his voice and wept at the grave of Abner; and all the people wept. And the king lamented over Abner." So, also, when the pious king Josiah was slain in the flower of his age, "All Judah and Jerusalem mourned for Josiah: and Jeremiah lamented for Josiah. And all the singing men and singing women spake of Josiah in their lamentations." We have, moreover, in the New Testament an example of the same kind in the primitive church at Jerusalem, when Stephen, "a man full of wisdom and of the Holy Ghost," was stoned to death by the Jews. This man stood conspicuous among the disciples of Christ on account of the miraculous gifts with which he was endowed, and the holy boldness and eloquence with which he defended the truth, for "being full of faith and power, he did great wonders and miracles among the people. And his enemies were unable to resist the wisdom and the spirit by which he spake." But when confounded in argument, they had recourse to violence, and cast him out of the city and stoned Stephen, calling on God, and saying, "LORD JESUS RECEIVE MY SPIRIT." And he kneeled down and cried with a loud voice, "LORD, LAY NOT THIS SIN TO THEIR CHARGE;" and when he had said this, he fell asleep. "And devout men carried Stephen to *his burial,* AND MADE GREAT LAMENTATION OVER HIM."

Here we find, that in the early infancy of the Church, good and useful men were suffered by divine providence to be cut off, when their services were more needed than they could be at any future time. God would teach us that he is not dependent on any instruments for the accomplishment of his purposes. The death of Stephen, probably, had a mighty effect on the minds of many who were present; and from among his bitterest enemies, there was one whom God had determined to make "a chosen vessel" to carry the Gospel not only to the Jews, but to a multitude of the Gentile nations.

And we learn from this part of Sacred Scripture, that God does not forsake his devoted servants, when surrounded by enemies, and while suffering the agonies of death. Stephen saw heaven opened and the Son of Man standing at the right hand of God. And he was enabled to die in the full assurance of hope; and, with his last breath, to imitate his divine Master, by invoking mercy for his murderers. And although we are not permitted to know in what state of mind our dear young brother met death, we have good reason to conclude that his covenant God did not forsake him in that trying hour. Very likely his last breath was spent in prayers for the salvation of his murderers.

That the death of Mr. Lowrie is a great loss to the Church, and particularly to the cause of missions, none will doubt. Religiously educated from his youth, and in a family imbued with the missionary spirit, he early turned his thoughts to the condition of the blinded, perishing heathen. With this object in view, he commenced his theological education. During his whole course, it is believed, his purpose remained unshaken; and all his plans and studies were prosecuted with a direct view to this object. Possessed of a vigorous and well-balanced mind, and of cheerful, equable temper, his progress in learning was rapid, and what he acquired, he retained. With him no time was wasted, for even his hours of relaxation from severe study were spent in some useful employment.

He was willing to encounter all the dangers of the deleterious climate of Africa, and would have made that dark region the field of his labours, had it not appeared to all his friends that he was eminently qualified for the China mission, that great country having unexpectedly been opened for the preaching of the Gospel. Our young brother accordingly embarked for that important field; but before his station was finally chosen, he met with extraordinary difficulties and dangers. In one of his voyages he was ship-wrecked; the vessel was abandoned at sea, and the crew and himself were exposed to a rough sea, in an open boat, for many days; and when they approached the shore, were, by a manifest interposition of Providence, enabled to land, when at almost any other time their boat must have been swamped.

After his arrival in China, he devoted himself assiduously to the acquisition of the very difficult language of the country; and there is reason to believe with uncommon success. But not contented merely to acquire the language, he deemed it very important to make himself acquainted with the literature, and especially with what may be termed the classical literature of the Chinese. From communications received in this country, there is reason to think that he was making rapid progress in this species of knowledge.

Besides the acquisition of the provincial dialect of Ningpo, where he had his station, he had formed the purpose of learning the Manchu Tartar language, which differs from that of China in that an alphabetical character is used; and it is understood that this is becoming more and more popular, and from its superior convenience, will probably prevail. From these and other considerations it is evident that our Church and the cause of missions has experienced a great loss in the death of Mr. Lowrie. It ought to be mentioned, also, that with other missionaries, he was, when called away, earnestly engaged in revising and correcting the version of the New Testament into the Chinese tongue. For this work he was eminently qualified by his learning, and by his nice discrimination and turn for accuracy in matters of this kind. When sent for to Ningpo, he had been for between two and three months at Shanghai, engaged with Bishop Boone, Dr. Bridgman and others in this work.

It is, then, neither unreasonable nor unscriptural that great lamentation should be made on account of his death. Though none can be expected to experience the same kind and degree of grief as his venerable father and near kindred, yet many others deeply sympathize with them in their lamentations; and it may be presumed none have felt this stroke more pungently than his brethren of the mission. To them the bereavement is indeed great and lamentable. But this feeling is not confined to the missionaries of the Presbyterian church; others will feel sorely that a heavy judgment has fallen upon them. This is manifest from the affectionate and excellent letter of Bishop Boone to Mr. Lowrie's father. He says: "This event has thrown my family, who had the privilege to enjoy his company for the last two months and a half, into the deepest affliction. Dearly as I know he was beloved by the mission with which he was connected, yet, I believe, no one in China mourns his loss as I do." And no doubt the same feeling pervades the whole of the missionaries who have had any opportunity of acquaintance with our departed brother.

We may, therefore, lament the death of such a man, so beloved, and so well qualified to be useful in the most important work which is going on in this world. But though we are permitted to sorrow, yet not to repine. When Aaron's impious sons were struck dead in the sanctuary, "he held his peace;" he uttered no complaint. And when Eli heard the prophet's prediction respecting the judgment about to be inflicted on his wicked sons, he said, "It is the Lord, let him do what seemeth him good." Perfect submission is consistent with the most heart-felt sorrow. Indeed, the deeper the grief, the more virtuous the submission.

This event, I think, is a solemn call of Providence to our whole Church. It is evidently a token of the displeasure of our heavenly Father. God, by thus taking away one of the most eminent of our missionary corps, evidently calls the Presbyterian church to a solemn consideration of their ways; to an earnest inquiry whether, as a body, we have done our duty; and especially in relation to China. Some twenty years ago, the writer heard a speaker at a missionary meeting in Philadelphia, say, "If a hundred missionaries should now enter China, at different points, and every one of them should immediately be put to death, this would be a cheap sacrifice, if thereby that populous country should be opened for the preaching of the Gospel." At that time, the most sanguine did not dare to hope for such an event in their day. But God, by a wonderful Providence, has set the door wide open. Not merely one, but five great cities, are made accessible, and the right of residence and Christian worship secured by treaty. In consequence, a number of the most promising and best educated men offered their services, and were sent. But did the Church appreciate the importance of this extraordinary dispensation of Providence? Did she arouse herself from her long sleep, and come to the help of the Lord against the mighty; did she enlarge her spirit of liberality, and begin to wrestle with God in fervent, incessant prayer for this empire, which contains one third of the population of the globe? She did not. Had it not been for the generous donation of a few individuals, the Board would not have been able to send out the promising men who offered. And even now, there exists a general apathy. A few churches and a few individuals seem to be sensible of the solemn, responsible circumstances in which we who live in this age are placed. Professors of religion are too generally occupied with their own concerns; every one is attending to his farm or his merchandise; few have any deep feeling for the ark of God. Each one will build and decorate his own house, while the house of God is desolate.

Let the churches, then, consider this awful dispensation, as one in which they have a deep concern. Let the solemn inquiry be made in all our churches, and through all our borders, whether they have not been delinquent in their duty to the missionaries in China. Yea, let every individual ask himself, Have I done my duty? Have I remembered daily, as I ought, those devoted men? Have I borne them feelingly on my heart to the throne of grace? Have I given as liberally of my substance to promote this object as I ought? Such inquiries, honestly made, would, I believe, bring conviction home to almost every bosom. What, then, shall be the result? Having done amiss, is it our solemn purpose, by the help of the Lord, to do so no more? Let us, then, take words and return unto the Lord who hath smitten us. "Let the priests weep between the porch and the altar, and let them say, Spare thy people, O Lord."

If it should please our heavenly Father to make this distressing bereavement the means of awakening all our churches to the solemn consideration of their duty, as it relates to missions in general, and to China in particular, then will this sore judgment be turned into mercy. Let all the friends of Zion wrestle with God until he grant this result. Let them say, "For Zion's sake I will not hold my peace, and for Jerusalem's sake I will not be silent, until the righteousness thereof go forth as brightness, and the salvation thereof as a lamp that burneth." Such importunity is never offensive. Jacob said to the Angel of the Covenant, "I will not let thee go until thou bless me." And God commands us "to give him no rest, till he establish, and till he make Jerusalem a praise in the earth." Let every true Presbyterian resolve that, during the year, now commenced, he will bear on his heart before the throne of grace, the perishing condition of the heathen, and the wants of our foreign missionaries, with far greater frequency and fervency than during the year which is past. And, as our missionaries may be recalled unless funds are provided by the Church for their support, let every man, and woman, and child consider whether God does not require of them to do much more in the way of contribution than they have heretofore done; and see whether, from the very day from which you commence a new course, God will not bless you in a special manner. "Bring ye all the tithes into the storehouse that there may be meat in mine house, and prove me now herewith, saith the Lord of hosts, if I will not open you the windows of heaven, and pour you out a blessing, that there shall not be room enough to receive it." Mal. iii. 10.—*Missionary Chronicle:* February, 1848.

A cenotaph was erected to the memory of Mr. Lowrie, which bears the following inscriptions, partly in English and partly in Chinese:—

THE

REV. WALTER M. LOWRIE,

A MISSIONARY

TO

THE CHINESE.

BORN FEB. 18th, 1819.
DIED AUG. 19th, 1847.

"I am a stranger in the earth."—Ps. cxix. 19.

SECOND SIDE.

IN CHINESE.

The American teacher of the religion of Jesus, Low-le-wha, Seen Sang, [i. e. Mr. Lowrie.] Born in [the reign of] Kea-King, 24th year, 1st month, 26th day. Died in [the reign of] Taou-Kwang, 27th year, 7th month, 9th day. Reckoning back in [the reign of] Taou-Kwang, the 22d year, 4th month, 18th day, he arrived at Macao, China. The 25th year, 3d month, 5th day, he reached Ningpo; in order to propagate the holy religion. How can we know whether a long or a short life is appointed for us? He had but attained the age of twenty-nine years, when travelling by sea, he was drowned by pirates. Of all his associates there is none who does not cherish his memory, and they have accordingly erected this stone as a testimony of their affection.

THIRD SIDE.

He was attacked by pirates near Chapoo, and being thrown overboard, perished in the sea.

FOURTH SIDE.

IN CHINESE.

The Holy Book says—It is appointed unto man once to die, and after this the judgment, for the hour is coming, in which all that are in the graves shall hear the voice of the Son of God, and shall come forth, they that have done good unto the resurrection of life, and they that have done evil unto the resurrection of damnation.

The shaft is 4 feet 6 inches high; 2 feet 7 inches wide at the bottom, and 1 foot 9 inches at the top. The stone is a hard and smooth kind of granite, capable of a tolerable polish.

www.ingramcontent.com/pod-product-compliance
Lightning Source LLC
LaVergne TN
LVHW020105110826
845151LV00001B/66

* 9 7 8 1 4 2 5 5 4 4 7 1 3 *